WARRING SOULS

Warring Souls

Youth, Media, and Martyrdom in Post-Revolution Iran

ROXANNE VARZI

Duke University Press · Durham and London   2006

© 2006 Duke University Press   All rights reserved
Printed in the United States of America on acid-free paper ⊚
Designed by Rebecca Giménez
Typeset in Quadraat by Tseng Information Systems, Inc.
Library of Congress Cataloging-in-Publication Data appear
on the last printed page of this book.

Parts of chapter 7 originally appeared as "Ghost in the
Machine: The Cinema of the Iranian Sacred Defense," in *New
Iranian Cinema: Politics, Representation, and Identity*, edited
by Richard Tapper (London: I. B. Tauris Publishers, 2004.
Reprinted with permission).

To those who have been caught, displaced,

and have died in the wicked webs of war,

and to those who in the face of adversity

seek truth and reconciliation.

Contents

ACKNOWLEDGMENTS

I would not have been able to complete my fieldwork in Iran without the help and trust of my family, friends, and colleagues, and it is impossible to name the many people there whom I encountered over the past ten years. But above all I would like to thank my family in Iran, who took me in and accepted me as an insider and graciously excused the mistakes I made as an outsider. I would especially like to thank Amir, Nazanin, Kati, Rosa, Ali, Reza, Sheedeh, Mansur, Naser, Ferry, Mahin, Erika, Fakri, Mahmoud, and Zari Varzi for patiently and diligently helping me to become proficient in Persian, for speaking honestly about life in Iran, and for accepting me despite the twenty years that I was out of the country. Also in Iran, for their invaluable help with my research I would like to thank Golnush, Peygha, Mahssa, Pouya, Mehrad, and Aideen for including me in their group of friends; Mehdi in Shiraz; Ahura Farokhmanesh, Nader and Suri Davoodi, Amir Nikpey, Fatima Jahanshahi, Siamak Namazi, Reza Shahran, Golam Reza, Mahsa Shekarloo, Violet Pakzad, Sohrab Mahdavi, Ahmad Kiarostami, Persheng Sadegh-Vaziri, Kaveh Ehsani, Sima Mir-Hosseini, Ursala Pakzad, Mrs. Jahanshaii, Ibrahim Hatamikia, Kamal Tabrizi, Parviz Kalantari, Mohsen Makhmalbaf, Samira Makhmalbaf, Seiffolah Samadian, and Mr. Mohammad Avini and his colleagues at Rivayat-e Fath, the Farabi Film Center (Mr. Attibaii, Mr. Safiri, and Mr. Esfandiari), Khaneh Cinema, the National Film Archives, the Museum of Contemporary Art, the Islamic Propagation Ministry in Shiraz, the Foundation for Youth Studies in Tehran, the Museum of Martyrdom in Tehran, the Tehran University Centre for Islamic Unity, the Museum of Anthropology in Tehran, *Zanan* magazine, *Tus* newspaper, Ms. Agaii at Chanel Four, *Seda Seema*, the publications editors of Rivayat-e Fath Books, the Federation of Iranian Mountain Climbers, all my teachers at Deh Kodah Institute, and the late Mr. Asgharzadeh and Kaveh Golestan.

My friends and mentors who have supported me throughout my work include Harvey Stark, Katrina Karkazis, Diane (Pata) Kelly, Kristen Claire McCrory, Pamela Alice King, Julia Zajkowski, Nancy Um, Nilufar Nouri, Haideh Salehi-Esfahani, Amy Taylor, Kamran Rastegar, Jennifer Larson, Leide Porcu, Farah Haniffa, Michael Glünz, Audrey Short, Arang Keshavarzian, Lisa Anne Mitchell, Jonathon Bach, Yukiko Koga, Tak Watanabe, Akari Maruyama, Paige West, Thea Hunter, John L. Jackson Jr., Tara Sussman, Gouthum Gajula, Dard Neuman, Sima Rizvi, Godfrey Cheshire, Robin Lauzon, Sohrab Mahdavi, Setrak Manoukian, Amitab Dubey, Narges Erami, Persis Karim, Ziba Mir-Hosseini, Richard Tapper, Samuel Roberts, Milan Milinkovic, Marilyn Young, Alan Hunter, Santos Vales, Harriet Wheeler, Mary and Patrick Killough, Cynthia Nelson, Eva Koch, Abdul Aziz Said, Kevin Moore, Mikkel Borch-Jacobsen, Mehdi Korrami, Walter Andrews, Richard Pena, Melissa Hibbard, Peter Chelkowski, Wendy Meryam Shaw, Faraz Sanei, Rachel Moore, Karen Vonnegut, Tina Chen, Molly Nolan, Robert Vitalis, Manijeh Sanei, Suzie Baxter, Jam Paydavousi, Parviz Paydavousi, Mina Gorgi, Collette Caffrey, Dominic Parviz Brookshaw, Homa Katouzian and Ron Nettler for their support in the UK; my committee members and mentors, Michael Taussig, Marilyn Ivy, Brinkley Messick, Ervand Abrahamian, and Walter Armbrust; Joyce Monges for all her support at Columbia; my colleagues at the University of California, Irvine; and Eric Hooglund who convinced my parents that it was safe for me to return to Iran alone; and finally to Ken Wissoker, Courtney Berger, Justin Faerber, Katie Courtland, and Naomi

Linzer, and my anonymous reviewers at Duke University Press for all their hard work, thank you.

I would like to thank the Fulbright Commission for funding my research and for having the foresight as the first U.S. organization to make the important step toward cultural and scientific exchanges with Iran. I also thank the Department of Anthropology at Columbia University, the Markle Foundation, the Social Science Research Council, the Iran Heritage Foundation, the University of London School of Oriental and African Studies, the Woodrow Wilson Foundation, the Center for International and Advanced Studies at New York University, and the Middle East Centre at St. Antony's College at Oxford University.

In loving memory of those who have passed away in the time that I have been on this journey: Keyvan Varzi, Eva Klein, Ferry Varzi.

Finally, none of this would have been possible without the love and support of my mother, Charlotte Varzi, who was a true pioneer when she set out from Michigan to teach chemistry in Iran as a Fulbright scholar in 1967; of my father, Massoud Varzi, who always encouraged me to write and who provided me with a story; and of my brother and sister, Jehangir Fuller Varzi and Kimyia Fatima Varzi, who have been venturing with me all along. And for my partner on this journey, Kasra Paydavousi, whose creativity, support, love, and guidance are invaluable.

The Journey

The tale *The Conference of the Birds*, by the Persian mystic and poet
Farid al-Din Attar (650–1220), details the journey of a group of
birds in search of a mystic leader, the Simurgh, who lives behind
the mountain Qaf in an inaccessible place hidden by veils of light
and darkness. The Simurgh manifests itself neither physically nor
through knowledge or intelligence. Only through the imagination
is the Simurgh made visible. This tale is a metaphor for a mystic
journey, which begins with a guide, the Hoopoo, who is both a messenger of the world invisible and a being practiced in divine warfare.
Hoopoo claims to have hidden knowledge of the Simurgh, and she
serves as a guide for the birds who choose to journey to the world
of the Simurgh. At one point in Attar's tale, the Hoopoo states:
"Do not imagine that the journey is short; one must have the heart
of a lion to follow the unusual road, for it is very long and the sea
is deep . . . Wash your hands of this life if you were to be called a
man of action. For your beloved, renounce that dear life of yours,
as worthy men. If you submit with grace the beloved will give his
life for you." In so speaking the Hoopoo wins the trust of the birds,
and for years they travel over mountains and valleys. But the journey
is a difficult one. The only way to understand what they suffered,

Attar tells us, is to journey with them. Along the way, many birds find the journey too painful and make excuses to quit. The Hoopoo weaves their excuses, along with her replies, into a web of mystical tales that forms the heart of this lyrical quest.

baten -> inner self
zaher -> public self

Divination

An Archeology of the Unknown

To live means to leave traces. GEORG SIMMEL

The holy prophet said: "Affliction caused by the tongue
is worse than that caused by the sword. Among all the
things the tongue deserves to be imprisoned longer than
anything else." IMAM AYATOLLAH KHOMEINI

History is preserved on the left hand, while each day the lines of
the future are forged deeper on the right. It is the little lines, barely
visible, that the big lines stumble over.

In speaking of the pre-revolution years, Iranians often describe
the wailing entailed in Shiite mourning traditions. For many Iranians who have survived the revolution and war, mourning is now
done in silence: a silence that leaves no traces. For some, divination has given voice to mourning, unearthing scars and pointing a
path past broken lines and over history toward destiny. It is a map
used to avoid roadblocks, a tour book of hidden obstacles. Divination, like religion, is invoked when one relinquishes control of

one's own destiny. It is also invoked in order to tap into the world of archetypes: *alam al mithal*, a world occupied by the likes of the Simurgh.

How can anthropology be more exact than divination or anything but another kind of mourning?

OCTOBER 1993, TEHRAN *"If you want to learn about your country, Roksana, you must read poetry: S'adi, Hafiz, Khayyam, and Rumi. Work on your Persian. Do not waste your time on anything else. Come to me, we'll read together," says my uncle.*

"Can poetry kill fear?" I'm afraid to concede that I'm scared here, sometimes.

"Poetry could save your life, Roksana. Remember that. It saved mine," he says.

My uncle's love for literature endangered his life by leading him to Sadegh Hedayat and other Marxist writers' salons, thereby indirectly influencing his decision to join the Tudeh Party. That decision landed him in jail after the revolution.[1]

"Does he talk about being in prison?" I asked my cousin as I watched my uncle's shaky hand lift a spoonful of rice to his mouth. The shaking started in prison.

"He will not talk about it to anyone, not even my mother. He wants to forget."

His eyes tell me that he will never forget, and not a day passes that he does not think about it. Every now and then, at gatherings, when people are chattering among themselves, I've seen him light a cigarette and stare hard into the smoke. He does not look sad but rather content, almost smiling. He watches the crowd the way a ghost might observe a gathering.

"Poetry will help you in your time of need," he says, his back turned to me as we walk slowly into the den.

We read Hafiz.

No one knows where the lover's house is found
It is everywhere that the camel bells are heard

I try to imagine an Iran of lovers, camels, and nightingales, but all I see are crowded streets, hands clutching woven green rubber shopping bags, dingy sycamore trees, tiny box-shaped cars honking their way through miles of traffic. The horns once kept me awake at night. Now they are an urban lullaby. My uncle smiles to himself and takes a long drag on his cigarette while he waits for me to grasp the meaning of the poem. He sits with one leg folded up, his elbow on the knee of his baggy pajamas. Sitting with my uncle in his den, reading Hafiz, I feel safe.

"I see how poetry saved your life," I say.

"No, you do not, because I have not told you the end of the story. You are only beginning to see how it might save your life." He extinguishes his cigarette and slowly gets up, a sign that I'll have to wait to hear the rest of the story.

"When I was a young boy we were forced to memorize a poem every week," my uncle tells me on my next visit. My father told me that my grandfather gave his children a gold coin for each poem they could recite from memory.

"In jail I sat alone with my blindfold and pulled nervously at my sleeves. One day I pulled a frazzled string from my shirt and tied a knot for every poem I recited in my head. That was my meditation, my prayer. That knotted string was like prayer beads, a tie to sanity; tying a knot to remember a poem kept me from thinking of the horrors happening around me." He pauses to light a cigarette. His hands shake more at night when he is tired. It takes him a minute to light his cigarette; he's never conscious of time.

"One day, the half-blind old man who brought us our food caught me tying and mumbling. He threw down my tray and ran to tell the revolutionary guards that I was praying and that I had either left my Marxist, atheist ways or that they had made a mistake. He was so loud with excitement that no one could deny him. About an hour later my blindfold was removed and I was transferred to a cell of men awaiting trial. I was freed a month later. Many of my friends never made it out." He sits back as if to recall each and every lost face.

"Do not mistake my words, Roksana, it was not that small stroke of luck that saved my life. The fact that using the string and reading poems saved me from further physical harm is only a coincidence. Every knot was a Hafiz poem that freed me from the confines of prison by taking me away. Hafiz was a Sufi; he lived in a time when Sufis were persecuted. He teaches us how to rise above obstacles. Hafiz takes us to a beautiful place where we can live safely in times when our physical life becomes impossible to endure. In the hours that my mind could have given way to the darkness of the blindfold and prison walls,

Hafiz took me to Shiraz, to full-moon desert nights, candlelit zekrs, singing nightingales, and dancing dervishes. He preserved my mind and took it to a beautiful place while my body was kept captive. Sufis have been persecuted for a very specific reason, Roksana, they do not believe that a leader or any other person should mediate their relationship with God."

"Hafiz is more complicated than I thought."

"Hafiz can teach you how to move obstacles, especially the ones that are in your mind, of your own creation, those images that bombard you daily, that chip away at your strength and make you insensitive, harden or destroy you. They are the worst kind. No one should be able to mediate your relationship with God or the world — remember that."

Poetry worked like a veil to protect my uncle from mental invasion and served as a tool for mediating the world physically and symbolically. I fancied myself a reliable mediator of my own world, as someone who grew up without having to engage in poetry or in metaphor to protect herself, until my uncle, after reading my stories from which the above is excerpted, asked me why I had censored myself. His comment shocked me. I did not consider my writing censored. "I censored everything to protect you," I replied defensively. But he had never asked to be protected and, surprisingly, neither had anyone else I had spoken to in Iran who knew that I was writing about them. My uncle spent four years as a political prisoner in Tehran's notorious Evin prison, and he was the first to warn me not to get involved in politics. I had thus taken his advice and stayed away from all things political, and in so doing I had somehow transformed everything into politics.

In Iran the social is political, and as one who is not adept at living this way the idea paralyzed me. As a result it was not Iran that was to blame; I had imprisoned myself in my own self-censorship (the worst effect of oppressive politics is when we do its work). I was an easy target: already adept at writing in metaphor, having written poetry all my life; practiced at hiding my identity; and attracted to Martin Heidegger's use of the Greek term *aletheia* — revealing while concealing — which, I thought, was illustrative of Iranian culture. But I was practicing projection. I had enforced something on Iranian culture that it had already infused in me. My uncle was right. In the end we are not only mediators of our own worlds where we see what we want to see, but we also create that world as it creates us in a simultaneous act of revealing and concealing. In this world we traverse the geographies of *zaher* (outer self) and *baten* (inner self) while constructing and dismantling through bi-khodi (self-annihilation) and khod-sazi or khod-shenasi (self-construction or self-awareness). As the war filmmaker Shahid Morteza Avini told me, "reality is not what exists, but what has the possibility to exist." This book is a journey through the various veils or curtains of reality to meditate on the many possible meanings of reality for the young Iranians in post-revolution Iran who were the targets of the Islamic project that attempted to construct a specific Islamic reality. The veil I refer to here, a *pardeh* (veil or curtain), is the Sufi mystical term for something that obscures reality or is a projection of one layer of reality.

Sufi mysticism is indelibly ingrained in Iranian culture through a tradition of poetry that has infused metaphor at the heart of the Persian language and in the everyday existence of Iranians (providing, among other possibilities, a beautiful way to avoid, obscure, defer, fragment, and repress). Here the veil is not what covers women's hair, but rather is the mist created to keep distance, to keep reality from becoming real, at the same time that it is the ether that becomes reality.

One can enter the scene of a Persian miniature at any angle and still not be on the same three-dimensional plane as the characters depicted. Mysticism, like a Persian miniature, never assumes that everyone will always exist on the same plane, even if they physically exist in the same scene. Like the mystic journey, as a movement in time and space that is neither linear nor monochronic, this book moves through different moments and themes in post-revolution Islamic Iran to look at how the Islamic republic was constructed, sustained, consumed, and transformed. In this work I aim to narrate the political poem of the Islamic republic through the lens of anthropology, framed by the mystical allegory of the journey.

To meet this aim I follow the chronology of revolutionary Iran from 1979 to 2000 to show the journey from bi-khodi to khod-sazi and to demonstrate how a visual world was created, consumed, and dismantled. I am interested in the role in which the image plays as a vehicle for oneness with God for mystics and, in turn, the ways in which moving and still images worked to create a state of martyrdom and ultimately a religious state. I begin this work by introducing the mystical interplay of the self (khod) as it journeys toward self-annihilation (bi-khodi) and back (to self-reconstruction, khod-sazi) through a discussion of Nizami Ganjavi's *Layli and Majnun*. Nizami's tale is a way for us to become familiar with the important themes of the mystic guide, the image, the idea of absence, the world of archetypes (*alam al mithal*) and of deception (*riya*), and the function of these terms in the Sufi journey toward the beloved (God).

On February 11, 1979, after months of a bloody revolution that raged on the streets of Tehran between citizens who called for the end of the regime of the shah of Iran, Mohammad Reza Pahlavi, and the shah's police and the military, Ayatollah Ruhollah Khomeini returned to his homeland of Iran and took power in Tehran.[2] The Iranian revolution was unique in its ability to unite the Iranian people to bring down a powerful, U.S.-backed army through the use of rallying measures such as imported cassette tapes, pamphlets, and clandestine meetings.[3] Just after the revolution, as Ayatollah Khomeini and the religious Right were consolidating power, the new Islamic cultural producers of the state began to construct an Islamic republic with a very specific emphasis on the mystical notion of bi-khodi, self-annihilation, and shahadat, martyrdom, that had been carried over from the revolution days and was fast becoming a precursor to Islamic citizenship.[4] This situation was heightened in 1980 when the war broke out between Iran and Iraq, at which time nation building became synonymous with martyrdom. In later chapters I show how war constructed Tehran as a space of revolutionary Islam from the time of Khomeini's arrival in 1979 through the war years and, in turn, how the government attempted to use a strong Islamic public sphere to turn youthful subjects into Islamic objects.

This book is about the intersection of religion, vision, and power, and whether the individual ultimately has the power to turn an image on or off. It is about ways in which reality is constructed between the surface or appearance of things, zaher, and the inner and individual senses of reality, baten. To what degree does the surface permeate and or construct an individual's inner reality and faith? This is a story of the struggle to be seen and unseen, between visibility and invisibility. I tell the story of the many young martyrs who died and then were seen later in the murals covering the city walls, and I tell of those young, urban, secular Iranian youths who hide behind the scenes, trying to lead a different sort of life and in so doing remain invisible to the powers that be.

While I write about a particular nation-state at various stages of its development, the story is really that of the journey of selves, khod, as they traverse two particular movements in time and space alongside that of the nation. I highlight a key tension in Islamic Iran between bi-khodi (self-annihilation) and the notions of khod-sazi and khod-shenasi (self-help or self-construction).[5] These two concepts would seem logically to occur independently in some chronological shift or rational order. For example: self-reconstruction, khod-sazi, might logically serve as an antidote to self-annihilation, bi-khodi. However, self-annihilation can only occur after a self is constructed and available for annihilation. The people and the nation-state go through bi-khodi and khod-sazi in tandem, dancing with one another as they whirl in and out of these polar movements, stepping on toes, changing partners, and colliding.

The movement toward bi-khodi in revolutionary Iran began with Ali Shariati's idea of a "return to self" and a khod-shenasi (self-knowledge).[6] It was seen as important that an individual gain self-knowledge, especially in terms of national identity, before embarking on a journey toward self-annihilation and, in some cases, martyrdom. Shariati's work was much influenced by and in conversation with Frantz Fanon, whose work on Algeria and colonialism

bi Khodi - self annihilation
Khod Shenasi - self help

focused on identity and self-knowledge—in short, the importance of keeping one's cultural and national identity and self-awareness in the face of racist colonial policies that aimed at assimilating "natives."

At the same time that Shariati was writing about a return to a Muslim self, another writer, Jalal Al-Ahmad, raised his pen against what he called "Westoxification." As he writes: "I speak of being afflicted with "Westitis" the way I would speak of being afflicted with cholera. If this is not palpable let us say it is akin to being stricken by heat or cold. But it is not that either. It is something more on the order of being attacked by tongue worm. Have you ever seen how wheat rots? From within. In any case we are dealing with an illness, a disease imported from abroad, and developed in an environment receptive to it."[7] Needless to say, his work would eventually provide Khomeini with a revolutionary discourse. Al-Ahmad's next work, *Lost in the Crowd*, details the existential transformation of a Marxist who rediscovers Islam, and in so doing it provides invaluable documentation of a moment in Iranian and modern Islamic society when the existential modern individual began to turn to Islam as a political force. His colloquial prose and sincere curiosity of Islamic practice endeared the book to secular Iranian readers who felt the double alienation of being both intellectually Western and also Muslim.

Yale historian Abbass Amanat points to the importance of Shariati and Al-Ahmad in pre-revolution Iran: "With historians' failure to provide any coherent and meaningful interpretation of the past, it is not surprising that increasingly, intellectuals, essayists, and dissident pamphleteers took over the task of interpreting the past. In the absence of any serious alternatives, Jalal Al-Ahmad's hurried, ill-conceived, and even paranoic thesis *Westoxification* and Ali Shariati's often myopic, and distorted, interpretation of Shi-ism left an intense impact on the historical consciousness of the younger generations in the late 1960s and 1970s. It is a small surprise therefore that with their sway over the minds of the revolutionary multitudes they should emerge as historical figures in their own right rather than interpreters of history."[8] What Amanat is perhaps really concerned with, but does not properly articulate, is the exchange of history for ideology. Unlike the writing of history, method and falsehood are largely irrelevant to ideology. In discussing the early days of the revolution, given the problem of the lack of decent revolutionary history, it is important to remember that in terms of anthropology, the project is not to discern the historic accuracy of the texts but rather to look at their social usage. Often, words or "truths" live in the realm of the social as ideology; ideology is what takes half-truths and philosophical ideas and puts them into the realm of social action. As Terry Eagleton notes, ideology is about "lived relations" and not empirical representation.[9] Social practices are real, therefore, whereas some of the beliefs that justify these practices may be illusory.

Ironically, the intellectuals that Amanat claims "escape from realities and abode in the realm of ill-conceived ideological fantasy," were more aware than anyone of the needs and desires of Iranian society. They were, for example, the first to question the historical grounds of the shah's myth. Without their initial broad-based critiques of the shah's regime and the imperialism of the West, the articulation of discontent, which is a necessary precursor to revolution, may not have occurred in urban spaces of power (the intelligentsia and the universities). Hannah Arendt asserts that a revolution is not planned, and even the outcome of a popular revolutionary text cannot be anticipated. Whether a text is philosophy, history, or fiction, it might easily change to ideology the moment it breathes life through the voices and lungs of the multitudes.

While Shariati was well known for his work on returning to the self, it was his work on martyrdom that had the greatest effect on the turn of events early on in Iranian Islamic revolutionary history. While bi-khodi can be defined simply as "self-annihilation," it is a slippery term that can in one instance refer to martyrdom, a final, physical death, and in another instance refer to "self"-annihilation and madness, which marks the death of a constructed self, or ego, without a physical death. The mystical definition is the transcendence of the ego, which may or may not lead to physical death. In chapter 1 I address bi-khodi as a metaphorical death of a constructed self, which leads to madness, in the character of Majnun; and, as we will see, this metaphoric death eventually leads to physical death. Later, after leaving the realm of literature, we encounter self-annihilation both as a mystical practice in preparation for physical death and as the actual event of death at the Iran-Iraq war front where young men come to fulfill a mystic call to transcend material life by martyring themselves in battle (chapters 2 and 3).

From the war front we move to Tehran, where bi-khodi becomes a practice of leaving one's self through transcendent mystical practice (both New Age and Islamic, or what I call "Sufi cool") as well as through drugs and suicide as an escape practiced both by former war vets and by the young people who came of age during the height of an era marked by martyrdom and defined by bi-khodi (chapters 4–7).

The tension between bi-khodi and khod-sazi is most pronounced in the generation of today's youth (and, increasingly, in that of war veterans). Over twenty years since the founding of the Islamic republic, drug use, suicide, and prostitution rates have skyrocketed among the very youths that should theoretically be ideal Islamic citizens. The nation is racing to transform this era of bi-khodi to one of khod-sazi or khod-shenasi through Western popular psychology (that which counters mysticism by saving the self), self-help courses, television and radio shows, twelve-step programs, and other desperate and mostly ineffectual methods. While the government attempts to provide programs that will aid young people in developing into healthy individuals, khod-sazi has become one of the most important components of young, urban Iranian life in the form of hypnosis classes, yoga, self-help books, Jungian study circles, and Sufi poetry reading circles, among other things. My analysis here of post-revolution Iran charts a semiotic malfunctioning that is occurring as Islamic revolutionary public policy enters a period of serious crisis in identity, governmentalism, and belief. This crisis translates into what the current generation calls an identityless (bi-hoviyat) or schizophrenic existence, perched between khod-sazi, with its meditation classes and self-help books, and bi-khodi, with its turn to ascension and transcendence through drugs and suicide that is leading some youths to the mountains of northern Tehran where they have found a new geography of death.

My approach to scholarship does not allow me to amputate parts of history to make my task easier. No study of post-revolution Iran is complete without the Iran-Iraq war years (1981–1989), and yet I knew from my past experiences in Iran (1991, 1993–1994, 1996, 1998, 2000) that the individuals at the center of my research, secular middle-class Iranian youths, did not want to think about or discuss the war. I studied the war, interviewed veterans and family members of martyrs, analyzed memoirs, and watched documentaries, and yet I continued to focus on secular Tehran youths who struggle with life on the margins of a religious state. Why these young people? They were the targets of the Islamization project that hinged on the war; now they are supposed to be an index for the success of the Islamic republic. What is hidden and buried by denial is not yet lost in them but remains just below the surface, a surface that is ready to collapse at any moment. I have had access to these youths, and many are members of my family. They are who I would have been had my family not left Iran a year after the revolution.

Originally I was drawn to a research question that came from a comment made by Abdul Karim Surush (a revolutionary turned reformist who trained in the philosophy of science). During a presentation in Seattle, Washington, he suggested that over the past twenty years Iranians have shifted from being Cartesian subjects to being Islamic subjects. On hearing this I raised my hand (he generally does not call on women, but after much coaxing from the crowd he finally called on me) to ask him what defined an Islamic subject; in response he told me it would take too long to explain. The next fall I applied for a Fulbright grant to research the issue of whether the state had successfully effected a massive change in the identity of its youngest subjects. The following winter I went to Iran on the Fulbright grant—the first such grant for research in Iran since the revolution.

Many of the parents I met in Iran told me that as a research topic this generation is a waste of time because there is nothing unique or different about them and, further, they are without identity—*bi hoviyat*. The Western media has exoticized Iran's Islamic nature while also pointing to areas where Iranian youths are just like those in America. Can young people in Iran be pulled out of the context of their existence, Islamic Iran, and be likened to American youth? Do young people around the world share some sort of universal "youth culture" that is a result of globalization, media technologies, and the Internet? Are the anger, the violence, and the disengagement of today's youth a universal phenomenon? Can we blame the media or the Web for giving youth ideas about guns and drugs? The Iranian government, along with many parents I spoke to, blame the corrupt culture of the West for the problems facing Iranian youth today. From a view outside Iran, sexual activity, drugs, and even romance may appear not to exist, and Iranians appear not to be addicted to drugs, no one is infected with HIV, and a woman's face is never seen. Needless to say, this is far from the case.

My concern was with the kind of information that surfaces in places of privacy, in the cobwebbed corners of an individual's mind. I was interested in how individuals experienced their realities and not whether they were representative of the majority. My interest was in how people occupy the same strict ideological space and yet live in completely different realities. What happens when young people are forced to try to occupy various realities before they have formed their own? To what degree does an ideological public sphere affect the identity and lives of those who live in it? What happens to those who stop believing?[10]

It is very important at the outset of this work to define my use of the word secular, and to clarify whom I am referring to when I call someone secular. When I refer to secular youth (Iranians born after 1979) I am speaking of youth from a wide background—those who may be practicing Muslims, Christians, Bahais, Jews, or Zoroastrians; those who are believers in these religions but not practicing; and those who are agnostic or atheist—but who also have in common the belief that religion is a private practice that should not be condoned, enforced, or abhorred by public policy. In other words, the main characteristic of secular youths is not that they are religious but that they do not want public law to be interpreted through religious edicts. Indeed, they wish not to live in a religious republic but prefer to live in a society in which there is a separation of church and state. The use of the term "secular" becomes a little trickier, however, when it comes to the generation that was in its twenties during the revolution. The people from this generation whom I define as secular are mainly from a group similar to that defined above, yet who come either from families that were secular both before and after the revolution or from a more complicated group whose members refer to themselves as reformists who at one time were dedicated Muslims with a goal of establishing an Islamic religious republic in Iran. These reformers experienced a political transformation that did not necessarily change their religious beliefs (though many are no longer believers or practicing Muslims) but that no longer defined their political goals and aspirations through an Islamic paradigm. Although they may still follow daily Islamic practices themselves, they do not believe that the entire country should be beholden to do the same, but rather that the choice should be an individual one. Some in this group are still religious, like Abdul-Karim Surush, and want to see an Islamic democracy; but, as he explains, this will mean a country of Muslims who practice their religion privately and exercise duties as citizens that are not defined by Islamic law. In other words, religion for him is no longer part of the public sphere but is, rather, a private enterprise. It is also important to note that many of these secular youths that I worked with were very spiritual people. As I note in later chapters, while they did not adhere to strict religious rules, many were spiritual in a way that was not at odds with their secularism (they may have prayed to an imam, visited shrines, practiced yoga or meditation, attended Rumi readings circles, or participated in a general "Sufi cool").[11]

Before going to Iran I sought out a methodology that would upset or shake up the hermeneutic relationship of anthropologist and informant while also downplaying the role of anthropologist as an observer by involving Iranian youths in the very process I was entangled in, that of studying them.[12] This, I hoped, would de-emphasize the subject/object divide so as to create a more comfortable environment (as opposed to an environment where the subject simply answers questions, all the while wondering how the material will be used or interpreted). I hoped that by exposing the "scientific black box," I could decrease anxiety or paranoia and create intellectual trust. I was often scared to ask the questions I really wanted to ask, afraid someone would say, "Why do you want to know?" Anthropological research in Iran involving questioning and observing students contained the usual anxieties that anthropologists have about misrepresenting or misunderstanding their subjects, yet it was also compounded by the anxiety that at any moment either the anthropologist or the student, or both, might be branded a spy.[13]

My first task in Iran was to put together a *dowreh* (circle or salon) of college-age students, both men and women, to discuss public culture, contemporary history, and life in the city and at home.[14] Starting with students I knew from past trips, I formed a group of intelligent and culturally active youths from Tehran's top technical school, Sharif University. I chose Sharif University because I already had contacts there and, further, I knew that those contacts fraternized with people outside of their sociopolitical sphere. The students I worked with had placed highly in the university entrance exams and many were in disciplines (like engineering) in which they were not interested.[15] These dowrehs, however, provided them with the opportunity to partake in the humanities and other areas that did interest them. My aim, however, was not just to have a "focus group" where I provided questions for group discussion while I took notes, but rather I wished to understand the ways in which these students thought about and consumed their public space and public culture. In order for them to understand how I approached my own study, and so that they could participate in informed discussions, I first gave them a brief overview of anthropology. I asked them to keep a journal, personal but also ethnographic. My project thus became their project as they increasingly grew more excited about examining their own lives. Because in their own lives they were at a stage of examining both their future and that of their country, it was a perfect time for me to gain insights from them and for them to learn skills that helped them become more introspective and self-reflective and to look within themselves to solve problems.

The journal notebooks also gave them an opportunity to voice their problems.[16] We discussed Michel de Certeau's idea that habit can lead to a kind of blindness, and together we tried to unearth things we take for granted, such as young women donning Islamic covering when they leave the house, to write about how it makes them feel, or when they last thought about it.[17] The students helped me put together a questionnaire for their peers, and in doing so they expressed the kinds of things they would and would not want to be asked as well as offering the topics most important to address. We did not limit our discussions to "Iranian culture" but rather included other matters that interested them, which led to a greater understanding on my part of how they interpret culture in general. For example, watching a Luis Buñuel film together led to an in-depth discussion about social change. "Is Buñuel advocating social change?" they asked. "Is he suggesting that we break all social rules? Is that the purpose of movements like surrealism?" In my response I stated that for Buñuel social rules are arbitrary, which does not mean that he necessarily advocates that we change these rules but that we be aware of their arbitrary nature and that we reflect on this rather than taking for granted that this is the way that things should be. Buñuel was their choice to watch, it was their videotape obtained from a bootleg source. A long discussion ensued about the freedom to critique without taking the next step toward social change or of being accused of a crime by "merely critiquing the status quo." Studying Iranian youth thus turned into a project on modernity and the reformulation of religious and national identity in Iran, as it was the most important thing on people's minds.

My relationship to Iran and my belief that reality is lived on many slippery planes that are not always visible, let alone able to be articulated, have dictated for me an experimental form of ethnography. As mentioned earlier, my own internal censor, coupled with a vivid imagination, will not allow me to make any authoritative claims on reality, and thus I use different ways and different voices to relay my ethnographic journey. Throughout this book, the passages that are set off in special text incorporate various narrative voices taken from fiction (that is, from characters and events that I created while staying within historic and ethnographic facts based on my own research) as well as from voices that are fictionalized (in a neorealist sense where people play themselves; that is, the writing is either taken from their journals or from stories). I also use passages from my ethnographic field notes and from entries quoted verbatim from either my diary (mostly from my first extended trip back to Iran in 1993, when I spent a year living with my uncle's family and was the age of the young people I returned to study ten years later) or from the journals of those students in my dowreh. All of these passages are used in light of the idea that life is a constant process of invention and that these lines and voices are as blurred as they are distinct. I also chose to write a fictional vignette in chapter 2, largely because it was the easiest way to get around my own internal censor. Fiction is the most effective way to protect the identities of those being described, where uniqueness and individuality are sustained within a rubric of fictional identity. The fictional vignettes are my understanding of a character and the events surrounding that character based on interviews, participant observation, journal entries, and archival research in Iran.

By creating a fictional soldier in chapter 2, I was able to create a more complete picture of the war as I understand it based on my research. If reality is what has the possibility to exist, as is claimed by the war documentary maker Shahid Avini, then fiction allows characters to be placed in territories that are realistically possible, but also in places where they are having conversations they might not have had or are doing things they might not have done. The fictional soldier, whom I name Amir, allows the possibility of the Islamic Basij (Khomeini's revolutionaries)[18] and the secular middle class to speak with one another. He is a mediator of two different worlds that have struggled and will continue to struggle to live together. Amir is a middle-class educated Tehrani who is drafted early on in the war when all boys his age were sent to the front. His character is based on conversations I had with a young middle-class Iranian who was drafted to the front and who respected the Basij even though he did not believe in the idea of reclaiming Karbala or in the idea of holy war. The vignette is based on war memoirs and *vasiyat-namehs* (last wills and testaments), on films from the point of view of the Basij, and on interviews I had with war veterans in Tehran and Shiraz. This is an important scenario to imagine if Iranians are to forge ahead in creating an Iran that will incorporate the two strictly distinct realities of the Basij and secular citizens. This has become especially clear in the last presidential election, when Iranians elected Mahmoud Ahmadinejad, a war veteran.

In the various passages and vignettes I interchange narrative voices in order to place the reader, the anthropologist, the Iranians, and the fictional characters on different Archimedean planes: from first person to third person and where observer and observed become shared experiences. The first-person form is used for fictional characters, excerpts from the journals and questionnaires I collected in Iran, and from my own ethnographic journals. The second-person form is mainly used for my personal perspective and allows me to give the reader a feel for what I experienced as an outsider and an insider. The journal entries are directly from the journals I collected from youth in Tehran. Again, special text is used to set off these modes of representation.[19]

Finally, mystical Sufi allegories are more than just useful in discussing Iran, they are also an integral part of popular culture (secular, religious, Jewish, Muslim, Zoroastrian, Christian, or Bahai). Most Iranians read or have heard the ideas and poetry of Hafiz, Rumi, Attar, and Nizami. Their popularity and integration into Iranian society is testament to the degree to which Islamic mystical culture and its poetry has permeated Iranian culture, regardless of individual religious practices. Even Bahai youth in Iran considered Hafiz and Persian mysticism a part of their spiritual identity. Many Iranians use Hafiz's poetry to divine the future, either by opening up the poetry book to a particular page or by drawing a card inscribed with a poem and then interpreting the poem. In the mountains of Tehran, where many young people hike on the weekends,

1. A man stationed at a popular hiking spot in the mountains of northern Tehran sells fortunes on slips of paper preprinted with poetry by Hafiz (along with its divinatory meaning). The papers, in envelopes, are then picked out by canaries and handed to the patron. (Photo by Roxanne Varzi, 2000)

there is a man with a canary and a box full of tiny envelopes containing Hafiz's poetry printed on little slips of paper. The man charges a fee to have his canary randomly choose an envelope and thus a fortune.

Often, no matter with whom I was speaking (a family member, college student, Muslim, Bahai, Armenian), Hafiz, Attar, or Rumi were used to make a point or to offer advice. My first introduction to these mystics was at home with my secular father and uncles who introduced me to Hafiz when giving me advice, helping me to learn Persian, or just passing the time. Later, as I delved into Western theories of visuality, memory, and postmodernity, I found my-self comparing and contrasting the mystical texts with which I was familiar (Attar, Ibn Arabi, Hafiz, and Rumi) with writers on Judeo-Christian mysticism (especially Michel de Certeau and St. Augustine). In terms of theory and in what I had experienced in the field, Islamic mysticism has become an important theoretical framework for my discussion of popular culture in post-revolution Iran.

It is important to keep in mind that there is not a single mono-lithic form of mysticism practiced by all Iranians, but I was able to discern a number of deviations and threads of forms—in particu-lar that of secular northern upper-middle-class Iranian youths and that of the state, as defined primarily by the Basij who fought the Iran-Iraq war. So, there is an important delineation that must be made in terms of how people define mysticism as well as how they define themselves in terms of mysticism.

The book begins with the ways in which Ayatollah Khomeini, one of the most important cultural architects of the Islamic repub-lic (its founder and spiritual leader) defined mysticism and how it was used to consolidate power. When Khomeini came to power, Sufi mystical practices that lay outside of the framework of the state were banned in favor of strict Islamic jurisprudence. Locks were placed on the doors of the Sufi lodges, and many Sufi orders and their sheiks either fled the country or went underground.[20] At the same time that there was a move to suppress mysticism, it was actually being used in a new way to glorify martyrdom. When Iraq attacked Iran in 1980, the government consolidated its au-thority as a religious state by sending young martyrs off to the war. The war with Iraq (even more than the revolution) was the largest mobilization in the history of the Iranian population, which was achieved primarily by producing and promoting a culture of martyrdom based on the religious themes found in Shi'i Islam and in Sufism.

Those who supported the revolutionary government and fought in the war as Basij, thereby volunteering to be martyred, generally follow the line of Imam Husayn (they join Hoseyniyehs and com-memorate Muharram). The women members of these groups are veiled, and also have *hey'ats* (religious gatherings) that are separate from those of the men. Many of these hey'ats are supported by the Bazzaris (merchants in the bazaar, who belong to the more religiously conservative groups). Many followers of Husayn saw Khomeini as a Sufi sheik and saw themselves on the Sufi path.[21] My choice to use mystical theories to talk about the war was founded on the theoretical connections I made through observation and my own intellectual choices, but the choice was substantiated later in meetings with Basij who confirmed my own connections. One such meeting was with Mohammad Avini, the documentary maker and veteran of the Iran-Iraq war mentioned above, who spent an entire evening describing for me the mystical atmosphere of the war front. Our conversation and the materials he gave me allowed me to write the chapter on Islamic documentary making at the war front.

"What do you know about Islam?" Avini asks me.

When I have sufficiently proven to him that I am more than a reporter and have an understanding of Islam that will allow a deeper discussion, he asks me what theorists I am interested in using.

"I see a connection between Kojève and notions of martyrdom practiced during the war. I have a feeling that Henri Corbin, who along with Sartre and Battaille, among others, sat in on Kojève's lectures on Hegel at the Sorbonne in the 50s and later taught Islam at Tehran University, may have made some early connections there that his students picked up on. I have found no paper trace of this."

"You are right, we call Hegel the Rumi of the West."

"How do you know so much about Western philosophy?"

"I have a degree in Western philosophy from the University of Texas. Let's talk more about Hegel and 'erfan (Islamic mysticism)."[22]

Later, while interviewing Basij in Shiraz, I would again be asked about mysticism, especially whether I was a follower of Husayn. My conversations with Avini and other Basij about mysticism confirmed my intentions to use it as both an ethnographic descriptive and a theoretical framework for discussing war culture.

The secular youth with whom I worked in northern Tehran who

do not support the Islamic republic (among other generations of secular Tehranis) are followers of Ali and go to Khaneqahs that provide zekr-Ali (a ceremony where Ali's name is repeated in order to achieve trance). Most women who participate in these groups do not wear a *hejab* (Islamic covering) at the gatherings (or if they do it is by their own choice), and men and women generally sit together in the same space.[23] Some young people do not necessarily go to Sufi meetings or even consider themselves Sufi, but rather privately read Hafiz, Mawlana, play the *daf* (frame drum) or *santur* (stringed instrument) and wear their hair long, sport prayer beads as bracelets, and participate in a general Sufi cool that has become popular in northern Tehran. The government has taken note of the popularity of Sufi mysticism among northern Tehran upper-class youths and in response it has begun to produce its own brand of pop mystical music (a recording of Rumi songs being the first) in order to appropriate or to compete with the Islamic practices that are outside the state's influence.

The mystical journey is something to which no Iranian is a stranger. It can have any number of starts and stops as it runs into problems, goes off course, and comes to conclusions outside of the search. This has been the nature of my relationship with Iran, as someone who was born there (to a practicing Catholic American and a secular Muslim Iranian) and who left at the time of the revolution, and as someone who would return at different periods, beginning with the end of the war, as a long-lost niece and finally as an anthropologist. The jagged nature of my journey was also the nature of my fieldwork, which now dictates the structure of this work.

CHAPTER ONE

The Image and the Hidden Master

It [the Iranian revolution] was a picture-perfect revolution.

PETER CHELKOWSKI

ISFAHAN, CEMETERY OF THE MARTYRS OF THE IRAN-IRAQ WAR, SPRING 2000 *Row upon row of young male faces, frozen in framed photographs, stare out from the gates of the cemetery. The technicolor backgrounds suggest innocent auras or angelic visions. Many of the boys have small tufts of hair above their upper lip in an attempt to look older—a more benign attempt than the one that landed them in this premature resting place. As you walk along reading each unique name, epitaph, longing, and desire to die written in last will and testaments—a declaration of loyalty to the nation and Islam neatly penned from Khomeini's writings—you sense the individual in the shadow of similarities. You continue row by row until you reach the back of the cemetery where you will turn around and return. It takes half an hour before you reach the end and can turn to face the front. The backs of the elevated picture cases face you now, and you expect to be safely protected from the stares, to have a moment of reprieve before you walk back through the crowd of dead faces. But your expectation of blank boards is instead met by hundreds of pictures of the same face, that of Khomeini—the shadow, the unmovable*

2. Photos on the graves at the cemetery of the war martyrs, Is-fahan. (Photo by Kimyia Varzi, 2000)

image glued to the reverse side of every dead boy's individual illumination—stares back at you. His is the ghost here that most haunts. He is the reverse side of every unique martyr.

In Khomeini's Iran the concept of the image functioned as more than just a sign; it was an actual actor on the political stage. Those in power knew the strength of the image to foster belief and to topple a regime. Ayatollah Khomeini told his followers at the beginning of the Iranian revolution in 1979 not to be discouraged by the lack of arms: "propaganda," he noted, "is as explosive as a grenade." [1] In Khomeini's Iran, the image was a site of special power that must either be contained or exploited. The cultural architects of this period created a perfect balance by politically exploiting some images while containing others by restricting visual subjects that could potentially undermine the Islamic program.

During both the war and the revolution the Western media portrayed Iran as an impermeable surface of images and imaginings:

3. Image of Khomeini that usually appears on the back of a grave is here superimposed on the front, cemetery of the war martyrs, Isfahan. (Photo by Kimyia Varzi, 2000)

a nation of angry fists and of crazed martyrs rushing the frontlines of battle with the Iraqis; a place where for years the black and red colors of mourning and martyrdom shrouded the nation. The foreign press devoured these images, created at the height of Iran's revolutionary fervor, and regurgitated them faster than the Islamic republic could produce them. While the Western press for the most part has misrepresented the Islamic republic of Iran, at the beginning of the war they actually played right into the Islamic project.

The state carefully controlled the perception of two different audiences holding two opposing ideas about the same place. What was constructed domestically was not the picture allowed for export internationally. And, while forbidden satellite dishes infiltrated this domestic project, thereby allowing Iranians a glimpse of the world outside the Islamic sphere, little about the Islamic republic's actual domestic scene was known outside of Iran. This strict division of domestic and international image production was especially true of the war. The government kept complete property rights to all war images by giving only a few and select foreign reporters permission to report on the war from the inside; they knew that the images were the true spoils of this war. As I demonstrate in the pages following, it was the war that ultimately defined the Islamic republic as an image machine.

In revolutionary Iran images were only acceptable if they promoted an Islamic lifestyle, the glory of the Islamic republic, or the sanctity of the imam. At first an Islamic public sphere was created in which Khomeini was the sole living human image. This was reversed years later, just before Khomeini's death, when most currency and stamps contained photographs of martyrs and revolution heroes but rarely pictures of Khomeini himself. Could this policy have been, as Peter Chelkowski suggests, a clever manipulation of the people to suggest that Khomeini is their chosen representative? Chelkowski bases this idea on observing the expectation that the people themselves will "out of love and devotion carry his portraits and decorate every conceivable surface with his image." [2] Khomeini projected his own image as that of the nation, and thus to love the nation was to love Khomeini. Hidden in every image that portends freedom was the ideology of subordination to a leader and to death: the absolute masters. [3] The situation was similar to the case in Iraq where, as Samir al-Kahil notes, "much as Americans experience in daily life the culture of consumerism and advertising, Iraqis experience the awesome power of their leader." [4]

Khomeini secured power through his own image by reproducing it everywhere, and his photographic image played as important a political role as did the man himself. Through these images the country would memorize his face, not just as a visual act but also as an act of blind habit. Moreover, not only was Khomeini's photograph looked at, but it also looked back. He was always watching, knowing, and most important: known. Susan Sontag claims that politicians never look directly into the camera,[5] but this was not true of Khomeini whose penetrating gaze, even after his death, still stares out at his subjects from the highest place on every public wall in Iran.

If, as Walter Benjamin notes, the aura as a "unique phenomenon of distance however close it might be, represents nothing but the cult value of the work of art," then Khomeini's photograph is the perfect cult object in its ability to create distance through his penetrating gaze.[6] In a regime of paint and paper (most images in Tehran were, and are, painted), Ayatollah Khomeini was the only living person to be represented through photographic film negative;[7] his was the only image worthy of photography and, in turn, of mass production.[8] As such, he becomes the all-seeing leader who appears everywhere because photography is easily mass produced. This was especially true of the war years, as documented in the fascinating and morbid book The Imposed War: Defense vs. Aggression, published by the Ministry of War.[9] As page after page reveals images of death and destruction and moments of religious zeal, the reader cannot help but concentrate on the one image that remains constant throughout—that of Khomeini. While not physically present on the battlefront, Khomeini is there in spirit in the form of his photograph pinned to every living and dead soldier's uniform (and later, as noted above, affixed to the graves of the dead).

In the opening credits of Morteza Avini's documentary on the war, soldiers march past a picture of Khomeini pinned to a palm tree.[10]

In order to understand this image regime we need to look at the important function of the guide in mystical Islam and ways in which the notion of the guide was utilized in the creation of an Islamic republic. In the first part of this chapter I concentrate on the image regime created by the cultural architects of the revolution, especially that of Khomeini who manipulated the mystical use of images to place himself as the sole guide and interpreter of such a regime. The image is an important device used by novices on the Sufi path to move from earthly love to metaphoric love and finally to divine oneness. The image is also tied to a larger world of images, the *alam-al-mithal* (world of images or archetypes), which can only be accessed by a seer with the kind of vision that is the result of alchemy, magic, dreams, and love.[11] In some Sufi orders it is fundamental for a novice to locate a guide who is practiced at *tawil*, Shiite hermeneutics, to navigate through the image world.[12] When the novice has mastered tawil, or comes closer to oneness, the exoteric guide is no longer needed because the hidden master that is connected to the alam-al-mithal is now found within.[13]

While the image is a vehicle to oneness with the beloved in mystical Islam, it can also function as a distraction on the mystic path.[14] The novice runs the risk of veering off the path by looking for the image from without and forgetting that the real beloved is within the seeker's own being. The twelfth-century Persian writer Nizami Ganjavi illustrates the danger (and mystical utility) of the image in his *Tale of Leili and Majnun*. In Nizami's story, it is the mental image of Leili that allows Majnun the ultimate spiritual experience of oneness with God, but this happens only after he forsakes her image in favor of what he has already internalized—her image. In researching war images, it is clear that some Iranian soldiers who came to the war on a spiritual path used Khomeini's image as a vehicle to oneness, yet they never arrived at the stage where the image is discarded in favor of true oneness. Most of the soldiers died before reaching the point on the mystic path where they realized that the image was no longer necessary, for the beloved was already within them. Death played the role of ultimate union.[15]

Nizami Ganjavi's *Tale of Leili and Majnun* can be used to help fully appreciate the historic role of the image in mystical Islam and in Khomeini's Iran. This tale was composed in Persian around 1188 in what is present-day Azerbaijan. Written in the form of a lyric poem, the story is based on an Arab legend of ill-fated lovers: a

4. Body of
a martyred
soldier in
the Iran-Iraq
war. (Photo
by Seiffollah
Samadian,
1981)

young boy named Qays falls in love with Leili, who has already been
promised to another man. When Qays is prevented from marrying
Leili he isolates himself in the desert to compose poems lament-
ing his love. The people of the community observe his actions and
they are compelled to give him a new persona—that of the character of a talented poet and a pronounced madman, Majnun. Leili
and Majnun are never united in life, but in death they are buried in
a single tomb.

In *Leili and Majnun* the journey to the core of abandon (and an
eventual union with the ultimate beloved—God) begins innocently,
a requited love that will take the inevitable archetypical tragic turn
when the lover makes the mistake of revealing his love publicly, to
the detriment of his social obligations as a student and son. As a
result he is forcefully distanced from his beloved, which begins his
journey of abandon and madness. Mystics often choose metaphori-

cal love in preparation for divine love. At the core of this tale is the platonic notion that the nature of love is an irrational desire toward physical beauty, if only an image, which ultimately will end in self-annihilation, bi-khodi. Jalal al-Din Rumi (or Mawlana), a contemporary of Nizami's and perhaps the most famous Sufi poet ever to live, believed this union and self-annihilation could only work if the fire of love burned within the image.[16] Rumi believed that only by killing the rational self, nafs, and becoming a martyr of love, shahid, can one become a witness to God's truth.[17]

We see the image function in this capacity as Nizami's story progresses and Majnun replaces Leili with her image. The image is what will allow him to move from physical to spiritual love. When Majnun is separated from Leili he incorporates her in his imagination as memory, and by doing so he makes her present in everything.

The degree to which Leili has become incorporated, mythical, metaphorical, and ethereal is most evident when Majnun faints during his only opportunity to be with her. He has already incorporated her, and her physicality no longer exists for him. Leili's presence takes away the distance necessary to propel him on his mi'raj (journey). What is described as madness or a visionary state is a way of envisioning and seeing the beloved. The beloved and lover can only be united or present to each other in the realm of the unconscious, which Majnun enters through fainting. It is the replication of the beloved's mental image that Majnun has incorporated at the expense of his own identity; Leili's image becomes his "reality." She is replaced by an image that moves from flesh to word. Leili's image brings her closer to him yet also keeps her at a comfortable distance, allowing for desire to take effect. Such contemplation of the image (mental or physical), like the repetition of a name, is a step toward divine union while keeping a foot in the "real" world. It is the image that is incorporated and consumed. This brings the novice closer to the world of image and sign, alam-al-mithal.[18]

The mystic Ibn Arabi states that it is the creative imagination that links the mystic to alam-al-mithal.[19] In the Tale of Leili and Majnun, the entrance into alam-al-mithal can only happen through a move of bi-khodi or self-loss, thereby killing the nafs. Like Majnun, the novice may seek the beloved through an object or being on the outside, not realizing that the beloved is an image that has already been incorporated within. Majnun discovers this when Leili comes to stand before him and threatens to replace the image of her that he has already internalized. The internalization of the image is what has allowed Majnun the ultimate presence of self—which Leili's material presence threatens to destroy. The image can no longer be real when she is present, and if the image is not real then the spiritual experience is less powerful.[20] Thus the image is not outside of him but within him. As Henry Corbin remarks: "So excessive is the nearness that it acts at first as a veil. That is why the inexperienced novice, though dominated by the image which invests his whole inner being, goes looking for it outside of himself, in a desperate search from form to form of the sensible world, until he returns to the sanctuary of his soul and perceives that the real beloved is deep within his own being; from that moment on he seeks the beloved only through the beloved."[21]

The first symptom of bi-khodi is a disregard for the protective barriers that society furnishes for the self. Shame and humiliation fade as the self becomes centered on a new self: an object of love. For mystics this is the first step toward truth, toward the stripping of cultural clothing and baring the soul. This happens when Qays is renamed "Majnun," as one who is not "self"-contained (bi-khod).[22] Revelation, an unveiling of self, is an important act in the mystical journey of love and abandon. The first physical sign of Qays's state is his use of and relation to language; an early symptom that identifies a breakdown of self is the loss of coherent speech.[23] Is reality just a discursive practice? Is the beginning of self-erosion a move to create distance from common signification, pointing to the role of metaphor? Are "real" objects, including nations and states, no more and no less than the effects of discourse?

The mystical voice becomes a poetic inscription of being or incorporation, the ultimate connection between words, reality, and desire. Of a piece with this is the move by desire to contain or consume the image by means of metaphor. The repetition of memory through symbols is tied to the issue of inspiration, through the collectively symbolized unconscious as represented by the world of archetypes, the alam-al-mithal. For Sufis the name, tied to an image or a nonimage, is the key to meditation and trance in the practice of *zekr*, where the various names of God are repeated in order to concentrate on becoming completely centered on His being.[24] For Rumi, love is a mi'raj, a heavenly journey to divine presence, to a state of selflessness, bi-khodi. This is the state that Sufis enter in the practice of zekr, where they replace their nafs, or self, with His name.[25] Rumi says that lovers are strange because the more they are killed the more they are alive. It is this symbolic death (of the nafs) that is paramount to the Sufi experience.[26]

When Qays leaves for the desert and begins what is perceived as his mad rants and poetic songs of love, he is named Majnun. He has become conscious of language's failures to be transparent, and he comes to stand beside his own name, highlighting its difference. The first step to bi-khodi is to abandon the proper name, discarding that which labeled and defined him as a rational being in society, accountable to that society for having allowed him to enter into signification by giving him the gift of speech.[27] However, while the signification may work in a practical sense, it turns out to be a hindrance to contemplation of the beloved: "One can only see the shell but not the kernel. The name is only the outer shell, I am the veil. The face underneath is hers."[28] These words resonate with those of Rumi when he says, in the opening of his famous text *Masnavi*, "the lover is the sentence, and the beloved, the veil." Majnun abandons his own "identity" by shedding his proper name, Qays, and by taking on a common noun, *Majnun*, to incorporate the beloved.[29] "He escaped from Leili in order to find her."[30]

In death the lovers, two lost souls, finally unite as one. The mask is removed and love in its finality becomes the consumption of self and other: the ultimate mirror of dead images. The subject and object of love become interchangeable.[31] The soul, keeper of self and love, is released in death. The lover reaches the state of ecstasy, of self-annihilation. For Ibn Arabi the annihilation of the self is the moment of divine epiphany, a notion that is illustrated when Majnun says that he no longer knows himself and has death inside of himself. He has forgotten himself and abandoned subjectivity in order to find truth.[32]

Majnun's journey is thus the journey of a transcendental subject toward truth. It is the juxtaposition of two different notions of truth: first, the restoration of self (khod or nafs) through memory and language, as revealing the truth; and, second, the mystical belief that truth emerges in forgetfulness that is a symptom of love and that results in self-annihilation. It is this journey of the self toward bi-khodi through the use of an external beloved, a master who will form a connection to the alam-al-mithal (through the use of his own image) that I now turn to in light of Khomeini's Islamic Iran.

THE GUIDE OR HIDDEN MASTER

In Attar's *The Conference of the Birds* the nightingale is the first to come forward with an excuse as to why he cannot continue the journey toward the Simurgh: he cannot be without the love of the rose. So the Hoopoo tells him: "Oh nightingale you would stay behind dazzled by the exterior form of things, cease to delight in an attachment so deluding. The love of a rose has many thorns; it has disturbed and dominated you. Although the rose is fair her beauty is soon gone. One who seeks self-perfection should not become the slave of a love so passing. Forsake the rose and blush for yourself, for she laughs at you with each new spring and then she smiles no more."[33]

The Hoopoo warns all of the birds that the surface, an image, is the most powerful of manipulators. The hardest lesson for the disciple to learn (because it is a lesson revealed only with time) is that the image betrays, decays, and manipulates reality, eventually leading the seeker astray.[34]

Khomeini was not only the interpreter and guide of this symbolic world, but he helped to create that world. There is no better example of a nation that is both a discursive construct and an image regime than the Islamic republic of Iran.[35] Khomeini wooed the nation with speeches and leaflets to bring down a powerful U.S.-backed army. He was a *ghazal* poet, and his speeches replicated Sufi ideals to explicate the relationship between citizens and Allah.[36] He asked the Iranian people which they preferred, union and submission to God or submission to the shah, and they chose the abstract ideal that was so prevalent in their secular discourses of love and poetry.

Khomeini's mode of speech is full of Sufi terminology, like *tariqa*, the path leading into the natural realm, or of being directed by angel muses.[37] Most important is the notion of the self, khod, particularly the nafs.[38] Khomeini warns the Iranian people that the nafs is dangerous and must be tamed; nafs must be transcended: "Who can escape this temple of the self, this idol-temple that is situated within man himself? Man needs a helping hand from the world of the unseen to reach him and lead him out. It is precisely for this purpose that the prophets have been sent and all the holy books revealed."[39] Khomeini thus stresses the importance of a guide, of tapping into the other world, the alam-al-mithal.

In Shiism the relationship of the novice to the alam-al-mithal is complicated by the promise of a hidden or absent imam, the ultimate sheik, the master who went into occultation in 874 and promised to return.[40] Khomeini played on the promise of this return and the idea of a hidden master by emphasizing his adeptness in tawil (Shiite hermeneutics) and thereby placed himself in the role of grand interpreter, all the while constructing his own grand narrative. For the great Sufi mystics the hidden master functions in a space of absence, creating nostalgia and a desire to move closer toward the master, which can only be done through self-annihilation. For Rumi, it was Shams al-Din Tabrizi; for Majnun it was Leili. The role of the hidden master is to facilitate a connection between the disciple and the world of archetypes that results in revelation.[41] As Ibn Arabi notes, "Such a relationship with a hidden spiritual master lends the disciple an essentially trans-historic dimension and presupposes an ability to experience events that are enacted in a reality other than the physical reality of daily life, events which spontaneously transmute themselves into symbols."

The move to absent the physical beloved in favor of a mental image is an important moment in Sufism that is born of the mystic longing or yearning to be reunited with the beloved. This longing is grounded in the theme of absence that keeps earthly disciples in constant search for otherworldly connections, meanings, and signs. This tie to the other world allows an essential symbolic understanding: it is the transmission into signs of everything visible; it is the notion of absence that will allow us to make the leap from Sufi understanding to recognizing how Khomeini used these ideas in his political movement.

Khomeini placed himself in the role of absolute leader of the Shiites, which gave him an unmediated connection to the alam-al-mithal. He claimed legitimacy through his ability to interpret signs from the other world, thus allowing him to forsake all masters for the hidden master within him (founded in his own genius in Islamic jurisprudence and tawil). His orthodoxy was a claim to recognize no earthly master.

Khomeini's move from revolutionary cleric to mystic guide became apparent during his exile in Paris.[42] Whether or not he had planned it, Khomeini's exile created a longing for his return (the return of the beloved). Through exported tape recordings of his sermons from France, he became the creative imagination and active intelligence that was the connection to the alam-al-mithal. Khomeini was the muse of dormant rebelliousness and of a religious fire that burned within his followers and his own image. In his political speeches to Iranians prior to the revolution he emphasized the importance of an absent master at the same time that he regarded God as the absolute master. An invisible master allows autonomy, and Khomeini was at once master, muse, and beloved. His image became the sign of the Iranian revolution, a sign for change.

Khomeini brought out the romantic myth of reunion with the beloved (a myth that is defined by many as Iranian but not necessarily Islamic). Ensuing from the rhetorical and subtle reminders of this mystic myth in Iranian tradition was a yearning and a need, which was replaced with an image—Khomeini's. His exile created a longing much as Leili's absence did for Majnun.

For Iranians at the beginning of the revolution Khomeini was already a new language, a new religion. His discourse complimented that of the revolutionary intellectuals Jalal Al-Ahmad and Ali Shariati, who were calling for Iranians to return to their roots.[43] The discourse of modern loss and natural longing began with the writer Jalal Al-Ahmad's *Westoxification*, which warned that modernity's disease was like a cancer killing the Iranian/Islamic spirit. Khomeini then appropriated this (Marxist-inspired) language of nationalism; he took Persian words and replaced them with Arabic, a language best known to the clergy as that of Islam (according to strict Islamic interpretations, the Quran is not to be read in any language other than Arabic). Some Persian words were too powerful to change and had to be utilized in such a way to suggest that they were always associated with the Islamic revolution; like the term *mellat*, citizen, which became Islamic Mellat, referring to an Islamic citizen in particular. Once appropriated, the word that graced the names of the shah's national bank, parks, and schools became a revolutionary term — one that could be interpreted as Islamic or as reminiscent of the nationalist Mohammad Mossadegh, or even used in the broader sense of simply an Iranian national.[44] The old vocabulary was used to create new structures.

Khomeini's word was incorporated and consumed (in much the same manner as that of Leili and Majnun and the analysis of the image in Shiite Islam). Love burned within the image of Khomeini; he became the first metaphor, a step, toward absolute love — a veil for God. His photograph, like Leili's image for Majnun, became Iran's reality while the country awaited his return.[45] As Corbin notes, "The degree of spiritual experience depends on the degree of reality invested in the image."[46] The time was ripe for the return of the imam, but the one in Paris, or the one in hiding? The line became blurred.

As the shah's regime buckled under the pressure of posters and cassette tapes (along with the help of Marxists, nationalists, feminists, and postmodern philosophers) the degree and power of reality invested in Khomeini's image became obvious. Khomeini

returned as an interpreter for an Islamic state, as preparation of redemption, to pave the way to God. His absence was so great and the
longing so strong that his return was overwhelming (as was Leili's
for Majnun).

The beginning of the Iranian revolution saw followers in the
streets repeating both Allah's name and that of Khomeini: *Allah-o
akbar, Khomeini rahbar* (God is great, Khomeini is our leader).[47] Fists
beat heaving chests and banners flew as Khomeini transported the
nation to the world of image and sign. The millions who marched to
the airport in 1979 to greet Khomeini is an indication of the mystical state, of the reality invested in the image. Khomeini "imagined"
the nation as a servant of God and as something closer to heaven,
and he did the same for himself as a mediator between heaven and
earth.[48] He placed himself between the people and God in order to
interpret, or rather to write, the rules of a religious state.[49]

THE ISLAMIC REPUBLIC

Khomeini's campaign to illuminate the evils of the shah's regime
and subjugate it to morality began in the early 1960s. At the same
time, Ali Shariati was convincing the people of Iran that the act of
intizar, of patiently waiting for the hidden imam, would not serve
the nation. "The hidden imam will not reappear of his own accord:
human intervention is needed to pave the way for his final coming.
People need to begin the imam's work of overthrowing oppression
and implementing universal justice in order to occasion his ultimate return and revolution."[50] Between Khomeini's juridical authority and Shariati's mass appeal, many in the general public were
convinced that the nation must rise up and prepare for the coming
of the imam, even if that imam was not officially the hidden imam.

Khomeini played on the popularity and expectation of the hidden imam to derive legitimacy directly from the people. Eventually,
Khomeini allowed his proper name to be replaced with the title
imam, and it was this title that he took to his grave. He did this
by redefining the modern Shiite conception of imam, by first de-

mystifying it and later by picking up on the mythic mystic notion to give himself absolute power. He began his rhetorical campaign by claiming that the prophet allowed for an open translation of Shiite law, provided that the right jurist appeared to help the people interpret meaning from the symbolic world. Corbin and Allamah Tabataba'i explain that Shiism inherently allows for interpretation, and that "laws that can guarantee the happiness of human society cannot be perceived by reason. Since according to the thesis of general guidance running throughout creation the existence of the awareness of these laws in the human societies is necessary, there must be another power of apprehension within the human species which enables man to apprehend the real duties of life and which places this knowledge within the reaches of everyone. This consciousness and power of perception, which is other than reason and sense, is called the prophetic consciousness, or the consciousness of revelation. Of course the presence of such a power in mankind does not mean that it should necessarily appear in all individuals."[51]

Max Weber says that while kings are divinely ruled by God, the charismatic leader is responsible to those he rules, a God-willed master who bears his responsibility by showing his people the way.[52] Khomeini was already a source of emulation, a mardja-i-taqlid (one worthy of imitation), and he was set apart from ordinary clergy by his unwavering stance against the shah. Here legitimacy is not derived from genealogy, but from acquired qualities and ritual acts that the individual possesses. Charisma can only be awakened or tested, but never learned.[53] Khomeini was a charismatic leader when charismatic leaders were in short supply and in great demand. He concentrated on goals and issues that appealed to the masses, eventually leading the young supporters of Shariati to bestow the title "imam" on the only ruler they believed to be a truly charismatic leader who could carry the revolution and lead the ummat (Moslem society) to a classless society.[54]

In life, Khomeini lived in a simple, quiet home in the hills of northern Tehran. In death he resides in a huge, ornate mausoleum that boasts a large mosque and an even larger parking lot. His tomb

5. Khomeini's mausoleum, road to Ghom, Iran. (Photo by Faraz Sanaii, 2004)

is as large as any reputably sized mosque in Iran, and it is covered in bronze and gilded in gold. Its existence sprouted synthetically from the desert dirt—nothing surrounds this concoction but endless stretches of desert plains. An airport was built nearby to ease the tribulations of pilgrimages to the site. The actual tomb is covered in a Zarih, a silver cage like those of the imams and imamzadehs: Khomeini is buried like any imam. Because in the Middle East bazaars tend naturally to spring up around mosques, the bazaar at Khomeini's site was preplanned by the government in order to speed the process of developing the area into a pilgrimage site. The prominently placed small bazaar sells everything from posters of the late imam to Cover Girl lipstick. Free tea is served from large scalding-hot cauldrons, and mourning music and posters of the late Ayatollah are sold from little stands.[55] Seventeen years after his death, the enormity of the place makes it seem like there are few visitors.

While Khomeini's mausoleum attests to his greatness and status as an imam, his house is preserved as a testament to his modesty and status as a man of the people. It is generally overlooked by the public, except for groups of schoolboys on fieldtrips or a stray mother and daughter on a personal pilgrimage. From the small courtyard outside of his house, the voices of the boys are heard as they run around the adjacent mosque loudly reciting the Quran. In the mosque and in the portrait gallery (full of envelopes addressed to Khomeini in different languages and bearing stamps from all over the world and dated roughly before the revolution) the largeness of his legend starts to become apparent. Thus it is surprising to enter the tiny courtyard of his home to find only one entrance to his personal world: a window, only barely transparent, where one must move closer and closer beyond one's own reflection before barely making out the imam's slippers placed at the foot of his chair, along with a robe, plastic flowers, and a roll of toilet paper. In this light Weber writes: "For the ascetic, the divine imperative may require of human creatures an unconditional subjection of the world to norms of religious virtue and indeed a revolutionary transformation of the world for this purpose. In that event the ascetic will emerge from his remote and cloistered cell to take his place in the world as a prophet in opposition to the world—he will always demand of the world an ethically and rational order and discipline corresponding to his own methodical self-discipline." [56]

Khomeini's greatest achievement was his ability to elicit a feeling of equality among members of a nation composed of seventeen different ethnic groups and six different religions, not to mention a highly stratified class system.[57] Every class, ethnic group, and religion came together under Khomeini to fight for justice. He created a group feeling similar to what Ibn Khaldun terms *assabiya* (unity): a Muslim nation that extends beyond the boundaries of the Iranian nation. Khomeini was able to articulate eloquently what so many were afraid to voice.

Once Khomeini came to power the diversity of the political groups that brought down the shah was wiped out in favor of one system: Islamic governance. Newspaper reporters asked Khomeini what form his new government would take. No particulars were given; instead he invoked the only person to have combined religious leadership with temporal power—the first imam, Ali, the father of Husayn. Later, after establishing the republic, Khomeini stated: "Everywhere the goal is the same: an Islamic government. It is possible, of course, that some people understand and accept the concept of an Islamic government without knowing the details of its functioning, but what is certain is that the whole of Iran . . . is unanimously proclaiming its demand for an Islamic government." [58]

Shortly before Khomeini's return to Iran, Said Arjomand interviewed him and asked the question on everyone's minds: "How should one relate what you have written in *Velayat-i-faqih* to the actual political organization of Iran and the management of daily affairs?" In response, Khomeini stated that his famous book on Islamic governance, *Velayat-i-faqih: Hukumat-i-Islami (Guardianship of the Clergy: Islamic Government)*, was about the principles of government, not its organizational structures. The main focus of the text is the fundamental principle of sovereignty as the right of the religious jurists. As he explained to Arjomand: "The details of the matter of actual organization will have to be dealt with by appropriate laws which will be enacted later," [59] although no one was quite clear about the meaning of "later" or what defines an "appropriate" law. Khomeini did separate basic laws (traffic regulations and urban planning) from sacred law, however, and wrote that it is "beneath the dignity of Islam to concern itself with basic laws." [60] Yet the basic question continued to be evaded.

Khomeini never wavered in his determination to implement the mandate of the clergy. As soon as he returned to Iran he began a project that required a drastic reworking of the state. The judiciary system was desecularized and brought under the control of the clergy, and the jurisdiction of the state was to be restricted to "laws beneath the dignity of Islam," such as traffic regulations and the economy. The legislative branch would pass laws, and the executive branch would implement them. The concept of *Vilayat-*

i-faqih was incorporated into the Islamic republic's first constitution—only now it was no longer the governance of the jurists but the government of the jurist.[61]

Implementing the Islamic government was a well-planned enterprise. The first step was the almost organic development of the komiteh (Islamic police), where committees (komiteh) of banditlike revolutionaries sprang up from the poorest masses to revive the old Sharia-style courts.[62] Nothing was written in law, and no criterion was directly attributable to the Quran; it was Khomeini's word, as a mediator between Allah and the people of Iran, that came to be law. The fluidity of the law gave the komiteh absolute power of interpretation to make on-the-spot decisions about lashings and fines based on appropriate behavior and dress. While the komiteh kept some semblance of Islamic order, the revolutionary council kept busy preparing for elections and drawing up a constitution.[63] As Arjomand notes, "Putting doctrinal emphasis on the continuous quality of the imamate . . . endows the jurist as the representative of the hidden imam, with supreme power over men and responsibility only to God." Under the jurist is a council of guardians with extensive powers to represent the Shiite religious institution and insure that the legislative and executive branches stay within the framework of the constitution.

The next move was that of a cultural revolution to desecularize the education system by purging Western-influenced individuals, tagootis, from the system. Throughout summer 1979 an intense effort at "Islamization" was enacted, which included new "Islamic" rules of behavior.[64] Soon, the government began to take a harder stand on the rules for appropriate Islamic behavior. As clerical power was consolidated, the memory of a "Persian" monarchial past became a threat, and thus all books related to monarchy, including those by William Shakespeare, were banned or burned. The country was thus purged of any Western or monarchial influence and sympathy. A dress code was instilled that physically identified the mellat (those who stayed as opposed to those who emigrated) as good Muslims and nationals. Men were forbidden from wearing ties, short sleeves, or anything too overly bourgeois or Western, and a mandatory Islamic dress of head and body covering was enforced for females above the age of ten.[65] Conduct between the sexes was enforced according to strict religious criteria—men and women were kept apart in order to protect them from the temptation of carnal passion—which only heightened the desire for union. The only acceptable union was that with God.

CHAPTER TWO

Mystic States

Martyrdom and the Making

of the Islamic Republic

Hello, my country:

What is this love, this spark that a delicate song brings to my heart and soul with such skill? Our delicate hearts that pulsate in the chest, ignited by fire in the bones: how can they end this lyre of love within themselves? A love whose pain runs in the flesh and veins like wild green ivy. Like the songs of spiders—maybe. These pains, these pains that bubble with love in a person, they swirl and boil, these are sweet pains—the result of a surreal trance. These pains with the colorless illusions that silence every tear, yet hit the ear with delicate songs of love. It engulfs the soul and opens it to rebellion. It rebels. A fine and delicate chaos.

SEYYED YASSER HASHTROODI

And then there was war, or the "sacred defense" as it is called. In mystical allegories there are no real wars, only the ones fought within oneself. But there are wars in the *Shah Nameh* (Book of Kings) and in other ancient Persian texts. These wars—Persian, Greek, and Roman—consolidated empires, expanded spheres of influence, and began an age-old practice that assured a cultural space and the legitimacy of "nationhood." When Attar's birds set out on their journey they saw themselves as a country, a bounded group of people. Their concern was with the legitimacy of their country, and they knew that in order to be legitimate and persevere as a nation, they needed a ruler.

So it was not their choice, nor their need for assurance as to the status of their nation's legitimacy; rather it was the leader who insisted that they engage. The war distracted the birds as their leader set about changing their notion of home. It was during this time that many of the birds flew west, and still others flew east. Those that stayed did not necessarily agree with the war, but they still believed that they must come together to defend their nation, which was now threatened, not from the outside as they thought but from the choices they made on the inside.

THE MYSTIC CALL, 1983 *The desert was a plump, warm, and soft mother who held her two warring boys on separate thighs while they slept, divided by a small gulf between her legs (no-man's-land). She stroked their foreheads with a warm, musty palm and blew their brows with sea breath that smelled of part exploded gun shell, part seashell. Crackling bombs and red flares, tripping on ecstasy, tripping upon a war.*

"Do you think they sleep?" a soft voice next to Amir asks.

"Who, the generals? Most definitely," he laughs softly, here among the Basij one can put down professional warmongers without the threat of being court-martialed. But one should still be careful. He wants to make a friend. He likes these men. They're not like the ones in Tehran. They are not military men; they fight for a belief.

"No, the Iraqis. You would think in all this silence we could hear them breathe."

"We cannot sleep, why would they?" Amir leans over and unearths his cigarettes. The light of the match illuminates his friend's face for a moment. He is young, with longish hair. The Basij come as is—sometimes without uniform or army haircuts, depending on when they volunteered and from where. It is a moonless, dark night.

"Would you like one?" Amir extends the pack.

"No, thank you." After a polite pause, the young man continues. "They are doing this because they hate us, they want land. It's a military operation for them, like work. We are fighting for our namus, our nation," he says, sounding more like he's trying to convince himself than to state a fact.[1]

"Do you think that Iranian soldiers who were drafted and do not believe in this war can sleep any easier?"

"There's no such thing, we all want to defend Iran and Islam — we all believe in this war."

"Yes, but, well, the Iraqi soldiers did not have a choice . . . I mean, I do not know."

"I'm a Muslim, I believe in peace, but I must also defend God."

"Are they not Muslims?"

"Are you defending them?"

"No," Amir says softly, giving up the argument before it's even begun. "What did you do before the war?"

"I studied engineering. I played tambour."

"A Sufi instrument."

"Yes."

"I played daf."

"A Sufi instrument," the young man chuckles. Amir can feel him smiling at him in the dark.

"Why did you volunteer to come to the front?"

"It's the express lane to martyrdom, to paradise. We have a much better chance of getting martyred here than in Tehran." Amir had expected something different, something spiritual but not quite so mechanic: martyrdom, beginning and end of story.

"How are you assured paradise?"

"Do you not read the Quran?

"Of course I do, but, well, it seems like an easy way out of our earthly duties."

"I'm still doing earthly duties, until Insh'Allah, God decides it's my time."

"What are those duties, but sitting here waiting to get martyred?"

"I'm using my civil engineering degree." Amir thought this boy was smart. He could tell from his accent that he came from a good upper-middle-class Tehran family.

"Doing what?"

"Making missiles."

"How can you be a Sufi and make instruments of war?"

"It's a holy war."[2]

After the revolution Khomeini banned all mystical practice for strict Islamic jurisprudence; in so doing he made moves to oppress emotion by allowing emotional catharsis only in the purist sense of the mystical definition—by glorifying martyrdom. When Iraq conveniently attacked Iran, the war provided Khomeini with the perfect opportunity to consolidate his authority as a religious leader by sending young martyrs off to the war. The war with Iraq (even more than the revolution) was the largest mobilization ever of the Iranian population, which was achieved primarily by producing and promoting a culture of martyrdom based on religious themes found in Shii Islam. It was the war that created and consolidated what we know today as the Islamic republic of Iran.

The idea of martyrdom came to represent and conflate the ultimate union of citizen and nation, lover and beloved, and servant of God and God. Martyrdom became state policy. Toward the end of the war, street names were changed to those of young martyrs so often that even the post office was lost. The ideal for an Islamic Basij was to die for the nation, which took on the role of an object of love and was replicated discursively in chants and war songs and ultimately inscribed in the names of the dead—young virgin martyrs.[3] The repetition of the memory of glorious death through symbols, especially chants, replaced a coherent language and thought process, bordering on what some might define as mad love or simply madness—majnun.

MARCH 1983 *While his kamikaze-like battalion prepared for martyrdom, signing government-issued forms of last will and testament, prostrating for prayer behind a mullah with an AK–47 strapped to his shoulder, and kissing each other good-bye as they wailed loudly for their soon-to-be widows and fatherless children—for their own eminent deaths—and while palm trees swayed in the breeze of fresh chemical warfare, Amir plotted his mental break-*

down. Instead of running at the oncoming Iraqi tanks with the raw energy of volunteer soldiers battling in the path of God, he would run the other way, screaming "no, no," which is all it would take to win him a one-way ticket on an old cement truck back to Tehran and into a psychiatric hospital. Unlike his father's generation of career soldiers, Khomeini's soldiers were fighting a war. Not since the Anglo-English invasion before the Second World War had Iran had to defend itself.

The revolutionary guard officers who arrested Amir at the Pakistani border the first time he tried to escape gave him the choice of "volunteering" (rather than being cuffed and conscripted). This generous offer was made to avoid a public show of resistance toward military service in front of other unwilling younger boys. Either way he was stuck, so he went along with the charade. Some of those boys were here now and could attest to Amir's voluntary arrival at the draft offices. The other boys, scared and unhappy about military service, also acted politely and addressed their nemesis as sir, only in lower, scared voices. For Amir, a lack of respect led to a lack of fear, making him seemingly more reverent and innocent.[4]

In keeping with Hegel's philosophy we see that history is and continues to be a bloodbath and a dialectical process. (According to Ali Shariati, Hegel's dialectic found God realized in human history.)[5] While the sources that lead from the inception of Hegel's influence on modern Iranian thought are not apparent, it appears in Kojève's reading of Hegel that Hegel's dialectics provide an interesting formula for the Islamic state.[6] Hegel's Christianity could easily be Khomeini's Islam as it is played out in the politics of modern nation-state formation. It is Hegel, through Kojève, who might begin to explain the phenomenon of martyrdom in Iran today, along with the reactions to the war and the impossibility of recovery.

THE SACRIFICIAL LAMB

In discussing martyrdom in Iran, it is important to make a clear distinction between the characteristics of sacrifice explicated by Western theorists such as René Girard and those that I believe to be at play in the Iranian case. Girard's concern is with the masking of violence, or the deferral of violence, inherent in a society through the ritual of sacrifice. His basic premise is that societies use sacrificial rituals to quell a violent urge that is inherent in human society. In the case of Iran, where a bloody revolution had occurred, there was a need to quell violence. The idea of a sacrificial crisis comes into play when the situation is kill or be killed, or what Girard calls a preventative war. In the case of Iran in 1980, a revolution could have quickly turned into a civil war due to the many parties contending for power after the ousting of the shah.

As Girard says, "Society is seeking to deflect upon a relatively indifferent victim, a 'sacrificial' victim, the violence that would otherwise be vented on its own members, the people it most desires to protect."[7] Had this aggression not been redirected to the outside, citizens might have turned on one another and the Islamic republic might not have slipped so easily into place. The government thus found an "other" to which to defer the violence—that of the Mujahidin organization in Iraq, and eventually the Iraqi nation.[8] This was a key move, because once the Islamic republic was formed and contained there was no chance for "othering" within the borders of the nation without instigating possible civil war.

We thus find some explanation in Girard as to why there is an initial need for war, but this explanation does not sufficiently analyze the important role that martyrdom comes to play in the culture of the Islamic republic over the course of the two and a half decades that it has been in existence, or what the state is really hoping to achieve through war. This was more than just a preventive war. The ritual of sacrifice, according to Girard, masks violence; it is a deferral of the violence that is inherent in a society so as to prevent conflicts from erupting. He suggests that the sacred embraces all those forces that are a threat to peace. Or perhaps sacrifice eradicates those forces that threaten the legitimacy of the regime. As Girard says, martyrdom's "vitality as an institution depends on its ability to conceal the displacement upon which the rite is based."[9]

Mysticism (the desire for transcendence), is used again during the war as a vehicle for excitement in encouraging reunion with God, when what is really at stake is protection of a bound and contained society. While the ostensible reason for martyrdom in Iran is a mystical desire for transcendence, or even what Girard would refer to as a sacrificial need, the most immediate concern (not always obvious to willing martyrs) is plainly a matter of national defense and political legitimacy. One Basij I spoke with, however, believed that "the war was not about getting Iraq, but about becoming closer to God."[10]

Ayatollah Khomeini was able to easily awaken the mystic desire because of the strong history and memory of martyrdom already present (because it was dormant as a political force) in Shiite history. Not long before the coming of Khomeini, Ali Shariati spoke about martyrdom. He espoused that through martyrdom all of the sacredness of that ideal and goal transports itself into the existence of the martyr. He writes, "True that his existence becomes a non-existence, but he has absorbed the whole value of that idea for which he negated himself. The martyr becomes sacredness itself. He had been an individual who had sacrificed himself for thought and now he is thought."[11] Historically, Shiite Islam centers on the martyrdoms of Imam Ali and Imam Husayn. These two martyrs hold an important and emotional place in Iranian culture. The death of these Imams are commemorated twice every year in Shiite communities, once on the nineteenth night of Ramadan, when Ali was said to have been killed in a mosque while praying, and again during the month of Muharram, when Husayn was killed on the battlefield at Karbala. Both occasions provide Shiites with a space for cathartic mourning.

ASHURA AND THE KARBALA PARADIGM

After the death of the prophet Mohammed, the Muslim *ulama* (community) stood divided over the question of succession. One group, the Shi'at Ali (partisans of Ali), believed that Ali, the son-in-law of the prophet, should succeed him since he was *ahl-e bayt* (part of the family). Everyone else supported Abu Bakr, the prophet's companion. Abu Bakr ruled for a while, and when Ali was finally permitted to rule (after being passed over several more times), he lasted only a few short years before he was murdered.

When Yazid became caliph the followers of Ali, who came to be known as Shiites, urged Ali's son Husayn to go to Kufa (in modern-day Iraq) and take power. On his way to Kufa he was martyred at Karbala by Yazid's forces. The battle at Karbala left an indelible mark on the relationship between Sunnis and Shiites. According to the Ithna-Ashari Shiite tradition, there have been twelve Imams since Mohammed, and every one of them was persecuted at the hands of a Sunni caliph.[12]

The strong memory of victimization and persecution lives on in the commemorations of the deaths of Ali and Husayn. Their deaths are commemorated twice every year in Shiite communities, once on the nineteenth night of Ramadan, when Ali was killed, and again during the month of Muharram, when Husayn was killed on the battlefield at Karbala. Muharram has become famous for its gory imagery in the procession of Shiite men who beat themselves with heavy chains, cut their foreheads, and pound their chests. In the villages and quieter parts of the cities, residents participate in the dramatic tradition of Ta'zieh (the reenactment of the events at Karbala), and even though the audience already knows the events, the reminder of Husayn's martyrdom elicits an emotional response. The death of Husayn is also commemorated frequently during the year at ceremonies known as rowzehs where the story of his life and martyrdom are sung and wept over.

On the nineteenth of Ramadan, all-night zekrs (meditations) take place in which a mullah sings the tale of Ali's martyrdom while the audience wails—the crescendos rise with each successive blow to the imam's body. Many Sufi orders associated with Imam Ali are extremely serious in their efforts to memorialize his martyrdom. These occasions not only create a space for cathartic mourning, but also reinforce the Sunni-Shiite split by conjuring feelings of victimization on the part of the Shiites at the hands of the Sunnis, and they foster a culture of martyrdom that has become synonymous with Shiism. Elias Canetti describes the events of Muharram:

The passion of Husayn is recounted from wooden pulpits, with as much detail and elaboration of the incidents as possible. The listeners are deeply affected; their cries of "oh Husayn, oh Husayn!" are accompanied by groans and tears. During the first nine days of Muharram, groups of men wander through the streets, their half-naked bodies painted red or black. They tear out their hair, wound themselves with swords, drag chains behind them and perform wild dances ... On the tenth day of Muharram the festival culminates in a great procession originally designed as a funerary parade to reenact the burial of Husayn. The passion play itself, which follows this long and exciting introduction, consists of a loose sequence of forty to fifty scenes ... there is no question of dramatic tension in our sense of the word; what matters is complete participation ... But it is not in theaters during the performance of the passion plays that this crowd undergoes its paroxysm. The "Day of Blood" (Ashura) in the streets of Tehran, involving half a million people, has been described by eyewitnesses: "500,000 people, seized with madness, cover their heads with ashes and beat their foreheads on the ground. They want to give themselves up to torture, to commit suicide in groups, or to mutilate themselves with a refined cruelty." No destiny is accounted more beautiful than to die on the day of Ashura, when the gates of all eight paradises stand wide open for the saints, and everyone seeks to enter there.[13]

Canetti's description of Muharram is poignant for a number of reasons. First, it was written in the late 1950s, just before the Muharram celebrations began to acquire new political meaning and well before the Islamic revolution of 1979. Therefore, unlike other accounts, it was not written to favor any particular details for or as evidence of the political importance of Muharram. What is most interesting about Canetti's account is the way it is placed into history. Indeed, it is noteworthy that the account is situated in a work well outside of Iranian or Islamic studies—Canetti's book is titled *Crowds and Power*, and the Muharram description is found in the chapter titled "The Pack and Religion," in a section called "Islam:

A Religion of War," under a subsection called "The Religions of Lament." Power, religion, war, and lament exactly describe the revolutionary era in modern Iranian history.

Even before the Muharram ceremony was revived as a political force, Canetti used Muharram as an example of a mass force that has the potential to foster power.[14] He writes as an ethnographer, from first-hand travel accounts, not from a social science perspective but from a desire to describe an experience—one that occurred many years ago through the eyes of one who was not emotionally involved. Given this framework, Canetti's account details some important points: Muharram has an incredible potential for power and violence, it is taken seriously and it closely resembles mystical trances (as evidenced in the trancelike flagellation and self-mutilation akin to the daggers with which dervishes are rumored to pierce their cheeks).[15] Canetti's description is of a crowd that, when caught up in the emotion surrounding Muharram, is ready to die for the mere memory of Husayn: "Emotionally the contemplation of the personality and fate of Husayn stands in the center of faith; they are the mainspring of the believers religious experience. His death is interpreted as voluntary self-immolation, and it is through his sufferings that the saints gain paradise."[16]

Shariati, writing on Muharram, explains via Heidegger the importance of Husayn; it is from Heidegger that he takes the claim that an individual is the sum total of all of his or her experiences and knowledge of the world. Thus, even though Husayn is met only in books and ceremonies he becomes a part of contemporary Iranian culture.[17]

The political power of Muharram became more than apparent in December 1978, shortly before the revolution. In late November the shah saw the potential for radical religious zeal inherent in the coming ceremony, and he effectively banned Muharram by not allowing permits to gather publicly.[18] This act only enraged people more, however, and the ayatollahs Shariatmadari and Taleqani urged the people to take to their roofs and chant, "God is great." Muharram began on December second with three days of

6. A photo of a dead soldier held by his son illustrates how images from Muharram became inflated with images of the war against Iraq. (*Kitab Kudak va nojavan, veejeh gesehayeh jang*, edited by Mahmoud Hakimi [Tehran: Ministry of Islamic Guidance, 1982])

violence. In Tehran, thousands spent the night on their rooftops shouting "God is great," while thousands wearing white shrouds to show their willingness to be killed violated the night curfew and poured into the streets. In the end an estimated seven hundred people died.[19]

Khomeini also took advantage of this passion play's potential for violence, both to justify the war against Iraq (based on the old Shiite-Sunni tensions) and to motivate the troops. The Iran-Iraq war institutionalized martyrdom as never before, in part because Khomeini played on the passion of Muharram and the Sufi understanding of abandon. For Iranians, the Iran-Iraq war, like the battle at Karbala, was interpreted as a battle of the righteous against the infidels.

When Saddam Hussein attacked Iran in September 1980, only a few short months into Khomeini's rule, the myth of Karbala had already been revived in the revolutionary discourse and in the speeches following the revolution to commemorate the death of its martyrs. With Karbala already on everyone's minds, it was no surprise that the Iraqi attack invoked a religious rage that Khomeini then made ripe for war. The attack gave Khomeini the perfect opportunity to keep the revolutionary zeal alive by redirecting the masses' attention away from his plans for an Islamic government and toward the "infidel" Iraqi nation. The timing could not have been better. Ayatollah Khomeini called on his new Islamic republic to come forth and defend the nation of Islam. For many, it would become a jihad—holy war.[20] As Medhi Abedi notes, "Traditionally jihad was understood to be justified for three reasons: to repel invasion or its threat, to punish those who had violated treaties, and to guarantee freedom for the propagation of Islam."[21] The notion of jihad is intermingled with the important notion of shahadat, or martyrdom. Without shahadat, there is no jihad; shahadat, like jihad, signifies witnessing and the state of bearing witness.

Khomeini made it clear the war was a spiritual one that the people, and not a professional army, would fight. It would be a sacred defense, a war of good against evil, of spirit against military might, where a human wave of believers would form a wall of defense against the corrupt technology of the Iraqi infidels. Furthermore, in practice Iran had no other choice.[22] When Iraq invaded, Iran was still in a state of revolutionary shock: Khomeini and the council of guardians were busy drawing up the constitution, and the army was in disarray (high-ranking officers were purged, while those posts were given to people with religious and not necessarily military qualifications). Instead of training an army, Khomeini armed the people. He claimed that if the people could not save the nation, it was not worth saving. Soon, the memory of Shah-Yazid was replaced by the new enemy: Saadam-Yazid.[23]

The transition from revolutionary zeal to war zeal was a smooth one. By 1981, in a television broadcast of Friday prayers at Tehran University, Hashemi Rafsanjani claimed that the public virtually begged to become shahids: "They cry, shed tears, and they implore their commanders, 'take me along on the nightly operations so that I may become a shahid.' "[24] As Rafsanjani told the congregation: "Once the bullet strikes the body of our warriors they are carried on the angels wings to paradise where they reside by the prophet and God."[25] "Boundless sermons invited warriors to consider Shahadat. Martyrdom, prayer leaders claimed, was the 'greatest reward' of the Jihad warrior (mujahid). 'It is the most lofty and honorable way to depart from the world, for death in God's way is the reward of Allah in the hereafter, as well as historical global honor and pride.' "[26] According to Khameini, "Remaining alive under the condition of subjugation to the rule of the superpowers is, in reality, death, while death through cutting the bloody claws of the superpower is life."[27]

What motivated those who joined the ranks of the Basij (the volunteer martyrs), many of them in the prime of their youth, to die for an abstract cause? It was more than just speeches at the Friday prayers. Within the first few months of war, a production of persuasion began, and everything from print to celluloid was used to illustrate the beauty of sacrifice.[28] Much of the production happened at the front in interviews, writings by the soldiers, and letters home, which worked both to inspire the troops and give first-hand testimonial that would ultimately encourage other men to join the greatness of dying a martyr's death. Martyrdom is nothing without remembrance and without the cultural industry that keeps the martyr alive after death, because what is promised is eternal glory.[29] Testimonials and memoirs written by the soldiers before death not only attest to the beauty of dying for one's country, but also assure, via a written text, that their lives will continue on earth (even more prominently) after death.

MARCH 4, 1985 *Bombs fly through the air, the sky is ablaze, there is no night . . . Amir looks up from the page to see if the other soldiers are writing in*

بابا
نامه
داده!

7. In traditional schoolbooks a well-known sentence reads, "Dad gave bread" or "Dad gave water"; this one reads "Dad gave a letter" (from the front). (*Kitab Kudak va nojavan, veejeh gesehayeh jang,* edited by Mahmoud Hakimi [Tehran: Ministry of Islamic Guidance, 1982])

their new government-issued journals. The Ministry of War and Islamic Guidance gave notebooks to the Basij to encourage them to write their memoirs. The short, stout representative from Tehran, with his bushy beard and large, square-shaped tinted glasses, suggested that they use poetic phrases wherever possible.[30]

What the hell am I supposed to be writing about? The beauty of blood — this great faith — the way mourning music inspires me to die like every Muslim martyr who came before me? The truth is mourning music makes me sick, Amir thinks, tapping the end of his pen against his nose. Aside from the occasional swoosh of an overhead missile heading for Tehran, the marshy land that hides Amir's battalion is quiet. Their only job now is to wait. But for what?

"Describe the feeling of love and joy you will experience as a beautiful angel carries you on her wings off the holy battlefield to a paradise from which you will look down upon your families and loved ones who will not mourn, but honor your lives," the robust visitor from HQ had suggested before heading straight back to Tehran. "Too bad he could not at least stay for tea," comments an awestruck eighteen-year-old in Amir's battalion.

Amir notices the captain watching him from the corner of his eye, waiting for Amir's response. He has been keeping an eye on Amir since the day he showed up. He is not like the other Basij who volunteered to fight at the front, most of whom came from poor families in the south of Tehran and the provinces. These Basij were illiterate or at best uneducated, and most were at the front for the promise of a better life, in order to submit themselves to God so as to free themselves from hardship. As far as the captain was concerned, Amir's perfect olive complexion, his well-polished and polite Persian, and the odd, almost foreign way about him did not suggest that he was motivated by the same things that motivated the rest of the Basij.

"Our mothers and wives will receive medals from the ministry. Women are even promised salvation through our martyrdom," the young boy continues with a gleam in his eye. Amir is not sure if the gleam in the young boy's eye is pure passion for martyrdom or pure insanity, although he has been in the unit long enough to start differentiating between the two. By unselfishly sacrificing their men, the women and children of the Basij are promised salvation and a lifetime pension.

My mother does not even know I'm here, Amir thinks; imagine the day when she's handed a pension and told it comes from her dead, martyred son who is supposed to be safely studying abroad. And then she'll receive the last will and testament telling her how my only desire in life was to martyr myself for God and country.

Most of the older men in his battalion are illiterate and have given Amir their notebooks so that he can write for them. Amir puts the point of the pen to the paper and writes,

> Fallen camouflaged into the folds of a tent
> olive green on olive green
> chameleon of war
> seeing, but not seen
> He crosses out the first line and writes:
> Swallowed by tent folds

Along with the journals filled with memoirs were the statements of last will and testament, *vasiat nameh*, drafted before the soldiers went to battle according to the instructions of the prayer leaders. These testimonials substantiated the combatant's thirst for martyrdom, because not only do they express the desire of a martyr's death, but also affirm the notion that this death was already predetermined, fated. As one Basij noted:

> "One martyr had wanted to come before Imam Husayn without a head, so a year before his death he had arranged his grave, without room for his head. He died without his head (it was blown off).
>
> One martyr who was born on Imam Ali's birthday asks to die that day. He does.
>
> One martyr asked to die without anything. Have you seen *Men in Black*? It was like the ending of that film. This martyr died and we never found his body. We are merely atoms. Death is not the end. Not for Shiites, anyway.[31]

The late Ayatollah Taleghani stated that because he had seen the truth and believes in the afterlife, he had no fear of death.[32] Rumi talks about a progression from inanimate to vegetable, vegetable to animal, animal to human, human to nothing—a return. When Muslims pray, they are prostrate to the ground to touch the dirt that they will become. The Quran says, "And say not of those who are slain in the way of God: they are dead. Nay, they are living though you perceive not."[33]

Meanwhile, in the camps there was trance, abandon—the promise of leaving the world for a better place.

WEDNESDAY, APRIL 28 *I did not think the Basij were really this crazy*, Amir writes.

I thought that they would cower once they reached the front. But those who orchestrated this mass martyrdom have already thought of that possibility, which is why they prematurely play mourning music and have pep rallies. If these kids were scared of dying, they would never show it. There's too much camaraderie for any one person to selfishly admit fear. No need for drugs—I swear some of these guys are tripping hard naturally.

When the sun begins to set the soldiers stop what they are doing—building small floats in the marshes, knee deep in water, preparing hand grenades or setting mines—to go to the nearest source of clean water and perform their ablutions. When they are through they listen for the call to prayer and begin the prostrations from wherever they are standing.

Amir leaves his chores and pretends to go wash, instead walking away from the water toward a small hill where he sits, pen in hand, watching the sun make silhouettes of the scattered men. He sits in lotus position watching the men become slow shadows moving into the delicate dance of prayer. He takes a deep breath, closes his eyes and begins his meditation. When he opens his eyes it is pitch black, except for the tiny fire the soldiers have kindled near camp. He gathers his notebook and pen and makes his way down to the fire where the men have already begun to form a circle. This morning, the second morning camped at this particular location, a group of khans (Kurds) had come to welcome them and bring them fresh yogurt and bread. As Amir comes closer to the circle, he can see a group of men in traditional Kurdish baggy pants and turbans, warming their dafs by the fire.

"Salaam Aleekum," Amir calls as he approaches, barely extending his arm to shake their hands before they have jumped up to give him the two customary kisses.

"Ya haq," they greet him. A Sufi greeting.

He gives them a half bow of respect and points to the dafs warming by the fire, saying, "This is a happy day." He smiles but does not tell them that he plays. Amir's captain watches the interaction, finally feeling at ease with Amir who appears to be excited about tonight's program. Perhaps he is one of them.

"Ya Husayn," calls the captain. The imam, martyr of Shiite Islam whose blood was spilled centuries ago on Iraqi soil in a town called Karbala, is invoked for inspiration.

"We will reclaim Karbala," calls the captain.

"Ya'Allah," answer the men.

"Allah-akbar (God is great)."

"Khomeini rahbar (Khomeini is our leader)."

Amir is both fascinated and frightened by the loud awakening of these usually mild-mannered men. He stands awestruck until someone takes his wrist and pulls him back into the circle that is forming. The men weave their arms over one another's shoulders until they are a wall of flesh, a circle of flesh, before they slowly and methodically begin to rotate the circle, stepping with their left foot first, quietly at first, softly humming, "Hu, hu." They sound like owls lost in the night. The dafs join in from outside the circle, quiet at first, slow, then building to a strong pulse that causes the men nearly to pound down their left foot in exclamation with each step. Once the rhythm is established, the men bow their heads in and out of the circle. A human chain rotating on a special axis around the fire, like the Sufis of old who rotated around the sun, they whirl as a unit, as one, and allow the drums to create a state of trance—zekr, the repetition of the Imams' names: "Ali, Husayn."

Later, Amir will write:

I have experienced sages who sit all day in silence, fakirs who draw swords through their cheeks to wow tourists and I have seen true masters make themselves disappear—but I have never seen a zekr turn men into a fighting machine.

Still entranced we broke the chain and let go of each others' arms, kissed one another on the shoulders and systematically turned to form a line. At the front of the line was the captain holding a Quran, high above our heads—the way one does when someone is leaving on a trip—it is held high enough for the person to pass beneath it, then lowered to be kissed before they pass again. What trip was this we were embarking on? I fell to the end of the line, so I could watch and be prepared for the next step. The men continued to walk straight—straight to the shore where they suited-up in wetsuits and waited along the beach.

The captain came up behind me and told me as a medic I am never to leave camp. I exhaled, perhaps too loudly; no one wants an unwilling martyr among the mad.[34]

Of our fifty men, no one returned alive. I am told they were joined by other battalions, thousands, tens of thousands of men that took off all along the shoreline of the Shatt al Arab straits. They will never tell us how many. We are led to believe that we are unique, a chosen few.

He puts down his pen.

"Your chances of martyrdom may be better in Tehran these days," the captain mentioned.

"They're bombing the city?"

"Scuds, 365-mile range."

What he does not tell his soldiers is what he heard accidentally on crossed radio wires—that civilians in Tehran have begun seriously to protest the war. Night after night, Amir is forced to wait on the shore and wave good-bye.

"God be with you."

"May you be martyred."

"May God accept my martyrdom tonight."

He can only hear them faintly, he cannot stand to get too close; he'd rather watch indescribable, unfamiliar silhouettes of expressionless bodies go off to battle, because it will not be long before the faces return, expressionless, indescribable, silhouettes.

DYING TO BE DISPLAYED

It is not the martyr himself and his desires that are important per se, but the role he plays in creating a desire, a need, a fear—a culture of survivors, bound by blood to the nation. Like mass production, war substitutes uniqueness for pluralities. In the wake of literally hundreds of thousands of deaths in the Iran-Iraq war, the Islamic republic aimed to emphasize uniqueness over quantity by painting billboards of specific martyrs, with real names, from real pictures. While these martyrs are not reproduced mechanically and in mass quantities like Khomeini's photograph, photography plays an important role at the inception of these images by arresting the real at the moment of its death in order to replicate it in a less-than-real form for public consumption. Almost every mural, stamp, and piece of currency produced graphically and in painting derives its image from a photograph that is doctored to create a billboard, poster, or postage stamp.[35]

The space of death needs two things in war-era Iran: a martyr and a photograph. Martyrdom is meaningless without memorialization, and memorialization is not possible without a photograph.[36] The painter cannot paint a man he has never seen. A sculpture park on the Basra River in Iraq displays eighty sculptures of dead soldiers produced in the likeness of their photographs. If one is not photographed in life, then he will not be memorialized (visually) in death. Photography is vitally important in bringing the dead back to life, or rather bringing death to everyday life, by providing an image that can be replicated by someone who never knew or ever saw the dead soldier.

قائم پوستر قم: پاساژ قدس تلفن: ۷۴۴۰۵۹ همراه/۵۵-۰۱۱۲۵۱۲۰/۰۹۱۱۲۵۱۲۰ ۳۱۳

8. A piece of martyr memorabilia sold on the streets and at the museum of martyrdom in Tehran. 2000.

In this age, the risk of losing one's soul to photography is highest in modern war.[37] The image, during the war in Iran, was born in death. With the help of photography and the war, a literal theater of death evolved that outlasted the war to sustain the theme of jihad and the sacred defense throughout the republic. The Iran-Iraq war provided the optimal opportunity to contain and manipulate the political power of images. Without a foreign press to sanitize the images, the cultural producers of the Islamic republic had full control over consolidating Iran's image regime. Martyrs provided faces whose dead displays did not threaten the authority of the ruler. The Quran states: Angels do not enter houses where there are dogs or pictures.

The Islamic taboo on representation resurfaced in Iran to "culturally" justify a visually Islamic social sphere.[38] The argument in Islam, however, is somewhat reversed: the belief is not that the soul resides in the reproduced image, but rather because the reproduced image is not a living being it has the potential danger of eliciting idolatry. The prophet realized the competitive power of an image; he feared that he might be replaced by a false idol. The Quran says: "Those who make pictures will receive the severest punishment on judgment day. Allah will say unto them, 'make alive what you have created,' and they will not be able to."[39] A mortal may not be able to breathe life into an image, but with modern technology she or he can surely animate an image to a degree where it will take on a life of its own. Success in controlling images could potentially lead to gaining the power of a prophet.

Plato warns that danger is not found in the material icon but in the human senses, which are quick to deceive. He who controls images controls thought, belief, and ideology. The power to control perception is the power of deception. In our modern age of distraction, the senses are easily manipulated. Moving images are especially dangerous because, according to Walter Benjamin, they encourage distraction rather than contemplation. In the cinema, the moment an image or frame of an image is displayed it also disappears in a flicker. A painting, however, remains stable and present for as long as the viewer chooses to contemplate it. This idea was not lost on urban planners in Tehran who made certain that the themes meant to evoke thought in the populace, (martyrs, revolutionary scenes, Quranic verses) were, and still are, always painted. A painting on a wall is not as easily mass produced as a photograph (which can be copied and glued to the wall), and a painting is more permanent than a paper billboard. In addition, rarely is there more than one of the same mural or painted billboard. This makes every mural unique, a work of art that will be looked at as if for the first time, in contemplation rather than habit (merely acknowledging something already seen). In Tehran painted murals, done mostly in Soviet social realism, are placed in a frame where a cosmopolitan viewer would normally expect to see a billboard advertisement. Like American advertisements, these billboards are usually found alongside the freeway where they receive maximum exposure. Khomeini however, could not plan for the present-day growth and speed of the metropolis, which turns fixed images into moving images by the speed of the viewer on the freeway. Even in their uniqueness, these billboards are not any more available for contemplation than a repetitive advertisement. The pace of the city is like the flicker of a movie projector where in the moment of viewing, the image has disappeared. At the same time, once something is seen, even if only for a second, it has the power to inhabit the mind.[40] The danger of images is their apparent ability to take over thought, and as Plato said, to deceive. This is a theme that resonates both in the Quran and in philosophies of modernity: the prophet says, "Remove it from my sight, for its pictures are still coming to me in my prayers."[41] Centuries later Benjamin, quoting Duhamel, says, "My thoughts have been replaced by moving images."[42]

In the end, the difference between the cultural producers of the war and the picture makers referred to in the Quran is that on judgment day instead of bringing images to life the war producers used images, especially moving images, to end more lives (by creating martyrs) than they could ever create. The martyr, like everything else in this world of illusion, becomes a symbol. The question is no longer why he wants to die; that is obvious in the charged emotions and mystical energy of the time. Instead the question is how is his death manipulated toward nation building? In light of this issue I turn to Alexander Kojève's reading of Hegel.[43]

LOVER / BELOVED OR MASTER / SLAVE?

For Hegel the issue of martyrdom cannot be discussed outside the context of the separation of church, family, and state. A citizen must ultimately choose between the family and the state. When the war with Iraq commenced, the Islamic state of Iran promised to protect and care for those citizens that chose to fight for and help build the state. The state promised to provide for families that gave a martyr but, as I discuss later, it cannot uphold this promise, which is a significant factor in its unmaking.[44]

According to Hegel, in a pagan state the family is chosen; in a religious state, the state succeeds. The same issue or ultimatum is at stake when Khomeini calls for martyrs in jihad. The Islamic state asks that the citizens give to the state what is most precious; to give oneself, one's son, or one's husband to God, ostensibly for freedom but in reality as a means of consolidating the state and "enslaving" the citizens. Man can neither renounce his family nor the state in the pagan world (Kojève 61). But, in the world of Islam, the state comes first; the state is the family, it is *namus*. At the beginning of the Iran-Iraq war, during the weekly Friday prayer services, teenagers were encouraged to ask their parents' permission to go to the front. Mothers were congratulated for giving up their sons, while families were consoled for their losses. Hegel sees this tragedy of being caught between state and family as the very thing that will bring the pagan world to its end.

The Islamic state succeeds in providing a higher cause for work (what Hegel believes is lacking in the pagan world) in the act of war and martyrdom (jihad and shahadat). According to Hegel, the pagan state is a human state that only perpetuates wars for prestige as opposed to a warlike state with real work.[45] Hegel's notion of true work is important to understand how martyrdom can be the only way to freedom. In the Documentary *Revayat Fat'h*, martyrdom and work become synonymous—a voice-over tells us: "It is night and the eyes of the prisoners of the world (aseer-ha ye donya) are tired, but in place of sleep the children of the last prophet are still working. They are the best slaves of God, in the road of truth. Be awake brothers, it is the time of wakefulness . . . the laughter of tears, the tears of laughter."[46]

Work is an important link in understanding the master/slave dialectic. Kojève explains that, for Hegel, mastery comes about when one works or fights for the state. He notes that in a pagan state citizens become private people, without work, which leads to their enslavement by a master: "When all is said and done, the former citizens become slaves of the sovereign. And they become slaves because they already are slaves. In effect to be a master is to already fight, to risk one's life. Hence the citizens who no longer wage war cease to be masters, and that is why they will become slaves of the Roman emperor. And that is also why they accept their ideology of the slaves: first stoicism, then skepticism, and finally Christianity."[47] While the martyr, the one who ends up dead anyway, is the real master, everyone else who participates from the side, the citizens who do not fight but become entwined in this Islamic/Christian (religious) state, in this culture or theater of martyrdom, are the true slaves. According to Hegel this is the slavery of the bourgeoisie and the condition of evil ("Westoxification," *taghout*) that Khomeini plays upon when he comes onto the political scene.

He looks tired and scared, thinks Amir, wishing he could tell him it was going to be OK—*wishing that Kazem wanted to escape as badly as Amir did. Little does Kazem know that Amir has taken him as a prisoner of war in order to save him. Only the prisoners of war are ever freed. He wants to ask Kazem: Where are you from? Why do you feel so passionately about fighting this war? Who convinced you this was a good idea? What would you be doing if you were not here? Whom do you love? How do you express your love? Who loves you and is waiting for you, sick with grief and fear? The poor kid probably thought this was all in the plans, Amir thinks to himself, as he tries to refuel and keep an eye on Kazem at the same time.*

Kazem curses the pain caused by his legs cramped by cold, wet wind or his stomach aching as the acid of anxiety eats the raw lining. This was not the hero's death he had imagined. This was worse than death: it was the same banal suffering he experienced day in and out in life. It had not occurred to him that a soldier would have to work and could suffer before death.[48]

He fantasized a beautiful boat ride, a quick confrontation, and recognition of the enemy, a few exchanged shots and a glorious moment when the bullet hits either him or the enemy. He returns heroic either way—alive or dead. Pain never played into his fantasy. In this fantasy the bullet does not cause pain but rather an intense sensation, a tingling—God's fingers tickling him with affection as he is lifted through the gates of heaven.

Few returned seriously wounded in his battalion. The wounded were usually too far gone and either left to die at sea or taken to a real hospital at a seaport like Bandar Abbas. He had never been in a war hospital, a friend had never died in his arms, but he knew suffering, he knew physical pain. He recognized just barely tolerable pain. He saw it first on his mother's face, contorted with muscles that squeezed harder and harder to hold out the bad times that were seeping in to stay in premature wrinkles as his dead baby brother was pried out of her trembling arms by health workers who feared the meningitis would spread from the contaminated corpse. Kazem knew the pain caused by sharp corners of a plywood box full of Chiclets and cigarettes on the lower back of a ten-year-old — indistinguishable from the heavy, dark, polluted air he moved in to hawk his wares. He thought he had escaped that pain: the unremarkable pain described as discomfort by those who had never experienced it. He sought vindication and self-worth in any future pain — not this awful unbearable discomfort. The farther they moved away from the front and veered off course, and the longer the captain took to give Kazem his chance, the more Kazem felt cheated of his rightful fate.

According to Hegel's dialectic, the outcome of the slavishness in the Christian world (and in Islamic Iran) is a desire for life sublimated in a desire for immortality or eternal life. As Kojève notes, "If the pagan master accepts the Christian ideology of his slave, an ideology that makes him a servant of his absolute master, of the king of heaven, of God, it is because, having ceased to risk his life and becoming a peaceful bourgeoisie, he sees that he is no longer a citizen who can satisfy himself through political activity. He sees that he is a passive subject of a despotic emperor. Just like the slave. Therefore he has nothing to lose and everything to gain by imagining a transcendent world, in which all men are equal before an omnipotent, truly universal master."[49] Khomeini's pre-revolution speeches that had rallied the nation against the despotic rule of the shah had an uncannily similar ring to Kojève's words; for example, when Khomeini states: "The leader of the Muslims taught us if a tyrant rules despotically over the Muslims in any age, we must rise up against him and denounce him, however unequal our forces may be, and if we even see the very existence of Islam in danger we must sacrifice ourselves and be prepared to shed blood."[50] Or, further, "My beloved ones summon up all your strength and open the bonds of slavery! One after the other, remove the treacherous pawns of the Shah from the scene of those who manipulate them and their like in Islamic countries. The way to happiness, freedom, and independence is barred by those pawns and those who manipulate them, so scatter their rank and save the country!"[51]

Khomeini does not tell his citizens to save themselves but to save the country, just as the Iranian POWs who are hoping to see God do not title their memoirs "Hello, God" but rather "Hello, My Country."

In making his point on the slavish master, Kojève writes, "Hence Christianity is first of all a particularist, family and slavish reaction against the pagan universalism of the citizen-masters. But it is more than that. It also implies the idea of a synthesis of the particular and the universal that is of mastery and slavery too: the idea of individuality . . . of that realization of universal values and realities in and by the particular and that of the universal recognition of the value of the particular, which alone can give man *befriedigung*, the supreme and definitive satisfaction."[52] Kojève continues to say that: "Christian man can really become what he would like to be only by becoming a man without a God—or if you will, a God-man. He must realize in himself what at first he thought was realized in God . . . he himself must become Christ."[53]

Khomeini pointed out that citizens and their ruler are not quite God but rather shadows of God: "The Islamic ruler is a shadow of God, what is meant by a shadow is something that has no motion of itself. Islam recognizes a person as the 'shadow of God' who abandons all individual volition in the sense that he acts only in accordance with the ordinances of Islam, so that his motion is dependent, not independent."[54] This view resonates with the Islamic notion of *taqlid*, or mimetic imitation of a master and his morals, behaviors, and living. Kojève explains that the synthesis of the particular and the universal is only affected in the beyond, after death. In the meantime, man must realize his mortality during his lifetime in order to go toward his death and afterlife. "And this means that the transcendent universal (God), who recognizes the particular, must be replaced by a universal that is immanent in the world. And for Hegel this immanent universal can only be the State."[55] This resonates strongly with Khomeini's notion of the *valiyat-fagih*, or an Islamic state. As Kojève points out, "What is supposed to be realized by God in the kingdom of heaven must be realized in and by the state, in the earthly kingdom. And that is why Hegel says that the 'absolute' state that he has in mind (Napoleon's empire) is the realization of the Christian Kingdom of heaven."[56] This notion works to elicit the service of martyrs, but in order to sustain the state (and key to understanding the Islamic nation) is Kojève's interpretation of Hegel, when he states that "there must be a real evolution, which prepares the social and political conditions for the coming of the 'absolute' state; and on the other hand, an ideal evolution, which eliminates the transcendent idea, which brings heaven back to earth."[57] In the Islamic republic, during the war, the transcendent idea is not eliminated, but emphasized. It is this heaven on earth that is both created and affected by a martyr culture and that surrounds the religious state.

Kojève goes on to explain Hegel's point that the only way to realize the Christian self is through work (fighting, risk of life). "The working Bourgeois, to become a satisfied citizen of the absolute state, must become a warrior—that is he must introduce death into his existence, by consciously and voluntarily risking his life, while knowing that he is mortal."[58] This is the comedy, the irony of the men who go to the front and are turned around after they have risked their lives by introducing death into them, only to survive. They have done this for the state; they have introduced fear into everyday life.[59] But there is more. There is the point at which the mystical goal of self-loss is illuminated in Hegel's philosophy. Hegel says: "It is from himself that he must free himself. And that is why the liberating risk of life takes the form not of risk on the field of battle, but the risk created by Robespierre's terror. The working Bourgeois, turned revolutionary, himself creates the situation that introduces into him the element of death. And it is only thanks to the terror that the idea of the final synthesis, which definitively satisfies man, is realized."[60]

Still debatable is whether one must physically confront death to introduce it into one's life. Georges Bataille believes that one must confront death in the sacrificial act. For Bataille sovereignty

9. A war veterans' mural in Tehran showing disabled vets who continue to fight as well as play. (Photo by Roxanne Varzi, 2000)

is waste, a purely gratuitous act like laughter, eroticism, martyrdom.[61] And yet the kind of martyrdom we see in Iran is not gratuitous because it is predicated on an economy of heavenly reward.

Kojève says that only a fictive contemplation of death can be had, for death reveals nothing—there can never be an actual confrontation, for death cannot be revealed to a finite being except in its fictive representation: cleaning the guns of shahids, films and war memoirs, being the one with the missing arm, witnessing a battlefield filled with dead bodies. For Kojève, the two self-consciousnesses in the master/slave dialectic must each confront death but also stay alive in order to prove their freedom. Life must be preserved while it is negated. This is achieved by creating a martyr culture: telling stories and making movies and billboards of dismembered bodies, men in wheelchairs, detached limbs, bloodshed—inscribing the fiction of death, an almost death, on the body.

For Girard, the returning soldier invokes contagion.[62] For Iranians, the returning soldier is something sacred—he is Kojève's fictive representation of death. It is the excess of martyrdom, the leftovers, the bodies (dead and alive) that will represent death and the fear of death to Iranians. It is the fictive contemplation that mecha-

nizes Kojève's slave role. It is in deciding not to fight that the in-
equalities appear. The nation must be made to confront its own
death, to fear that death and choose the slave position.

According to Hegel, this assures death's role as the absolute
master. Death rules. The leader of the religious state is then a veil
for death/God/master all at once. He is the shadow of death. He
is merely an effect of the slave's freedom, the slave who freely decides to submit because he is afraid of his own freedom. Kojève
asks: Does the slave experience freedom in experiencing his own
death? How could he, if he does not survive death? It is the country that experiences death through the theater of war. The citizens
experience what they think is freedom, but what really is a fear of
death and in turn enslavement to the master. Girard says, "As soon
as the judicial system gains supremacy, its machinery disappears
from sight. Like sacrifice, it conceals as it reveals — its resemblance
to vengeance differing only in that it is not self-perpetuating . . .
The judicial system has a monopoly on revenge." And so the Islamic
republic during the war had a monopoly on death.

Revolutionary terror, according to Hegel, is what causes citizens
to manifest their freedom by being guillotined. Martyrdom in Iran
is not so much an attempt to deflect violence, as Girard would have
it, as it is a move to enslave the nation while allowing it an ostensible sense of freedom as it "freely" submits itself to an absolute
master: death. Through Hegel's absolute state we come to understand how the nation is a site of both death and absolute mastery at
the same time that it allows a sense of freedom.[63] The state is death;
it is the constant possibility of death, the protection from death,
heaven on earth: namus. The nation (even namus) becomes a veil
for the absolute: it masks fear as it creates it. It is this condition
of the absolute nation, created through a martyr culture, that has
enslaved the imagination of modern Iranians, transforming them
into shadows, unmovable images of the state they represent: impending death.

JANUARY 1986 *The food here is awful and most of us live on sugary tea and
biscuits. They say faith provides more fuel than food. Every day someone is*

martyred and every day I wonder why it was not I. Our battalion has given so many martyrs that we're almost obsolete. We could easily have martyred our whole unit at the front today but thank God our battalion leader has some sense; he says that it is pointless to get killed without a strategic purpose and that we should wait for a proper offensive moment to get militaristic as well as spiritual value. So, we spend the day sitting in our tents listening to rowzehs of Imam Husayn and to Khomeini's speeches on tape. It is too dangerous to leave our tent.

I'm trying to drown out the lecture on the other side of the tent so I can write. There's really not much to say. Even now, in the tent, there is silence.

Amir puts his pen down and looks up to see why the men have fallen silent. Someone commented that the group is out of water for tea. Everyone is dead silent, each contemplating whether to volunteer to leave the site, head toward the river, closer to the front, toward the waiting Iraqis hidden in the marshes, and get water.

They're probably thinking how Imam Husayn would have done that for his troops.

As Amir writes the sentence a sense of urgency comes over him, a need or desire to go to the water.

I am the last person in this unit who wants to die in the supposed path of God, but I suddenly feel the overwhelming urge to go to the river. Maybe I just want to one-up all these scared hypocrites.

Amir stands quickly, placing his little notebook in his rucksack, before swinging it onto his back. He grabs the teapot and runs before he has time to lose his nerve. He can hear them calling after him, protesting, screaming that he is their last medic. Something stronger than their protests propels him toward the river—it's as if his very life depends on getting there.

"We need you to stay alive," they shout, without moving from the open mouth of the tent. The dark hollow of the tent resembles a mouth frozen in a silent scream. Amir lets the voices fade as he runs closer and closer to the water. Just as he is about to reach the riverbank a deafening explosion rocks him to his knees. He covers his head and begins to pray. He thinks the Iraqis have spotted him on the beach and are trying to kill him, but the silence behind him suggests otherwise.

Amir slowly removes his hands from his helmeted head and raises his neck, then chest until he is sitting up on his knees, like a soldier surrendering, a man pleading. He turns to look behind him where all that remains of his unit's tent is a smoldering heap of canvas and flesh.

He is overwhelmed by tears that do not fall, shaking that has yet to start, sadness, anger, and finally the depression that comes from unexpressed anger that is turned upon oneself: as though he has already been through all the motions and what is left now is numbness. He turns toward the Shat al-Arab straits and sits back on his heels and begins to weep.

Amir wakes lying in a fetal position in the same place he fell at the explosion, only now he is covered by a blanket and surrounded by a group of men who sit cross-legged around him, forming a chain of protection.

His legs shake: From the cold? From fear? It would take weeks for his fingers to stop shaking and years for the eyebrow twitch to disappear. A sound unfamiliar to him, a gasping—the result of his attempt to fight the sobs, begins to crescendo not unlike the motorboats as their engines begin to rev louder and louder—the call to battle, the signal to depart. The sound now has meaning; he can attach faces to the sound. War becomes personal when sound becomes visible.

"God saved you because you were the only one willing to martyr yourself for your battalion and get water. You are a hero," they tell him.

Did God save me? Does God agree with me that this is crazy? Perhaps He is not egotistical and crazy enough to desire people to needlessly die for Him? Why would He put us here in the first place? Dying seems like escaping God's real purposes for us, whatever they may be.

"You are a hero," another soldier repeats.

A hero of chance is what I am, Amir thinks. You cannot save people who do not want to be saved. A hero is someone who can face life day in and day out—not someone who renounces the hardships of daily life to achieve their singular spiritual salvation—or escapes life's hardships through death.

Amir lies in his tent and writes in his journal, using the recent trauma as an excuse not to speak with anyone. What they do not know is that he was already traumatized. He was traumatized the moment he heard a young man say he wanted to be martyred, then watched his dead body return with an awkward half-smile, half grimace. We cannot change our minds after death, Amir thinks. That's it, the finality of finalities. For them anyway. I believe in Karma. He takes the journals of men who are illiterate, some he recovered from his former battalion, some he was given, and in each one he writes:

This was not my choice, I was fooled. I do not want to die. Pray I return alive.

He makes up different names, writes in different styles and signs off with the name of the operation: Karbala Five.

He tells himself that he is not afraid. He is more angry than afraid. He did not choose to die. He was conscripted and forced to put himself in this position and now he'd do what he could to get out of it. The rest was in God's hands. If he wanted Amir to live, he would.

CHAPTER THREE

Shooting Soldiers, Shooting Film

The Cinema of the Iranian Sacred Defense

IRAN-IRAQ BORDER, EARLY 1980S *Morteza Avini hugs the 16mm movie camera tightly to his chest, covering every inch of it with his mammoth body as he runs across the front line, dodging bullets and bombs to reach the fallen body of his soundman.*

"We need a paramedic," he shouts, but no one can hear. The bombs send deafening thuds as they drop. Soldiers, who in their panic have lost their ocular vision, feel their way around the sand dunes.

When he reaches his crew member the only sign of life is the sound meter that waves furiously back and forth in response to the dead silence and deafening crashes. He switches the machine off and takes the man's wrist to feel for a pulse. The movie camera is still strapped tightly to Avini's chest where his soul suffocates under the weight of another dead friend.

The four remaining crew members help carry their colleague to the morgue. Not one has lost his faith.[1]

Morteza Avini's film series *Revayat-e Fath* (Witness to Glory) is the longest-running documentary on the Iran-Iraq war, and as such it was the lens through which most of Iran viewed the war and its aftermath. The serial was shot live at the front, edited there and in

Tehran, and then aired on television across the country every evening of the nearly decade-long war.[2] The program was conceived by Avini at the beginning of the war when he joined the Jahad-e Sazandegi organization as a volunteer cameraman.[3]

When he arrived at the front, Avini's immediate concern was with the effect of Iranian television propaganda on the war. He saw a large discrepancy between what Iranian television was broadcasting to the public and what was really happening. For example, Iranian television claimed that "the minute an Iraqi saw an Iranian Muslim fighter he cowered in fear and ran." According to Avini, however, "this approach was a mistake, as our soldiers were not ready for the fight; they thought it would be easy. We should have pumped up the image of the enemy to get our soldiers ready. If we see the enemy as someone who is weak then there is no point in pumping up our own power; we need to see them as powerful in order to call up our own power and be prepared to fight. If we see the enemy as weak we have no reason to be strong. Even with all of our media, we have never been able to know the enemy."[4]

The Iranian government worked to convince the Iranian public that Iran was winning the war and that young men were volunteering in droves. Indeed, they offered the impression that volunteer soldiers came to the front in such large numbers that they had to be turned away. The government also painted the picture of an offensive rather than a defensive war. According to Avini, "Television filmed dead Iraqi bodies and showed the freed cities. Viewers found this to be sick rather than inspiring." Most Iranians only supported the war insofar as it was a defensive act, and this propaganda, according to Avini (and as confirmed by a number of civilian Iranians I interviewed), actually turned Iranians against the war.[5] At the time Iran was on the defensive with few volunteer fighters, and the ones who were fighting were dying so Iran needed soldiers more than ever.[6]

Avini responded by starting a film series to illustrate the beauty and true purpose of the war in order to encourage young men to volunteer at the front: "The film shows you how to get closer to God. We made a film that kept the war holy. We made these films in order to entice people to go to war, and not to entertain and inform the public."[7] The goal was to mobilize forces for the front and incite martyrdom and *mobarezeh* (struggle).[8] Avini began his effort with what he called "truth films" (*majmu'eheyeh haghighat*), out of which evolved the series *Revayat-e Fath*, which aimed to tell the whole truth about the people who fought the war.[9] Avini's goal was to be a witness to the soldier's faith and to film that faith in order to represent it to the general public. According to a member of the crew of *Revayat-e Fath*, "War is when you go forward, get land, and go back and lose land, but he [Avini] wanted to understand better what the reason for war is."[10] For Avini it was all about faith. According to soldiers interviewed by Avini, "Even with iron the enemy can never get past our faith."

FILMING FAITH

How does one become a witness to something as ethereal, personal, and invisible as faith, and then represent that faith to the general public through the lens of a camera? Avini's documentary project is more concerned with creating or bringing to the fore an Islamic reality than it is about witnessing faith. Avini's notion that "reality is not what exists, but what has the possibility to exist" is what compelled *Revayat-e Fath* to become the strongest component of the revolutionary project to create an Islamic reality.[11] In effect, therefore, the project was a simultaneous act of shooting soldiers and shooting film; of creating an Islamic reality while documenting that "reality" for propaganda purposes.[12]

Avini's philosophy of documentary filmmaking emerges from a mystical Islamic philosophy that divides reality into *baten* (inner) and *zaher* (outer) dimensions. When he states that "reality in the Quran is what is composed of the inner self, but today we interpret reality as that which is seen on the outside,"[13] he is talking about exposing the inner reality where faith is found, and as such creating a new surface, zaher, that projects the way an Islamic reality should appear. In this respect, Avini's work is instrumental to Khomeini's Islamic project that aimed at projecting his version of a proper Islamic reality and the proper civic duties of an Islamic citizen. Avini's documentary series was a fundamental part of creating the surface reality of Islamic revolutionary Iran. Unlike the makers of Islamic public policy, however, he took seriously the concern with baten, the space of faith, and the issue of getting at what true belief meant for, and how it was experienced by, the average Iranian soldier. He believed that faith could be witnessed and filmed and in turn could encourage the faithless to become believers. For these filmmakers, the idea of the documentary was not defined in terms of replicating "reality" so much as turning it inside out, taking what is inside, un-filmable, and invisible and finding a language for it in film. In this effort they were constructing a new surface reality that would eventually find its way to the very heart of the matter: faith.

MYSTICAL DIMENSIONS OF FILMING FAITH

In film the mystical image world, *alam al mithal*, comes alive in the projection of images onto the stage of life. Unearthing and projecting deeply buried images is a project of tying the spiritual world to the material world by allowing the camera to be the mechanical organ of perception that Ibn Arabi espoused would bring a novice (using the image as a vehicle) closer to God. Just as Khomeini's image was used as a vehicle for mystical love, the film images of the sacred defense were also used as metaphors or examples for how a young man might commence on the path to God. Thus, like Sufi tales or allegories such as Attar's *The Conference of the Birds* that represent the hardships and beauty of the mystic path or journey, *Revayat-e Fath* aimed to show the mystic journey (including the hardships) as it was to be for real people on the path.[14] The documentary series encouraged disciples to forgo material existence and bear the hardships of the mystic path, as did Attar's tale. Indeed, the voice-over of the series is full of mystical language, including *aref* (mystic), *baten* (inner reality), *alam* (world), *haqiqat hasti* (truth of existence).

The mystic Ibn Arabi's creative imagination is about opening the soul to perceptions not readily conceived by reason. Mystics believe that a veil obscures our vision of the world and that practices such as zekr in which the disciple enters into a state of trance brings one closer to the true representation of the world, the representation that God gives us. Celluloid manipulates light and shadows and thus allows film to act as a "shadow of God," a moving image that is not real but rather a mimetic image with the purpose of bringing the viewer closer to God through the world of images and representation.[15]

Avini's brother, Mohammad, now runs the Rivayat Fath production and publications. In our interview, Mohammad speaks of the war in terms of mysticism. He says that Morteza is a mystic and against war: "This was no war, it was a holy war. Cinema should be against war; defending religious ideals is not war, it is a sacred defense."[16] And as he further notes, "it was not about taking Iraq; but about becoming closer to God." His description of the front portrays a mystical atmosphere where the soldiers "loved mystics like Hafiz, whose poetry they read nightly at the front."

Being a Basij was not a job but a vocation, a calling. According to Morteza it was about tafakur, an invitation from above. The foreign press depicted Iranian soldiers as crazed boys who rushed the front lines merely to be slaughtered. But, according to veterans of the war, these [Basij] were not simple people, no, they knew about the world. They had a purpose, a goal, hadaf, they did not just go to go. People thought the Iranians were like sheep led to slaughter; this is not what it was about. These men were not interested in material life, they were not attached to children and wives; they were attached to religion.[17] The Basij I interviewed in Shiraz say that the war film audience who did not experience the war firsthand will perceive the Basij as "idiots who were needlessly out to get killed; fanatics whose minds did not work or who did not have a purpose and were lost. Whether or not it was a choice, they were pulled into the war. That's not how it was at all. They came with purpose and reason, it's only when people came to the front and saw the Basij for themselves that they understood, empathized and felt why the Basij were there."

Mohammad Avini says that for his brother, "it all went back to

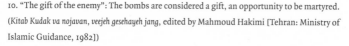

هديه دشمن

خواب خواب بودم. يادم نيست چه
خوابی می‌دیدم، شاید خواب مدرسه‌ام را،که
ناگهان باصدای پی در پی گلوله‌ها از خواب
پریدم. بقیّه هم از خواب پریده بودند. برادر
کوچکم گریه می‌کرد. نمی‌دانستم چه
شده، این گلوله‌ها ازکجا شلیک می‌شود و
چرا؟ آن فدر صدای آنها نزدیک بود که فکر
کردیم همین حالا روی سرمان می‌ریزد.جان
درفکر گلوله‌ها بودیم که برادر کوچکم از
یادمان رفت، صدای گریه‌اش میان آن
صداهای گوش خراش گم شد. عاقبت رفتم
واو رادرآغوش گرفتم تا آرام شود درحالی که
خودم می‌نزسیدم وبی خواستم گریه کنم،
همسایه‌ها وحشت‌زده ونگران آمده بودند
درخیابان وباهم‌ْ حرف می‌زدند. خبر رسید
که عراقیها حمله کرده‌اند. اماچرا؟ آن هم
ساعت یک بعداز نصف شب، بدون هیچ
خبری. ما که به آنها کاری نداشتیم. شهرما،
مهران، نزدیک مرز عراق بود و آنها هر چند
وقت یکبار تیراندازی می کردند اماتا حالا،
ما به آنها حمله نکرده بودیم.

10. "The gift of the enemy": The bombs are considered a gift, an opportunity to be martyred. (*Kitab Kudak va nojavan, veejeh gesehayeh jang*, edited by Mahmoud Hakimi [Tehran: Ministry of Islamic Guidance, 1982])

the imam; he was an eccentric person. He transformed people. My brother's spiritual transformation goes back to him. The strange thing is that the imam stopped writing mystical works at the age of twenty-seven or twenty-eight. He wrote poetry, but not mysticism; he has *hadis*, like, reason and love but not mysticism. And yet it is with a mystical mindset that people went to war. The existence of the imam was like that of the sun, all the rays around him were like him." [18]

Many men I interviewed saw Khomeini as their spiritual guide as the war was starting. They saw themselves as mystics on the path. Mohammad Avini recounts those days when a small group began to read Khomeini's books about Shiism and religious philosophy. He

من مرگی را انتخاب میکنم
که زندگی ساز باشد

11. "I am choosing death in order to build life": Poster available for sale at the commemoration tents in the streets of Sannandaj, Iran. 2000.

says that these students of the imam were not political. According to Mohammad Avini, the war was an experience (like the journey), "a gift" given to the soldiers by their imam. He says, "the Imam taught us how to live, to see the world, and the boys at the front experienced these teachings in a stronger way, especially the experience of death."

Khomeini taught the soldiers about the function of martyrdom in mysticism, explaining the difference between *shahadat*, martyrdom, and death. As Mohammad Avini states in our interview: "They learned that there is no fear, because one cannot fear that which they want: to be closer to God. Martyrdom had roots in this culture, but it had a moment, each year."[19] Khomeini allowed the people to experience martyrdom outside of its historic moment and thus to look at the world in a different way. "The boys at the front became part of this school of thought that was grounded in Jalal Al-Ahmad's book, *Westoxification*, where he says that we abandoned martyrdom."[20] Mohammad saw his brother's cohort as a group of believers who were practicing what they believed; he explains that faith is not a theoretical science but practical knowledge that can only be gained through practice: "Before the revolution Khomeini wrote many *resaleh amaliyeh*, traditional Islamic books that give advice on how to live; instruction books for life." The resalehs were all that Khomeini could offer his followers before the revolution, but after the revolution he offered the biggest resaleh ever: the war front.

In *Revayat-e Fath* the front is represented as holy as any place of religion or religious learning. In one scene we see clerics in combat gear, riding mopeds through the front to distribute Qurans. From the front, the scene cuts to Mashhad where the film crew interviews *talebs* (seminary students): "What's more important, your studies or the war?" "Islam is here," the students reply, "One hundred percent. This is studying, and we are teaching and getting rid of the enemy." The film then shows a glimpse back at the front where soldiers are seen praying and reading before going back to Mashhad, where a taleb explains the connection between Fikr (Islamic thought) and the front: "The truth is, that faith is at the front as much as at the Hose (seminary), we are warring for Islam, which has roots in Fikr." The camera then goes back to the clerics on mopeds, who are asked, "What do you do at the front?" In response, they state, "Well, on one hand we're there to answer questions, give their spirits power. There shouldn't be a separation of being at the front and at the Hose. Taped lessons are sent from Ghom. When we have listened to them, they send more, so we do not leave our lessons. It is not the same quality as being at the feet of our teachers. May god forgive our sins."

According to Mohammad Avini, in our interview, "The front was the place to experience life, because death is life's biggest experience. Khomeini told us that the spirit of Islam is in this war. The war front was the best place to practice faith. It takes sometimes seventy years on the mystical path to come close to transcendence. The front is an expressway to heaven." In the series, a soldier says, "I kept thinking that I was in the sky and cut from earth then I reminded myself that every step of this journey brings nearness to death, and I remembered that martyrdom is not death, but life."[21] The cameraman goes on to describe the morning of his friend's martyrdom: "When morning came, a freezing cold wind came and entered through our skin to our heart. My voice trembled with the wind as we prayed and we knew that the twelfth imam would take our prayer and that Imam Khomeini would always remember us. We, *da'ah ahd*, made a deal with prayer. I knew the twelfth imam could hear us and went to God to tell him I had read this and that the friends of Khomeini promised to stand here. We trembled, I was so happy I wanted to fly, I hugged the soldiers, we kissed, especially Ali. Little did I know I would not be the one to die, that it was Ali that was meant to go—that morning was Ali's victory morning. Ali could smell heaven; he knew he was on his way. When Ali was dead all I could feel was nothing and the memory of one of Khomeini's sermons."[22]

At the Ministry of Islamic Guidance in Shiraz the American film *Men in Black* is used to illustrate what happens in the moment of martyrdom: "Remember the last scene, how they move away from earth and become very, very small, well, that's what it's all about." One becomes a mere molecule, or the dot of Rumi's metaphor.

There was a sense that being present at the front allowed a soldier to see with an open heart. Stories circulated widely of the ability that soldiers had to foretell their own deaths.[23] The Basij in Shiraz tell me of a soldier who in his last will and testament says that he does not want his body to be found after he dies, and indeed they never found his body. Another man, a painter, whose work now hangs in Shah Cherag in Shiraz, painted a portrait of Imam Husayn using orange as the primary color. His friend asks him, why orange? It should be red for blood. He tells him to wait, that it soon will be. He turns at that very moment and is struck by a bomb, causing his blood to spill all over his painting, turning it red.

For the men who volunteered in Avini's group, and for their fellow Basij, belief is not a theoretical science but a practical knowledge: "You must practice to believe and the front is the perfect place to practice belief. Everything becomes a metaphor for the front, and the front becomes a metaphor for everything else. The path the mystics pointed out, the path the imam pointed out, is transcendental, you need to transcend worldly qualities, like fear; it's a practical matter that should be experienced in practice. What you read and learn in books, and memorize; learning, including religion, will not be rooted in your soul, it's something you must experience, not learn theoretically." [24] This is not a discursive act but a practical one that is about imitation: to be present in the presence of God.

If this is all about practice, then how does one assure oneself that habit will not take over faith? Avini states: "Revivals of the soul: constant revival will not allow habit to take over. Adat Amal ro az haghighat toheed meekuneh. Habitual practice of prayer is necessary to keep faith alive, without repetition it dies out. At the front, one was always in a space of prayer. Faithfulness: to lose life for love." [25] A soldier interviewed in one episode says, "We get our strength to pummel the enemy from prayer." [26] A Basij in Shiraz tells me, "The Basij, who are usually thin and weak find their strength elsewhere, in prayer, they live for the heart not the stomach, they put their hands on their hearts, they're from the south of the city, they do not have a lot but they work with what is. Even after their friends gave up or were martyred they were able to laugh." [27]

KEEPING THE REEL REAL

Veterans of the war at the Ministry of Islamic Guidance in Shiraz claimed that because the war was spiritual it was not something that could be visualized: it was not material, and therefore not replicable materially (through film). [28] "It's impossible to really relay the war because it was a war of spirit and religion. You cannot easily show the truth of it. You cannot talk about it or see it with the naked eye. You cannot put it in physical or monetary form because it was a spiritual war and not a war for power. If we speak of it, it strays from the truth." Like faith itself, it must be experienced and not merely known or learned.

At the same time that some members of the Islamic cultural project were claiming that it is impossible to show the spiritual reality of the war, they called on cinema to do just that. The aim and goal was to show the spirit of the war. "Avini was able to capture the spiritual aspects of the war by exploring the reasons that a soldier would choose to be flattened by a tank in the line of duty, rather than to show the tank killing the soldier. He claims that the documentary went after the soldier's and other people's spiritual identities, as opposed to filming the material reality of war." [29]

According to Mohammad Avini, in our interview, "War is certainly a reality, but what happens at the front is another truth. The truth is what must exist; reality is something that does exist. Reality belongs to God; only He can show us what is inside and out." War is the physical reality with which religion blends to form a surreal reality. By manipulating the surface reality in order to expose what is hidden, the filmmakers of Rivayat Fat'h partake in a surrealist enterprise, utilizing montage and decoupage to put forth a representation of what might be real and in turn recreate the surface. [30] This echoes Dziga Vertov's belief that it was not enough to show fragments of truth, but that these truths or fragments had to be thematically organized so that the resulting whole represented a truth. [31] The producers of Rivayat Fat'h discuss the persuasive elements of the project in terms of a particular culture that they were promoting; a culture specific to the war: "Television used the usual cultural framework to show the war, but the war culture itself was different and it changes history." [32] Avini's mission was to promote a culture of martyrdom in order to encourage men to fight in the line of the imam. Their particular aim in recording the war was to show the truth of this martyr or Basij culture. [33]

Complicating Avini's project to move against the earlier propaganda created by Iranian television at the beginning of the war was the fact that some of its message was already evident in soldiers who still believed in that depiction of the war, and who continued to propagate it themselves when interviewed by Avini. In watching

Revayat-e Fath a contradiction can be seen in what Avini claims he is trying to achieve (in reversing the earlier attitude) or rather in just how deeply the TV propaganda was ingrained in Iranians who came to the front. Not one Iranian soldier (in the first episode) talks of the power or might of the Iraqi soldiers, but instead the soldiers continue to speak within the framework of the earlier propaganda by claiming that an Iraqi soldier cowers in the presence of an Iranian soldier of Islam. In the film, one older man says: "*Allah akbar* (God is great), *ruhieh nadaran* (they don't have the guts), they ran when they saw us, by the time you say 'Ya Fatima,' Zahra or the name of Husayn is spoken, they tremble, thank God."[34] So this is an instance where earlier propaganda is replicated, despite an effort to counter it. Had Avini desired it, he could have cut out these particular scenes. Was he being true to the principles of documentary, of truth films, or did this propaganda perhaps have a place in his project?

If we accept the notion that the filmmaker's work is to create a specific reality rather than to formally document, then should not the claim to a particular genre like documentary (that which represents "reality") become a contested one? If these films are both documentaries and creative constructions of a yet-to-be reality, then why not place them in the neorealist genre? The question of representation is an important one in anthropology, and the question is certainly carried over to film in terms of the medium itself and its ability to properly represent reality. So, what exactly is reality?

Anthropologists agree that anything that is represented, no matter what the medium of representation (film or text), is done so through the subjective channel of the one who is making the representation; in so doing, therefore, nothing is completely a pure imitation of the original. Making choices of what to show creates a reality. According to Avini's writings, "Reality is what is created in the representation of something's likeness, *Ingar*, something similar; this in turn is what creates the world and God's world is reality."[35] The way something is shown constructs reality. Showing an Islamic ideal is real in terms of Avini's definition of the real (that which has the possibility to exist). By showing this Islamic ideal, he brings it into existence. "Documentary films are supposed to be close to reality, so reality must be defined. Neorealism shows everyday life, the bad things, the surface, just what you see and nothing beyond. People who respect artists look at their work as an element of the artist's soul and not as real life."[36] And yet, neorealism is about the liminal space between what has the possibility of existing and what does exist. Neorealist films are marked by their portrayal of human tragedy, poverty, suffering and human agency, the will to power, the ability of the individual to transcend hardship (or at least the spirit that tries).[37] For the Italians neorealism represented a move against an onslaught of government propaganda, whereas many Iranians in post-revolution Iran see it as merely more propaganda under a different guise.[38]

According to Avini, "neorealism shows ugly truths and what is wrong with reality on earth; we show beauty."[39] He notes that Iranian filmmakers like Amir Naderi and Mohsen Makmalbaf show the pain and ugliness of war, where as he tried to show its beauty.[40] "With neorealism, reality becomes whatever is physically present and that is all they think about; life is about the problems they find."[41] What then is "real"—the ugliness, or the beauty, or both? What is the truth? Is it the truth that matters in the end or the effect that these documentaries have on the viewer: that is, encouraging a boy to give his life to the state?[42]

Why is it so important to the project of filming the war that these films be defined as purely documentary and not neorealist? For one thing, neorealism calls on people to play themselves, which then directly implicates a faithful Muslim in the act of riya. Riya, which literally means deceit, is about making a public display of one's piety such as muttering prayers loudly. Riya allows for appearance to exist without belief.[43] Neorealism presents a problem in Iranian cinema because it encourages riya; it asks people to act out what they believe. Riya presents a problem for filmmakers who are trying to witness and film faith, as the act of intentionally displaying faith is inauthentic in this aspect of Shiism. The problem with doing this, however, is that riya presupposes the idea that true faith cannot be seen and that any attempt to construct it on the surface is deceitful. How does one film faith without opening a space for riya? The key is to find a way for faith to surface without it being the intention of the subject to project it onto the camera. Filming faith thus becomes filming daily gestures and then framing them in such a way that points to religious intention.

TECHNIQUE: PROJECTING REALITY—
THE NEO IN THE REEL

The crew of Revayat-e Fath went to great lengths in order not to encourage riya. "Without equipment and material things, our technique and our character were the only things that stood in the way (of direct representation)."[44] Their concerns ranged from the relationship of the camera to the people being filmed; interference by their own subjectivity or character; the effect of the other filmmakers present; and the possibility of incidents that would or would not encourage riya. "The microphone encouraged riya so we eliminated it. We spent a lot of time in the villages preparing our subjects for the camera, getting used to it until they could be natural in front of it (until they could forget it was there). We'd spend hours without running the camera just speaking with people, until they got comfortable with the camera, only then did we hit the on button and let the tape roll. Once a group of villagers circled the camera and one by one started speaking into it, yelling, screaming: the tears dripped from under the visor of the cameraman, the soundman held out the microphone while he cried; even I was crying. We let them get everything out."[45] Avini here creates the picture of a film crew in tears, which suggests that subjectivity, feelings, and thoughts are being manipulated and played on as the crew are filming and recording people's misery (without objectivity).

The crew interviewed soldiers about their dreams, showing the brotherhood among them, emphasizing all the good admirable qualities that Islam is supposed to promote without concentrating on "clichéd" displays of piety.[46] To do so, the crew used specific interviewing and filming techniques to ensure that the project remained in the realm of pure documentation and not become an encouragement of riya. To this end they wanted to prove that the project was not fictional or neoreal, negating any argument for riya. They believed that the best time to film was during battle when the men had to concentrate on what was happening; at times of rest the soldiers became actors.

An argument that is made repeatedly in writings and in conversations with group members of *Revayat-e Fath* is that because they were not properly trained filmmakers, there was no way that they could possibly know how to construct fiction or neorealist films and therefore were merely recording what was really happening: "We tried to do non-clichéd work. We had no experience and brought forward only what was in our souls."[47] They claimed to take film from whatever happened without aiming to create a scene, or frame. They merely lived with the war and filmed what they lived: "Scenarios, frames, we did not follow the laws of film; this was all natural."[48]

This argument creates a myth that without proper training one cannot possibly manipulate film. The only training that the crew was given was a set of lectures by Avini on the art of interviewing.[49] "We interviewed and edited our film in such a way that the interviewer is not visible; the audience only sees the soldier speaking directly to the camera. This made it intimate, personal and sincere for the audience [potential martyrs]. We tried to take film when soldiers were not looking; we never filmed the interviewer so it feels like the soldier is speaking directly to the audience."[50]

Given that interviewing was the only training received by the project members, they utilized it in important and telling ways. By not filming the interviewer the audience is given the impression that the soldiers are actually speaking to them rather than replying to specific questions or comments put forth by someone outside the camera frame. The impression is that the interviewees are coming forth with their own stories and information, when in truth they are being led in certain directions by an "absent" interviewer. There is also the impression that the crew members are merely rolling tape, but on close examination the numerous jump cuts in the sequence of various interviews show that the interviews are cut and edited. And the truth is that *Revayat-e Fath* is well edited. The opening sequence is telling. It begins with an establishing shot of a mosque (presumably Karbala), along with the voice of a famous rowzeh khan who sings, "Anyone who craves Karbala step forward." [51] Another poetic voice-over is accompanied by military music as a slide wipe reveals boots of soldiers marching in a parade. The next cut reveals hands drumming in the forefront, while in the backdrop women in chador sit along a parade route. A very poetic voice-over harkens:

Awaken oh citizen of the city of love, awaken.
Get ready for your pilgrimage inspired by love, awaken.
Put on your robe and raise your banner, sing aloud.
Anyone destined for danger come forward, come forward.
Anyone who craves Karbala step forward.

The next shot reveals more boots, then the soldiers' faces, over which is superimposed the text of the rowzeh khan's song so that the audience can sing along ("Anyone who craves Karbala step forward"). A small circle with the head of the rowzeh khan also appears superimposed on the footage of the marching soldiers, and his voice states: "From heart and soul we are the servants of the wise sage Khomeini." In response to this statement his audience in the background responds with a *salavat* (praise upon the prophet Mohammad and his decedents; a notably Shiite reference to the imams Ali and Husayn).[52] The sequence then ends with a shot of drums playing a military march. Some of the episodes in the series open with the credits rolling over a shot of the soldiers at the front, who walk under and kiss the Quran before motoring off to war. This act is part of Shiite tradition to ensure a safe return when leaving for a trip—only these men hope not to return.

In all, the large number of cuts in what amounts to five minutes of film is striking; and meaning comes out in editing. "Avini knew what he wanted, what types of personalities and stories and he went after them."[53] In editing, the films became life. For the most part Avini had to edit the film on site because there was not enough time to go to an editing studio in Tehran (a twelve-hour trip by car) and then return to the front. "We did not edit the way some-one trained in film might. For example, we were filming a bridge-building project in which we tried to interview one of the soldiers who said, 'Not now I'm working.' We left that scene in the film, to the chagrin of a film student who later asked why we had not edited it out. We had wanted to show how hard the soldiers work and that their work was more important to them than being on film. The film student thought that we had forgotten to edit it, and that every-thing needs a storyboard ahead of time. We never set-up shots, we had no storyboards."[54] Is not war the ultimate storyboard?

According to those working on the project it was impossible to direct the war in terms of filmmaking conventions: "Of course we cannot direct the war and tell them where to bomb for the sake of the film. At the front it is impossible to direct a film, you can only record, if there had been a director directing, we'd have missed a lot, so the cameraman was the director.[55] We never worked with a tripod, it grounds us and we needed to move. Our equipment was heavy and kept us back. A camera is a useless device in war, when there is an explosion you need to look away from the camera for a minute to see what or where it hit (as if the camera too might blink). Things happened so fast that there was no time to direct and so the director and cameraman became one person. Events and the camera did not always meet each other, which is why the camera has to become part of the cameraman's body, his eyes, this is not an easy thing to do."[56]

Avini, like Vertov's *Man with a Movie Camera*, held the camera close to his body, truly believing that he had become one with it (if not for any other reason than to protect it physically from the dangers of war). "The camera became alive, it walked around and asked questions," he stated. And yet, "the cameraman and the cam-era were not part of each other: if a bomb fell, the cameraman would look up, so we had to make the camera the actual eyes of the cameraman, part of his body. The cameraman becomes part of what happens, they put their souls into the film. The feelings of the filmmaker were apparent in the speed of the camera's spins on shots, the way the camera is angled. The camera had become a part of the cameraman's body; it moved, questioned, felt."[57]

In one long shot the course of a missile is followed through the air to an invisible explosion; along the way the camera runs alongside two soldiers, past a wailing ambulance, through a sand dune, and then over to a group of soldiers hiding behind a truck. All the while the camera ducks in and out of shots, bouncing up and down, looking one way and then another so that what is seen is ahead of the cameraman.

Although Avini claims that becoming part of the camera erases the subjectivity of the cameraman, in another sense it brings pure subjectivity to the film. If the camera truly becomes the eyes of the cameraman, then it only sees what he does; rather than being set on a tripod rolling film. But Avini offers other evidence, as noted in this passage from his writings: "There were people at the front directing the soldiers, and this was fake. The microphone encouraged soldiers to speak as if they were on TV. The soldiers would dance for the camera and the commentator would say: 'look at how they sacrifice themselves,' and shahadat, martyrdom, would be taken less seriously. Sacrifice became an overused word. All the villagers, everyone, described soldiers as martyrs and it became less valuable. Television turned the place into a circus. Reporters ruined the atmosphere of the war; when they were present, soldiers were less serious and started joking around. They encouraged riya. These other directors showed so many people sacrificing themselves that the value of sacrifice decreased. If we were to merely show a large number of people sacrificing themselves, emphasizing the numbers rather than the uniqueness of the individual, it would decrease the value of martyrdom, so we show individuals.[58] At the front we were after reality, not our own thoughts and opinions, we should have been making propaganda for the imam (Khomeini) and the pasdar. It's not about whether or not war is good. We were Basij, not artists. We had decided that our work was of a documentary nature and thus cleaned it of any notion of news. We tried hard not to make this a television type show, especially like the news (there's a third world epidemic where we are hooked on television)."[59]

Even given Avini's intentions, *Revayat-e Fath* is not simply one hour of rolling, unedited reel without commentary.[60] Rather, it possesses a filmic and narrative poetry in the quality of its commentary and editing, thus making it more than a record of reality. The commentary, for example, uses poetic language dubbed over the action of the film, which is reminiscent of the documentary *The House Is Black* by the Iranian poet and filmmaker Furugh Farokhzad.[61]

In one shot (which is shot at night with only a small headlight and thus lends the scene an eerie green-blue hue), we see men preparing to go to battle at night on the beach. As they walk around the beach loading the boats and hugging each other good-bye, one face is particularly haunting as it looks directly into the camera in a close-up. A commentary is laid over the sounds of war, stating that these are the martyrs who are preparing for truth, they give themselves over to truth, the night of an offensive is the night they enter the world of martyrs, this is the night of Ashura. In another scene, men are shown doing daily rituals against the backdrop of war. Against this picture we hear bombs and a voice-over: "They're so relaxed they forget this is the scene of war, they're standing and fighting in the line of faith." Yet another scene shows men sleeping, reading, and praying while the commentary states: "They are preparing for martyrdom, some praying, some writing, some exhausted." Why the use of such poetic voice-over material? As Avini tells it: "Some things need explanation. Beautiful language makes a beautiful film. Even still, the images were more important than the voice-over. The beautiful language of explanation makes the war more beautiful, we got criticized for the dialogue, but we had to make the images more important than what was being said."[62]

Another extremely important element of *Revayat-e Fath* is its invitation to the audience to participate, first throughout the hour of the film's screening, then later at the war itself. Again the ideas of practice and religion come together through the use of various oral traditions particular to Iranian Shiism that are infused in the very structure and play of the program.[63] For example when the rowzeh khan appears, so do two lines of text that he calls for members of his audience (soldiers in a mosque in the film, people at home watching the program) to repeat, thus allowing the audience members to say the words.[64] This act brings the sense of a religious gathering both to the film and through the film, and thus effectively into people's homes within the context of the war. As such it is a very effective method to get the audience to participate, which in turn will influence them to somehow feel involved and to believe. It also couches religious practice in the context of the war and preparations for martyrdom, so that the viewer can feel at one with the soldiers.

What, then, is the nature of documentary, and how do the producers of *Revayat-e Fath* theoretically engage in defining their project as such? It would seem that they use the favorite anthropological trump of authority and authenticity.[65] Avini's authority, and that of his crew, is grounded in the authenticity they gain in being members of the Basij who came prepared to be martyred. They were not only present at the front, but they were there in the proper frame of mind (which then becomes the proper frame for filming). Being a Basij and a soldier at the front living the war is used as an argument for authenticity in representation. Avini and his colleagues felt that they needed to suffer the way a soldier did in order to truly represent that suffering. They argue that not only did they lack the training or proper equipment to manipulate filmic constructions but also they did not have the time to do so, as they too were busy participating in the war and only had time to "record" the scene. "In the time of battle there was not time to think about art."[66] As Basij participating in the war as soldiers, they automatically represented reality because they were reality; it was the only way to understand and get at what was happening at the front: "Anyone who was not at the front in the line of the imam like we were could never properly represent the front or show the war the way we did. You must be a Basij to understand the mission; we knew the ways of the front better than our own cities." The men who worked on *Revayat-e Fath* came to the front like the rest of the Basij; with the goal of being martyred. "Life in the end is death, this becomes obvious," says

Avini. "Our pay is martyrdom." [67] "They cannot destroy our faith with metal. Death for us is martyrdom." [68]

"Filmmaking at the war is its own kind of combat or struggle, as is life." [69] Only one member had film training before joining the project, as the qualification for working with the group was not training in filmmaking but rather the preparation to join combat. [70] Avini himself was not trained in filmmaking but in architecture; [71] he also was a lover of Sufi poetry, a painter, and a "student of the imam's." [72]

"We made a film that kept the war holy."

"I was at the war, I saw it all, anyone else is just reflecting." [73]

"We were part of the Basij, at the front, we were part of the war. We were part of the harshness of war: no food, bombs: we had to live the war." [74]

At the same time that Avini and his crew laid heavy claims to authenticity, it was their aim to eliminate subjectivity or at least to erase individual subjectivity. [75] This was not in contradiction to the issue of authenticity or authority, mentioned above, which is based on being part of mass Basij culture and not predicated on the individual subjectivity that resides outside of this mass experience. Avini says that "an artist's gift comes from God, without God it is lacking. Western art is about the self and individual, it is devilish and selfish." [76] His ideal is to become part of the whole, to be a channel for God's gift by erasing individual subjectivity and at the same time keeping the subjective reality of being a Basij at the war front. [77] Members of the Ministry of Islamic Guidance in Shiraz quote the great Sufi poet Rumi, "Anyone who is close to God can see the world through God's eyes," to explain that the Basij "are a different sort and want to be closer to God, and not the material world." In doing so the Basij erase their own subjectivity, through bi-khodi, in order to become closer to God.

Avini also claims that the cameraman's subjectivity is erased: "The cameraman had to clear his soul in order to keep his subjectivity from entering the film, and the best way to clear the soul was to be at the front." [78] At the front one becomes part of the collective war culture, which has its primary aim in erasing subjectivity and no longer has claim to individuality. Preparing for martyrdom is the ultimate bi-khodi, loss of self and ego. This means that the film is not funneled through the subjectivity of the cameraman because he is a Basij and the Basij's aim is to erase individuality, his self through bi-khodi. As such, this hermeneutic play or twist makes all filmwork at the front automatically devoid of the cameraman's subjectivity.

Fear was the last indicator of human subjectivity: only an individual can feel fear; a fighting machine or one who believes they are being taken to a better place does not have fear. "From the point of view of spiritual experience, fear should not exist, it's not allowed. If I became afraid, I asked for God's forgiveness and after a while the fear left. Most of the boys at the war were like this. There were bombs everywhere, mostly from unseen forces, but the boys marched ahead, straight ahead, ignoring this, without fear. They all had pre-destinies and pre-destination does not allow for fear. Fear had no meaning. If you take all these people from the micro to the macrocosm, and look at it from the point of view of the fear of God's wrath, then what worldly fear could be worse? If you give yourself without fear to God, then the devil will break. Fear would disappear; physical fear would leave for some of the guys: some had no human emotions."[79] In one episode of *Revayat-e Fath* a soldier says, "The enemy wants to scare us but our calm will not allow this to happen, and it only shows how little the enemy knows us."[80]According to everyone I interviewed, these soldiers genuinely had no fear. "You cannot have fear and be martyred. They did not have any hope of returning. There's no return, just a cleansing of the soul."[81] In another comment, from the series itself, a soldier states: "For us, it is about the victory of the imam. Fear: if we do not fear Satan, he will disappear like the wind. We go forward with faith [not fear]."[82]

At the same time that Avini's project was getting underway, a major controversy was brewing over how even fictional films were to portray the war. In 1983 a concern over the "production of action-packed war movies made with poor scenarios, unable to show the truth about the sacred defense," led the Ministry of Culture to start a War Movies Section at the Farabi Film Foundation.[83] Around seventy amateur film directors were trained as war-movie directors, including Mohsen Makmalbuf and Ibrahim Hatamikia who are now internationally recognized feature film directors. This new film initiative was similar to *Revayat-e Fath* in that it emphasized experience (as a soldier and a practicing Muslim) rather than theory (training as a filmmaker) as a basic qualification for making movies about the war. A filmmaker thus had to be a Muslim who had served at the front. Avini had definite ideas about fiction films; he noted that they "are less serious because the audience knows they are made up, whereas documentary is serious, as people know what they see is real. A filmmaker cannot know everything so fiction films are left wanting. An artist is recording his or her own art, and not reality. There were men at the front who wanted to see themselves as players in scenes they'd seen in westerns. In order to present a reality that is accepted, one must not present something that is too artificial seeming."[84] According to the filmmakers of *Revayat-e Fath* the cinema (be it fiction or nonfiction) should always show the true reality of war.[85]

In order to represent the true nature of the war (the Islamic elements), filmmakers used less action and more narrative in order to promote the spiritual aspects of the war rather than show it as a series of cold-blooded strategic maneuvers. This strategy created a new sort of war machine that, like a tank, had a slower-moving wheel and an arsenal (a reel of images) for ammunition. This war machine, or projector, held the nation captive to a passion play that they were (and still are) intimately involved in, where they were made to believe that their very freedom and flesh was at stake.[86] In an interesting circularity, and a play on the ideas of fiction and realism, was the fact that for many returning soldiers some of the best work prospects available were as extras in war films, because loading missiles into tanks was the only thing they were trained to do. In this way neorealism is turned upside down, as soldiers become actors in the fictional account of their realities.

The film *The Horizon* was one of the first movies made after the initiative to imagine the sacred in defense by transforming representations of Iranian soldiers from war mongers to spiritual warriors. Although the film achieves this transformation, it does not entirely negate the representations of war-mongering soldiers but instead relegates them to the world of the enemy, the Iraqis, who though also Muslim are portrayed as infidels. The Iraqis are characterized as clean-cut, cigarette-smoking, suave Westernized strategists who sit in their highly technologized war machine (a battleship geared with massive control panels and surveillance technology) watching and waiting for the Iranians. While the Iranians, in a small boat on the other shore of the Persian Gulf, are depicted as bearded revolutionaries with long shaggy hair wrapped in red bandannas and dressed in black as a reminder of the black shirt worn on the commemoration day of Ashura.[87] Their very bodies and souls oppose the traditional concept of a machine; theirs is a war of flesh and spirit (Khomeini's words are echoed here—a human wave of believers), and theirs is a spiritual war in which they do not aspire to be what one Iranian soldier accuses his partner of having become: a war machine. Their battalion is called the Imam Husayn Battalion and their little motorboat The Ashura.

As I note in an earlier chapter, reclaiming Karbala was ostensibly the single most important goal of the war as well as the event that allowed the war the status of a scared defense rather than a military offensive.[88] Even a cursory look at Iranian war films produced by the state reveals the degree to which the Karbala discourse permeates every aspect of the war.[89] While the dramatic tradition of Ta'zieh (the reenactment of the events at Karbala) is never fully reenacted in the films I reviewed, the thematic use of Ashura in the war, and again in cinema, makes the war itself a performance of Ta'zieh. In this sense Ta'zieh is doubled in the cinema, which reenacts the reenactment, bringing many mimetic layers to the ghost-memory of martyrdom in Shiite mourning. Ashura is an absent moment that history makes present in the very call to jihad—a call for martyrs. During Ashura, Ta'zieh replays events already known to the audience to remind them of the martyrdom of Husayn and thus revive dormant passions. In the play, like the war, "a devoted warrior, inspired by the fire of his faith, faces a large army and a treacherous adversary. He is killed in battle and he is bitterly lamented. His death however fulfills a prophecy."[90] Indeed, his death becomes a powerful mourning date that resuscitates the ghost of Imam Husayn, who after the Iranian revolution (a celebration date) has turned every day in Iran into Ashura.[91]

There are scenes in *The Horizon* that resemble the Muharram ritual of *sineh zani* where the soldiers move in a slow circular dance with one arm extended into the circle and the other arm hitting the chest. Toward the end of *The Horizon*, as the troops of the Imam Husayn Battalion are preparing to attack the Iraqi fleet, the film moves completely away from plot-driven action and into a trancelike sequence that begins with a young man wearing an Ashura headband and combat gear, sitting cross-legged on the beach with his arms extended to receive a blessing: the gift of death. Just as the leader begins to rub ointment on the soldier's palms, the hypnotic sound of dafs come in followed by a chorus of, "Die, die, die, go to this death, leave this earth. Die, die, die," sung as each successive soldier, dressed in black scuba gear receives his blessing and joins the circle. Black against the black night, the soldiers walk under the Quran, kissing it twice, before disappearing into the gulf of dark water.

In the scenes that follow, the divers become an eerie personification of death that moves through the water, with nothing but oxygen tanks and AK-47s to attack a mammoth, technologically advanced Iraqi warship. A storm sets in as they descend into the water. If the Iranians believe themselves to be closer to nature and slaves of God, then the storm can only be a prophetic announcement of death. Back at Iraqi headquarters everyone is relaxed, certain that the Iranians will not try anything in bad weather. Meanwhile, the Iranians have slipped on board, unnoticed, and like ghosts in the machine they begin to rewire the technology of the Iraqi war machine. The first sign of their presence is a computer crash, because the radar did not detect anything.

Like ghosts, like the spirit of death itself, the Iranians slipped right past the radar: a triumph of spirit over technology. "The Iranians cannot possibly be on board, check the radio," demands the

Iraqi captain. When the Iraqis turn on the shortwave radio, a slow melodic voice singing Surahs from the Quran is heard over the airwaves—a softer version of the religious music heard on shore. "They're praying," whispers an Iraqi soldier. Praying and fighting thus become synonymous, because the war for the Iranians is one of spirit. They are soldiers, and slaves of God, who can slip past radar undetected, move through a storm, and amplify prayer. And, by amplifying prayer, they are announcing death. Like the grim reaper, they board the ship and start taking people to their deaths—silently, one by one. The moment an Iraqi soldier sees an Iranian diver—tall, dressed in black like a masked apparition of the night—it is already too late and he knows he must die. The Iranians have literally emerged from the darkness of night; only mourning music announced their arrival. As Paul Virilio writes: "War cannot break free from that magical spectacle, because its purpose is to produce that spectacle: to fell the enemy is not so much to capture as to captivate him, to instill the fear of death before he actually dies."[92] The Iranians thus enslave their enemy by the fear of death, just as they are enslaved by their leader. Meanwhile, a camera shot pans the dark beach where hundreds of Iranian soldiers sit listening to the same Quranic music that is being played for the Iraqis. The soldiers are already mourning their comrades, at battle, even before they wash ashore as dead bodies. The call to war, jihad, presupposes a call for martyrs, shahid, and mourning.

After the war, cinema becomes a device for mourning the dead of the war.[93] But before it is able to fulfill this function, it must create the circumstance that elicits the need to mourn: first Ashura and the death of Imam Husayn, then the war and countless deaths. In many instances war cinema is created out of the rubble of war, from the looted images that come to make meaning of what has been pillaged and lost. But in the case of Iran's war the cinema and war created each other in a simultaneous act of shooting soldiers and shooting film. The fiction created a reality in the same instance that reality fed the fiction.[94]

Despite the problematic definitions of "reality" and of genre that these films may or may not occupy, they remain invaluable because they are one of the few resources that elucidate the war culture constructed by the Basij. There are two main themes that permeate both fictional and nonfictional accounts of the war by Basij filmmakers: Ashura and mysticism. These ideas appear both as themes of various films as well as characteristics that permeate the films by virtue of their having already permeated war culture (like naming a motor boat *The Ashura*, or the act of soldiers retelling the story of Husayn's martyrdom in a documentary interview). Not only were these themes important at the front, but as noted earlier they were already part of public discourse during the revolution and thus readily available for use during the war. They were the most powerful themes surrounding the war and revolution, and because they permeated everything from public discourse to filmic representations it is hard to say which came first.

In Shiraz at the Ministry of Islamic Guidance, three men reminisced about the war years during my interviews there. One of the three was a Ta'zieh player before joining the war, and he stated that "it was perpetual struggle—mystical—it was Ashura everyday at the front." Whether their view of the camps is propaganda or can be used as ethnographic detail, the picture they paint of the war is clearly that of a battle that "rages alongside the ghosts of the soldiers of Karbala."[95] Mohammad Avini attests that the war was about Imam Husayn, "it was very Ashurai." Indeed, the biggest battle was called "Karbala 5 in 1365," and they called the nights before big battles the Shab-e Ashurai, where, like the nights of Ashura, they would cry for Imam Husayn and themselves before going into battle.[96] The men in Shiraz claim that they were seeking Karbala, a holy land. Theirs was a spiritual war unlike that of the army, which they describe as a war machine.

As another interviewee at the Ministry of Islamic Guidance explained to me:

Every day is Ashura; every ground is Karbala. Now we have a distance from the feelings surrounding the front, but Muharram is something we can still feel every year during its time. At the war we felt that feeling every day; it was always Ashura. A shahid's presence takes you straight to Ashura, it's mourning, it's the experience of Ashura. Every time a brother or friend is martyred you felt like you were in Imam Husayn's Karbala. We were part of Imam Husayn's caravan. It's the truth of a period in Iran's life, now, Ashura is a day in history and Karbala is a place in history, for some it is still alive, especially the kids who were chemical weapon victims, or hurt in the war; they still interpret their lives in relation to Karbala. This is not so of the general public. For the public it is more of a ceremony than an actual truth and ceremony is a big deal. The culture of Ashura is alive, but not the truth of it; it has become an empty ceremony.[97] Our movement began with the purity of the power of the Basij; the pasdar and Basij coming together. Everyone was in love, wanting to get close to God; to God and to Karbala and to die as martyrs like Husayn. Fourteen hundred years. After Karbala nothing will wash this memory but blood.[98]

Another man I interviewed added:

It's the same with war culture: every day the memory dies. It is not the political point of view that is losing color but the existential character. This Ashura war culture is not of the same ilk as routine daily culture and therefore it is hard to keep alive in the sphere of daily life. To do so, there must be both memory and repetition. The memory is there, but the zekr, the repetition, is dead. Memory never leaves if repeated. Memory survives only in repetition. The war is now a memory, and just that: it is the fire under the ashes. Shiite culture is unique. People may say all this is a memory, but it will always be burning under the earth; for Shiites, it can always be re-lit. Everyone who lives in this country has a readiness for the intensity of Ashura; it's always there."[99]

Through the help of media projects like *Revayat-e Fath* the memory of Ashura was projected beyond the war front into every Iranian television in every city in Iran. While this television serial was watched by millions of people at the beginning of the war, many became less inclined to willingly watch the horrors of the war, especially once the bombs began to be heard in Iran.[100]

WINTER 1987, TEHRAN HOSPITAL *They turn corner after corner through long halls that are dark and quiet. Finally the nurse's light falls on a mass of women and children huddled together in a small room, some bleeding and crying, others dead silent. Nilufar is handed alcohol and a box of matches for the one remaining candle, "In case it goes out."*

In the silent room the women's black chadors blend with the darkness to erase their bodies making visible only eyes and noses. Nilufar places the candle in the middle of the room where its light catches the edge of a metallic object on a woman's lap: a large framed picture of a young man. When the woman sees Nilufar looking, she instinctively raises the picture to her chest, as if poised to offer it were she not clutching the edges so strongly. She will never let go. Her eyes are patient and stubbornly expectant. Not a word is exchanged as another picture emerges from another black chador. Nilufar's eyes pass from one woman to the next as they raise their pictures: a wave of young faces, rising from the dead.

In the silence Nilufar can hear herself think, the tick of the radiators and fizzling bombs. With each new crackle of a far-off bomb she imagines the young boys rushing at the front lines, dying to be martyred. The women's pictures and the faces of the soldiers on TV begin to blend. Why is it, thinks Nilufar, that when they fail their suicide missions they return heroes, but when women fail they are branded insane?

In the hospital the dark is death's breath hovering over those on life support who need electricity to survive. For every moment of peace the electrical blackout gives her, it takes a moment of life from the others.

The government thinks that if they turn off the lights in Tehran then Sadam Hussein will not see where to bomb. Though it feels like the middle of nowhere and has cut itself off from the world, Tehran cannot erase itself from maps; it is caught in the web of war's radar that can scope for life and detonate, even in the dark.

Within a few months the reality that Avini was projecting from the front was beginning to take shape physically in the reconstruction of Tehran into a permanent display of martyrdom and revolution.

In this is a reminder of the Hoopoo's warning in Attar's tale, that the surface, an image, is the most powerful of manipulators. As I stated in chapter 1: the hardest lesson for the disciple to learn (because it is a lesson revealed only with time) is that the image betrays, decays, and manipulates reality, eventually leading the seeker astray.

CHAPTER FOUR

Visionary States

Inhabiting the City, Inhabiting the Mind

The relationship between man and space is no
other than dwelling.

MARTIN HEIDEGGER

Where there is space, there is being.

NIETZSCHE

*The city is mapped by death. Around every corner death appears as a cagelike
funeral contraption laced with strings of lights (on nights when there is electricity) that holds blurred snapshots of now-dead boys. The inky images slip
out and move like ghosts through the city, taped to the back windows of taxis
and trucks, haunting as they announce imminent death to a yet untouched
street.*

*Larger-than-life posters of war martyrs, whose eyes bleed ink in the rain,
stare down at her as she tries to find her way through a labyrinth of changing names.[1] Black like the martyr's eyes, she's covered from head to foot in the
mandatory Islamic covering, soaking wet and invisible to oncoming cars that
hydroplane past her—unable to differentiate her from the dark, wet night.*

12. Images of martyrs done in mosaic, Rey, Iran. (Photo by Roxanne Varzi, 2000)

Cars are not the only dangers. The komiteh, Islamic police, are said to be like rats, afraid of the rain and yet they prowl the streets.

She is trained to check every emotion and make herself invisible, to blend with the city and become a ghost. Tehran is a city of living and dead ghosts.

This is Tehran as seen from the inside and the outside, as I see it, walking through the streets, covered in black, death on my mind, on the tip of my tongue. Tehran stays with you and inhabits your mind, even after you are through inhabiting it. Later, in Istanbul on a street corner, I ask my Turkish friend when the young boys in the posters covering the side of a building were martyred. "That's our national soccer team." She laughs at my mistake. I continue to stare at them as if they are dead, however: death is imbedded in every thought, in every public image of a young man displayed. Miles away in another time zone, Tehran continues to occupy my mind's eye.

Revolutionary cultural policy in every sector of the Islamic republic (visual and print media, Islamic rules for behavior and the education of youth) is aimed solely at creating and projecting an Islamic identity on and to the public. Producing an Islamic identity is inextricably tied to the project of creating an Islamic social space; in a revolutionary state space is as much a part of ideology formation as ideology is a part of spatial formation.² The Iranian government has created a visual state that promotes an Islamic ideology, thereby keeping to Henri Lefebvre's axiom that what may be seen defines what is obscene. In such places, the ultimate foundation of social space is prohibition. This is especially true of Tehran, where restrictions and bans define a bound public space.

In the previous chapter I noted how Khomeini's project of Islamization manipulated the images and documentary themes of the war and the revolution to create a mental and physical ideological space in which to construct Iran's Islamic "reality." By exploring the intricate dance between the state and subject (the subject and object) as they work on and against each other in a battle to see and be seen, in this chapter I will examine the ways in which social Islamic space (zaher) is experienced (baten). In the end, do we occupy space, or does it occupy us?³ This chapter illustrates that the relationship between Iranian youths and the Islamic public space they inhabit in Tehran is a constant struggle as public space attempts to colonize young people, while these young people in their consumptive practices are constantly transforming that space for their own purposes.

CREATING AN ILLUSION

If power is bound by its visibility, then the power of Iran's clergy was made visible by the Islamic surface they so quickly created.⁴ By the time the generation of youth born at the beginning of the revolution was fully cognizant of its environment, Tehran was already transformed into an Islamic revolutionary space: Islamic covering for women was fully enforced; old monuments were replaced by revolutionary ones; and billboards of Muslim clerics and other Islamic visuals covered the city. Tehran is a typical revolutionary city in its ideological re-adaptation of space. From the old regime's cabarets and nightclubs appeared sandwich shops and bakeries; the Pahlavi Cultural Foundation became the Foundation of the Oppressed; the famous vineyards of Shiraz started producing grape juice in little triangular packets. Basij billboards display sayings

13. A mural done in the style of Soviet social realism, showing a Muslim soldier praying. This mural is painted alongside an Armenian church in downtown Tehran. (Photo by Roxanne Varzi, 2000)

14. An image of Ali Khameini, southern Tehran. (Photo by Roxanne Varzi, 2000)

of the Ayatollah—Namaz, Namaz, Namaz (Pray, Pray, Pray)—printed in neat block letters, each word an echo of the former, a constant reminder to pray that stands alongside other Islamic visuals that cover the city. Here there are strict social rules: women and men who are not related are not allowed to interact socially; boys and girls are segregated in school; and, until Khatami's election, entertainment such as chess, music, and theater was forbidden.

DIARY ENTRY, WINTER 1993, TEHRAN *Some mornings it's nice to know that it does not matter what you wear because no one will see anything but a tired face. I throw on my rupush over sweats and a T-shirt and pull my unruly hair into a barrette and cover it with my russari.*

"You did not bring a meghna-eh?" My friend Yasmine asks at the bus stop. She's taking me with her to college today.

"They make me feel claustrophobic. Do not worry, I'll pin my russari like a meghna-eh."

Light traffic echoes like curt snores through the sleeping streets.

When the bus comes, Yasmine shows me where to board in the back with the rest of the women. "Women ride in the back. Sometimes a ticket collector takes our tickets; otherwise we must walk to the front and hand the driver our ticket before boarding in the back. If it's really busy, we simply pass the ticket up from person to person until it reaches the driver. The worst thing is that the bus only allows five seats at the back for the women, while the men get most of the bus to themselves. They're usually all sitting, while we're packed together like sardines."

Our bus is long and brightly colored, pink and yellow. When we reach Taj-rishe Square, the main traffic circle in northern Tehran at the foothills of the mountains, surrounded by shops, restaurants, and a large mosque and bazaar, we switch from the bus to a shared taxi that makes runs up the foot of the mountain to Melli University.

University students are required to wear a strict black form of hejab called a meghna-eh, which tightly lines the face with an elastic border, thereby hiding any trace of hair, ears, and forehead wrinkles. Luckily, the man on gate duty was too nearsighted to notice that my russari is not a meghna-eh.

After passing the gate guard, we go through a curtained area, like airport security, where women guards check for makeup, sloppy hejab, lack of

15. A young woman walks quickly past a mural; her head is down, concentrating on her steps and not the mothers and dead martyrs beckoning to her from the walls. (Photo by Nader Davoodi, 1998)

socks, transparent hose, and plucked eyebrows—depending on who's looking we make it through without difficulty.

"Last week," Yasmine tells me, "the student ahead of me in line was forced to wash off all her foundation. They even have nail polish remover available."

Before heading to class we slip into the women's prayer room, where among prostrate students we find a place to stand to remove our heavy winter sweaters from under our rupushes.

"A lot of girls come in here to reapply their makeup after getting past the guards. Last week the komiteh barged into class and checked everyone for hejab. Three of my classmates had reapplied their makeup after going through the gate. The komiteh took them to the office, lined them up inside, and told them to wait there. The minute the komiteh turned to leave, the girls ran. So, now the komiteh watches us all the time from the windows in the rooms behind us," Yasmine tells me, pointing to the window behind where we are sitting. *"It's the window of the Islamic guidance office."* [5]

Even the bodies of the citizenry that move through the city create an ideological space.[6] Bearded men and black-clad women create the necessary look of an Islamic state and reinforce the relationship between belief and vision. Citizens dressed in black become a backdrop for the colorful billboards. Black clothing is required of all bodies — including those of tourists as well as women heads of state and female diplomats. In Iran, discourse forms the body; this is true of the Islamic body, which is the ultimate site/sight of the state's political rhetoric. Islamically clothed bodies become instruments (the site/sight of well-disciplined Islamic subjects) through which a social law maintains its hold on subjects and regulates them (by objectifying them). Youths who never experienced anything but this strong Islamic dress code were already consumed by and made a part of the objective dominant Islamic space before the possibility of rethinking that space (one cannot retrospectively rethink something that was always there). These youths formed the habit of dressing Islamically, starting from the time they became old enough to actively participate as individuals in public life.[7] This particular habit exemplifies the everyday experience of tactility where, as Michael Taussig states, "unconscious strata of culture are built into social routines as bodily disposition."[8] If social space is supposed to form the subject in the subject's tactile encounters with such space, then there is no better way to encourage space to transform identity than by making the subject physically inseparable from social space. This physicality of contact emphasizes what Walter Benjamin calls the "thingness of the city." Feeling the physical confinement of Islamic dress is a much more productive method of propagation for the state than erecting a million posters. Posters are more easily ignored than the feel of a hejab that is in constant need of adjustment or the effort to avoid tripping on a long hem and the effect of being trapped in a black, heat-absorbing tent on a hot summer day. Thus the subject becomes object by incorporating the object in the act of seeing, where the eye becomes more than a detached observer; it touches and absorbs that which it observes.

Experiencing the city as uniform and experiencing the self as part of that topography is the ultimate inclusion. The way Tehran youths see themselves is the way they view their landscape: average; similar to everyone else; and, more important, part of the objective space not as individuals but as fellow citizens.[9]

When a woman looks in the mirror she sees a part of the state, part of the public space. In the Islamic republic of Iran women's bodies become a part of the object (Islamic space), which is constructed so that ideology will seep into the very being of those who traverse it. Just as Khomeini's image floats on the backside of every dead martyr's picture, the state finds a way to superimpose itself on the individual so they cannot easily be visually, physically, mentally, or ideologically separated. This is a contrived, forced merging that does not evolve through experiential synthesis. This merging occurs a priori, before the possibility of resisting the dominant version of space/vision.[10] The mindscape and cityscape have merged. Law becomes habit.

This dominate space can be part of the imagination as well, if the person who occupies such space is willing to engage in it as part of their reality (as do most Basij and followers of the state). Otherwise, it is not part of the imagination of those who choose to ignore it, like many secular youths whose imaginations run counter to it. The memory of the city does not, therefore, show encounters but rather scenes in which we encounter ourselves in a "topographical consciousness."[11]

SUMMER 1995 *Remnants of a fleeting dark blue bruise the sky as night seeps into its veins. The city turns to neon as the sun drowns in its own last bright effort. It is in this light, the in-between, as the sun declines and gives one last bright wink, as the neon flutters and stretches and yawns, before the moon shows her face, that I catch an uncanny sight reflected in a passing shop window: myself, covered from head to foot in black. I have to look again, to slow down, take a few steps back and test whether the tall woman in black who just passed the reflecting store window is actually me. My bag, my eyes, my hand, reaching up to wipe the sweat from my brow cannot be denied. But this does not look like me—this person, like everyone else, looks like part of the landscape, but certain clues cannot be ignored: somewhere in there I am.[12]*

16. An ID picture showing the required magneh (head covering) for government offices and schools.

17. The chador, shown here in a Tehran bazaar on Ashura, is worn for prayer, in a mosque, or by religious women and government workers. (Photo by Roxanne Varzi, 2000)

According to some theorists of modernity this century has privileged the sense of vision over other ways of perceiving, like touch: As Taussig states: "The unremitting emphasis of analysis here is not only on shock-like rhythms, but on the unstoppable merging of the object of perception with the body of the perceiver." Taussig also describes the physicality of the mimetic experience of becoming part of the object of perception: "Copy and contact are steps in the same process, that a ray of light, for example, moves from the rising sun into the human eye where it makes contact with the retinal rods and cones to form, via the circuits of the central nervous system, a (culturally attuned) copy of the rising sun."[13] When thinking about space, the subject/object dichotomy does not exist because the subject becomes part of the object (and vice versa).[14] This is what occurs between cities and citizens.

City planners are not the only ones who invent the spatial existence of the city. At the same time that the city works to invent subjects, they too are working on the city, mentally and physically. The city is eternally written and rewritten by pedestrians, who write a text that they cannot read; viewing a city from above is like reading a text.[15] It is a complicated two-way street. The act of walking is a space of enunciation, a type of rhetoric: de Certeau states that "the long poem of walking manipulates spatial organization . . . it creates shadows and ambiguities . . . it inserts its multitudinous references and citations."[16] Walking selects and fragments the space traversed; it skips over links and omits whole parts, "it practices the ellipses of conjunctive loci."[17] Every day the city is born anew. Even the words that dress the city change: billboard advertisements, street names, and newspapers. Only the practice of metaphor remains outside the grid and the acceptable routine of the city. Migrational and metaphorical, the city slips into the clear text of a planned and readable space.

A city reveals itself to a stranger only in the first encounter. Once the imagination begins to work on a space, it creates a new space, one that may be different from the original perception of that physical space.[18] Representational space is appropriated by the imagination and overlays physical space, making symbolic use of its objects (which might as easily mean rejecting these objects). Only as a stranger, a lost newcomer, do we pay attention to our surroundings in order to navigate them. Once we know where we are, we begin to navigate unconsciously; it is in the realm of the unconscious and in habit that we experience the city the majority of the time.[19]

There is more to experiencing space than what meets the eye.

CREATIVE CONSUMERS: REMAKING SPACE

Space, like the commodities that occupy it, is not always used as originally intended by the producer. Space is not only transformed in the mind's eye but also through physical daily use. One of my favorite examples of daily use is the graffiti I found at a popular hiking spot in northern Tehran: *Shahram dear, please call me.* Here public space is used as a message board for what is not allowed in private space. Perhaps the graffiti was written by someone who is not allowed to leave a message at Shahram's home, because, most likely, this person is a girl and it may not be socially acceptable for her to do so.

In Tehran, the most creative consumers of the city are the youths who have developed an entire system in order to operate around the komiteh. Such youths have found that the most important components of survival (transgression) in Tehran are a fit body, a fast car (or a clever driver), and knowledge of geography.

Tehran is an enormous metropolis that has grown eratically without maintaining a consistent center. While it seems to grow like a boundless amoeba, the Alborz mountain range acts to close it in and has thus forced it either to spill out into dry, remote areas outside of the mountain valley or on top of itself (which is problematic because Tehran rests on a major fault line). While the mountains contain Tehran in their tight grip, they also provide an escape for those who are fit enough to climb above the usual walking paths. In the winter, ski season provides one of the only public social outlets where youths can fraternize with the opposite sex and meet people outside of their own neighborhood or familial relations. While the Islamic police tightly controls the ski slopes,

18. "Shahram dear, call me": Message written on the wall in Darband, a favorite weekend hiking spot in Northern Tehran. (Photo by Roxanne Varzi, 2000)

19. Mixed messages: Others speak through omission. (Photo by Nader Davoodi, 1998)

20. Up, up and away . . . we're no longer in Islamic Iran. After a steady climb up toward the mountains, Tehran loses its Islamic veneer. (Photo by Roxanne Varzi, 1997)

strong skiers can make their way above the last lift station to a place where veils are easily removed and coed gatherings are possible. Thus the space of nature, especially that unbridled locale of deep nature so antithetical to the metropolis — the mountains, the Caspian region, hills and deserted areas — provides the ultimate space of freedom.[20] Young people use the city in other ways as well. The old, beat-up patrol cars of the komiteh have a hard time going uphill, so someone in an even slightly better car can merely take a turn up one of Tehran's many steep streets and the komiteh cars will not be able to follow.

It is important to note here that the northern part of Tehran, in the foothills of the Alborz, is inhabited mainly by the upper class, while the south (further from the mountains) is inhabited by poorer Tehranis and squatters. The south has fewer skyrises whereas tall apartment buildings mark the north. As one literally rises above the city, whether hiking or in an elevator heading up toward one's home, it is interesting to watch how revolutionary public space is for the most part left behind. For those who can rise above it, Islamic Tehran turns into the visual representation of any secular city located in a mountain valley; of course, this is not so for those who live at eye level.

TRAFFIC JAM, SUMMER NIGHT, 2001[21] *Black jeans, black T-shirt—could be Tehran, could be New York—hair slicked back with oil, cologne strong enough to attract women, taunt the Islamic police, and give an anthropologist an allergy attack. Jordan Street. Thursday night. Cruising.*

Neon bulbs dangle from the little roadside flower stands that look like big white bubbles and, at night, like giant light bulbs. There is only room for one behind the small counter, where a man stands deftly wrapping the flowers and twisting a rubber band around their stems. He hands the cellophane-wrapped flowers to the young girl whose perfume overpowers the scent of all his flowers—indeed, it overpowers him. She gives him a tip but barely thanks him. As one who is poru (selfish), she is already in character.[22]

The Kansas deli is hopping; there is as long a line to get out the door with take-away as there is to get in the door to order or to be seated. Inside, groups of boys and girls sit at tables below old black-and-white photos of 1940s Tehran: horse-driven carriages alongside old Fords; snow-capped, pre-global-warming mountains; space on makeshift sidewalks and in the streets; and unveiled Iranian and European women waiting in line for roast beef sandwiches—this is the past.

Jordan is a long street that runs north from Argentine Square to a major four-way intersection that in turn continues north, west, and south. It is a two-way street, or rather two one-way streets with an island of grass that separates the north-south stretch from the south-north one. There are few places to turn around, and should the traffic become unbearable a driver might be forced to sit in place for hours—which for some is its charm. Like a crowded bar at happy hour, Jordan hosts a traffic jam every Thursday night by youths who come showered, coifed, and ready to be stuck in traffic in hopes that their car might get jammed in next to a car full of interesting members of the opposite sex.

Seven girls are piled into a boxlike, crème-colored Peykan car. One of the two girls jammed into the front passenger seat has to lift her "seat" every time the driver shifts gears. Segregation. The boys are piled and packed into a sleek new Jeep, the bass on the stereo pumps techno loud enough to nearly drown out the insults and jokes—the flirtations, in short—that are exchanged between the Peykan and the Jeep. The boys ask for numbers but the girls taunt and flirt coyly until the light changes or the traffic jam is suddenly cleared and they have no choice but to throw out the window pre-prepared makeshift slips on cigarette boxes and other offerings in hopes that the wind will carry them to a place of pollination . . . to the possibility of a phone call. The Jeep slowly begins to move as one boy comically opens the door and jumps out of the car—all the while still holding onto the moving door—in order to retrieve a wayward slip of paper with a magic number neatly penned in purple ink.

Approaching the midway point of southbound Jordan Street, the girls lick lipstick from their lips and pull their scarves forward to cover their foreheads and wisps of hair that were neatly and purposely pulled out earlier in the evening. The boys turn off their music, pull the tape out of the deck, and place it in a back pocket (the Basij always check the glove compartment) before returning to their individual seats. No one hangs out the window; the middle seats that had emptied are now filled because the window seat is no longer the most desirable.

Three plain-clothed Basij stand alongside the neon orange construction cones set up alongside the road in order to create a bottleneck to check passing cars. Two of the eighteen-year-old Basij have guns slung across their shoulders. The third boy has a walkie-talkie that is directly linked to the komiteh, who at any moment might be asked to appear with a van or car to transport the guilty youth to jail.[23]

The girls do not smile or say hello when the Basij pull them over.

"Where are you headed?"

"To our aunt's house." The driver looks straight ahead, avoiding eye contact when speaking with the Basij.

"All of you together? You are not all related."

"It's her birthday and it's women only."

"What's the address?" He writes it down; he might have to raid it later.

"ID's please."

The boys are less fortunate. They have to step out of the car while it is searched. They are patted down roughly, like criminals, and questioned. They are told that long hair is for homosexuals and that they have lost sight of God, and that perhaps it would be best for the Basij to help them back by sending them to the mosque this evening to speak with a very influential hezbollah. They pay off the Basij and leave. Others are less lucky.

Two months later, Jordan Street is host to a religious ceremony. This does not, however, stop the regular cruisers from showing up to scope out members of the opposite sex. In the old days Ashura was a solemn but social event. There were elements of mourning but also celebration. Yet during the war it became more solemn than social as Islamic rules and the punishments for not following them were strictly enforced, and emphasis was placed on the martyrdoms of the imams rather than on the post-Ta'zieh and sineh-zani feasts.

TA'ZIEH: PLAYING WITH PASSION *Tonight's Ta'zieh boasts a record number of people, mostly older religious folk and youths. Inside the amphitheater men and women are segregated on either side of the stage, and it appears that there are far more women than men. The men that are in attendance are mostly over the age of fifty, while the women are of every imaginable age from three to eighty. When the three-hour performance ends we head back to the car via the park attached to the amphitheater. Outside the amphitheater, in the park, some hundred dashing young men wait for the girls to come out after the play.*

"Given my great distaste for Ta'zieh, I came out to take a nap in the car, you should have seen the scene—there were a hundred boys looking for girlfriends." My friend's husband tells me.

"How was the play?" I ask a boy who passes by.

"Did not see it," he calls back, too busy tailing a fast-gaited girl to talk to me.

"What did you think of the Ta'zieh?" I ask another boy.

"I'm not so into Ta'zieh."

"So why are you here?"

"You know, hanging out."

"But why here at the Ta'zieh?"

"Everyone's here," the boy says moving his hand over his shiny, gelled hair.

"You really went all out for this," I comment, nodding to his chic black jeans and black button-down oxford.

"Yeah, well it's for Imam Husayn!" he snickers.

"Shit," he turns his head, sensing something is wrong before I register what is happening, and runs off. I look off in the direction from which he is running to find a komiteh officer, decked-out in combat boots and baggy military wear with a gun slung over his shoulder, busy shooing away the crowd. The crowd disperses quickly, in the course of which it naturally falls into line with the sineh zani (flagellation) procession making its way up Jordan Street.

On Jordan Street the pick-up scene continues as young women in elegantly flowing long black rupushes and pretty satin black russaris flirt across the way with boys in large SUVs with banners reading "Imam Husayn we love you." Most of the boys stand alongside the road, ignoring their religious peers who whip chains across their backs in tune to the rhythm of an impressive steel drum and cymbals.

In the case of Jordan Street, sineh zani and Ta'zieh are transformed through participation by youths whose intentions for and expectations of the ritual differ from its original intent and purposes. Sineh zani becomes an opportunity to fraternize and occupy space with an excuse that one would not ordinarily have for loitering, while Ta'zieh allows youths the opportunity to find a large number of the opposite sex, of similar age, in one place.[24] Like the chador, which is used to cover satellite dishes, Islamic ritual is also used at times to excuse and cover other acts.

JOURNAL ENTRY, FEMALE TEHRAN COLLEGE STUDENT, SPRING 2000 The susul (spoiled) boy from upstairs is playing a loud noheh tape and flying a black flag outside his house.[25] He does this—as we have witnessed each time he brings home a different girl—every day. He pretends to have hey'ats (religious gatherings) in the afternoon in order to bring women home and not be bothered by the komiteh. He thinks he's fooled us and we see him as a pious young man, ha!

We had another neighbor who had an auto dealership, a nouveau riche from the south of the city who moved uptown. This guy fought with his wife every day, and finally got a new wife . . . but until last year we were witness to all of their fights. At times the police had to come. This neighbor was in love with his first wife. First he'd hit her hard then go into the street and cry.

Muharram: He had a beard and he spent money for alms and hey'ats and food to give and bought his susul wife a lacy black chador and red lipstick and her orange hair would fall out of her chador and for Imam Husayn he'd give his soul . . . crying, beating his chest, you know the deal. They would put flags up and have loud dasteh and sineh zani without our consent. All of us neighbors were given nazri (alms) to keep quiet. So he thought with nazri that all of his sins were forgiven and he could start his bad work again the next day until the next Muharram.[26]

This transformed usage of ritual (and ritual wear, like the chador) is what de Certeau calls a secondary production, or something that is hidden in use. De Certeau uses the example of colonizers who introduce objects to colonial subjects, who in turn use the objects differently than their original intended use. The idea of secondary production is a valuable one, as noted above in the ways in which youths consume space, but it is also an important notion in (tired) debates about "Western" versus "Islamic" modernity. When the Islamic revolution first attempted to purge the country of Western elements, they conflated anything "modern" with "Western," as most modern technology was at the time produced by the West. Now the idea of "modern" has been redefined as something that is also Islamic. For example, modern technology like the Internet can be used for Islamic purposes (especially its propagation), which in the course of use transforms the technology from an evil Western entity to a new Islamic tool. The fact that an Islamic country is on the Internet (in what many believe to be a sign of "secular" "Western modernity") does not mean that the country is necessarily buying into Western notions of modernity.

Cyberspace can be anywhere, in any language, at any time. In the beginning Internet usage in Iran was only permissible for the clergy in the town of Qom, for the explicit use of proselytizing Islamic doctrine, introducing Shiite thought, and discussing Hadith with scholars in other parts of the Muslim world (in cyberspace the Muslim world could include New York or London as easily as Qom).[27] Just as colonial subjects who reappropriate certain colonial objects do not condone colonialism, the fact that the objects are unmade or remade is in itself a form of resistance to the producer of the object.

The Islamic republic of Iran, where certain commodities and practices are either restricted or mandatory, provides a ready example of secondary production. A state of imposed normality makes transgression a norm.[28] If this were not the case in Tehran, the city would appear like an endless funeral procession of solemn, black-clad citizens mourning a life in prison. Just as the state can claim a computer is Islamic, a woman can use a hejab or chador for secular purposes. While the Islamic republic enforces its cultural discourse through ritual and dress, these things used in unintended ways reinvest the power in the ritual or the covering from the hand of the state that imposes it to the citizen who uses it. Thus it is through improvisation that the average citizen makes his or her way around a social sphere of strict prohibitions. But even improvisation has its rules.

FIELD NOTES, 1993 *Black-robed, floating through a crowd of similarly cloaked bodies, mannequinlike faces stare back at me. I drift through the crowd like a black cloud, my eyes covered by forbidden sunglasses.*

My music is hidden under my russari. It moves me, dictates my speed, my rhythm, my thoughts — it blocks out the sounds of mourning music, snickering men, and honking horns.

It's late; the sun is setting when I walk through the front door. I start undressing the minute the garden door slams behind me. I pull my russari off my head and let it hang around my neck while I unbutton my long Islamic coat. It opens and spreads like wings and flaps behind me as I run up the steps. I undo my Walkman from my belt and pull the strings from under my turtleneck. I'm like the satellite dishes on the rooftops in Tehran covered by old chadors — as if the physical cover could change my rhythm, content, or shape — the way I think, act, my reception, or the things I do under cover. "They'll catch you," says my aunt, looking at my Walkman disapprovingly.

"How? I'm covered."[29]

From the perspective of a stranger, the required Islamic clothing transforms the surface of Iranian women's bodies into part of the visual landscape of an Islamic city.[30] To the untrained eye, the average Tehrani woman appears to be strictly adhering to Islamic dress codes. To look closely, however, is to see how the ways in which the woman wears these clothes and her small alterations to them (half an inch on the hem, a bright-colored scarf) differentiate her from the monotonous Islamic visual landscape. Even Islamic dress provides room for interpretation. Altered and played with, clothing meant for a specific use can be utilized in ways that transform its planned effect so as to allow for resistance. The ways in which women transform the mandatory uniform in order to assert their individual aesthetic desires point to markers of class, age, and geographic location. By changing her appearance, a woman changes the look of the public sphere. Improvisations mark the wearer within a framework of social and cultural rules and types. Even in a place where political affiliation and class are supposed to be unitary, or at least appear to be that way through a dress code, women have found ways around the dress code to defy what it is supposed to represent: the deportment of good, middle-class Islamic citizens. For example, during the 1980s colorful coverings were only worn by women in the northern part of the city (where less-religious citizens lived); a Chanel scarf was an indicator of a woman who had either been abroad or had friends who went abroad and could afford such luxuries. Youths who defied the dress code, even by an inch, obviously belonged to secular families, while women who chose traditional covering at the university usually came from families supportive of the Islamic regime. In northern Tehran there were more chadors used on roofs to cover forbidden satellite dishes, or used to hide liquor in transit, than were seen being worn by women in the streets.[31]

These tactics of consumption are the ingenious ways in which the weak (in this case those being disciplined by the state, women and youth, regardless of financial or educational status) make use of the strong (the government), thus lending a political dimension to everyday practices.[32] So these are improvisations, small transgressions against a law that has become habit. For Benjamin, however, this is not enough: the real revolutionary act would be for habit to catch up with itself. Transgressive physiognomic play would be to take a certain space and incorporate it, and in the process change it so completely that it becomes one's own work and not that of the government.[33] This is not only about transforming things physically, but also about the way in which one's mind is transformed or fixed to see or imagine what one wants to see or imagine. Such an effort entails a hyperawareness of one's space, where the experience of the space must be anticipated (having already been there and knowing what to expect) in order to avoid or dismiss it in a concerted effort not to look. While Taussig suggests that transgression is waking up to a full awareness of one's presence as an active subject among a world of objects, transgression in Iran is about being consciously unaware in spaces one does not want to be in: to walk through the city like a sleepwalker or somnambulist. (Or even the very opposite, like a Buddhist practicing mindful awareness: awake and aware, but detached.) So, instead of the automatic pilot merely being woken up to its own automaticity, the transgressive act is to be consciously unaware or awake to one's automaticity in order to quell a habit, and yet detached in order to resist participating fully in a space that is undesirable. In this action, Tehran becomes transformed into something other than its original purpose (for the government a space of Islamic propagation).

JOURNAL ENTRY, FEMALE TEHRAN COLLEGE STUDENT, SPRING 2000 She's right. I've never really thought about it but I guess there are certain places we avoid driving by without much thinking: we would never just drive down Vozarah [near the main komiteh jail] as a group of boys and girls, not unless we want to spend a night there—not unless we are masochistic or hard up for entertainment . . . though I know friends who are, and who do drive by there just to taunt the Basij, to be taken in so they can mock them all night and then say they were caught. We do a lot of these things without thinking. When Roksana points them out I notice that we do certain things, but I never think about it . . . like not driving past Vozarah with boys, like turning down the music in certain parts of town.

In an earlier visit to Iran when my Persian was less fluent—just after the war, when Rafsanjani was president and Tehran was plastered in revolutionary posters—I would ask my cousin to translate the posters. Instead of literal translations, I was often given explanations laden with opinion: "Oh, that's not an important sign; it says that prayer is like a dewy spring garden. Government garbage." Sometimes, my cousin would barely look at the poster before translating it. Like most Tehranis she no longer read the text, even the image-text, because she has come to anticipate propaganda in anything displayed in public space.

A few years ago I began to record propaganda in public spaces. My interest in propaganda immediately branded me as an outsider to my northern Tehran peers: what decent Iranian would photograph a government billboard or, for that matter, even stop to look at it? My cousin, who had no idea what my project was about, offered to help me "record Tehran," and so we sped through the empty highways in search of sites. Along the way he pointed out old important architecture, ancient monuments, and pre-revolution sites (like the shah's palaces).

"Do you want me to stop so you can take a picture?" he would proudly ask.

"No, thanks, that's not what I'm after." He would then shrug his shoulders and knit his brows, surely wondering about my motivations. When I finally asked him to pull over on the shoulder of the highway so that I could photograph a billboard of a young girl wiping the blood off a martyr's forehead, my cousin caught onto my project and became enraged.

"Why do you want to show the rest of the world our fanaticism? This is not Tehran—these are forms of government propaganda."[34]

If this is not Tehran, then what is? How is the city, already a text, translated into another text? How can my cousin drive past these billboards every day, experience them and see that they physically dominate public space, and still claim that they are not Teh-ran? How is it that he can live in this city and not see what is most obvious?

In Iran people learn to ignore or simply not register images that are part of the public sphere. They walk past them as though they are merely old rotted buildings, present and yet invisible. Space is navigated unconsciously, already appropriated by the mind. Through mental mediation Iranian citizens are easily able to move away from the state-produced space. And, in this way, Iranian life runs counter to automaticity at the same time that people seem to be functioning by habit: an individual in Iran is constantly calculat-ing, evaluating, making decisions, and turning on and off the in-strument of vision (be it in the mind or physically turning away) in an attempt to be seen and unseen. They mentally block what they do not want to be a part of (like the visual landscape of an Islamic republic) and force themselves into places they do (like the women who rushed into the soccer stadium, where women are not allowed, after Iran won the qualifying game for the World Cup). Hypervigi-lance (the ultimate cocktail of hyperawareness and denial) comes naturally for people who have lived through a war and revolution.[35]

Hypervigilance, hyperreality, hyperspace: the ability to be in two or three different places at once—or not at all. Spatial reality in Teh-ran resembles the Internet: it is hyperreal, full of text, images, and places to surf (to travel to), but only at the click of the mouse. Like hypertexts, parts of the city (those image fragments that create the city's montage) can be clicked on and off. Benjamin and de Cer-teau saw the city as a discursive and physical space; but what they had yet to experience is the new technology of hyperspace that is not just about writing but about traveling—clicking. Just as writing is a metaphor for experiencing the city, one could use the motion of clicking the mouse to move from space to space, from aware-ness to hyperawareness to numbness, as a way that a generation raised using computers might experience and perpetually reinvent the city.[36] In Tehran, pockets of space are experienced like hyper-texts: omnipresent but not always clicked into activation.

One type of Tehrani may experience the city as a space of martyr-

dom and nationalism: a place that evokes a sense of patriotism replete with Islamic banners, sculptures of tanks, and fountains of
blood. The city may evoke a sense of pride in an "Iranianess" that
is different from that of another Tehrani who in the same area sees
only Bulgari jewelry ads, greenery, and mountains, and who takes
pride in the urban geography while forsaking nationalist rhetoric
because she no longer sees what she is so practiced at not seeing
(that which she wishes not to see). I know this from talking to
people, from asking them what they see and experience when they
walk through Tehran, but I also know it from my own experience.
It was not until I stopped concentrating my research on war visuals
did I realize that I was practicing, unconsciously, the art of seeing
what I wanted to see, of clicking from one hyperreality to the next,
of making Tehran into what I wanted it to be. One day after a period
of time when I had been exclusively concentrating on the lives of
secular youth in northern Tehran, I realized that I had completely
left the world of Basij and the war; a world wherein at one time I was
so fully steeped that it defined Tehran for me.[37] My lack of interest was enough to transport me from revolutionary Islamic Tehran
to a cosmopolitan consumer capital where shopping and hanging
out at burger joints was a way of life for many youths. The minute I
stopped paying attention to the war propaganda, it almost ceased
to exist.[38]

These hyperrealities did not appear organically out of consensus; they emerged on the scene through time and experience.
The physicality of revolutionary Tehran, however, was constructed
"overnight." Many new parks, freeways, and public buildings, especially mosques, were constructed after the revolution.[39] Those
who protest that Tehran was a sprawling metropolis before the
revolution, have yet to see the new freeway system, the apartment
buildings, the revolutionary banners, the ways in which public
space is allocated and used, the revolutionary courts and holding
pens for disobedient youths all over the city. Hyperreality is a journey through space where the individual is the only pilot in control
of the mouse that clicks to "anywhere" and nowhere. Today, because of new technologies, social spaces (through the hyperspace

of the mind as well as the Internet) superimpose on one another and thereby further complicate the already complicated study of the everyday.[40] The effect of modern technology is thus reversed: no longer does technology encourage rote mechanization, instead it now encourages quick-paced thinking and clicking.

Early theorists of modernity feared the empty, automated, and rote living that resulted from industrialization. Marx's observation about the reification and objectification of people and the animation of objects is at the heart of any discussion of tactility and the city. In the case of oil-rich Iran in the 1970s, it was the threat of an industrial modernity that reified oil workers and animated the oil that Khomeini employed as a call for an awakening.[41] Modern living had already trained Iranians to tune out when necessary. Ideological projects like China's Cultural Revolution or the Bolshevik revolution would not find success in fully postindustrial, media-savvy societies where people are adept at shutting off signs (and moving through hyperrealities in order to supersede physical reality) or, more pessimistically speaking, are asleep (or desensitized as a result of sensory overload). Iran's revolution forced youth who were raised under its regime to be creative in order to find freedom. Tehrani youth look for pockets outside the dominant physical space where space is mental and not buried in the polemics of physical time and geography—much like Ibn Arabi's imaginal geography, the alam-al-mithal described in chapter 1. Thus it is not surprising that modern, postindustrial Iranians would not fully succumb to the propaganda project at play after the revolution.[42] More than twenty years later, the republic of images is just that. And yet, even lost in thought, the physicality of daily exposure, tactility, must have had some affect.[43] If the mind does not occupy a certain space but the body does, is that space then fully occupied by the subject? Can that space still somehow touch the subject? Even if one's mind is shut down or attempting to click to another reality, the city must leave its mark, just as pedestrians leave their tracks.

CHAPTER FIVE

Shifting Subjects

Public Law and Private Selves

11:30 AM: SHARIF TECHNICAL UNIVERSITY, TEHRAN, ISLAMIC MORAL CHARACTER CLASS (REQUIRED), SPRING 2000 *"What is an Islamic character (akhlaq)?" The chador-clad professor rhetorically asks the classroom of women. She continues lecturing the handful of students about the two selves: one that is formed of matter and one that is not.*

"There are things in the world that can either be sensed by the five senses because they are made of matter, and other things, like kindness, that cannot." The professor's chador sweeps the ground as she walks over to the window. "We have proof that the window exists because we can see it. Kindness also exists but we cannot see it. Our spirit exists after our matter dies."

A student asks: "So what happens to our soul when our matter dies?"

"It remains."

"So how are these things like kindness tied to us as individuals if they are not a part of our physical matter?"

"The memory exists even if the actual event or person passes. So, kindness is not a physical attribute, but the memory of it remains. Let's use the Iran/Syria soccer game as an example . . . it's long over but we have a memory of it. Does that mean that it does not exist? We are informed always by a higher source. Our foot walks; we know this not from our foot but from our brain.

Our brain is a higher source of knowledge than our foot. Everything is relative to something higher."

"So, how do we know if someone is a real Muslim? What makes one a real Muslim?"

"When you believe truly; you do not think about it."[1]

At the outset of the revolution, Ayatollah Khomeini called on the good Muslim people of Iran to join in building an Islamic nation by producing more children. As a result, two-thirds of the Iranian public (a majority of the consuming public) is today below the age of twenty-five. The revolutionary project to create Islamic subjects was aimed mainly at the generation of youth that grew up exclusively in the Islamic republic of Iran (and thus born after 1979). The project spanned general education (concentrating on elementary education), public space, and the media. In the last chapter I described how the government attempted to use public space to formulate ideological subjects. Again, paying attention to ways in which the public sphere, or surface (zaher), is meant to affect the interior space of faith and belief (baten), in this chapter I examine more closely public laws of conduct and the intersection of public Islamic culture with private secular culture in northern, upper-middle-class Muslim Tehran. In so doing I show how strict rules for social behavior helped form a collective public identity that is at odds with private, individual identities formed outside the strict guidelines of the state.

PARTICIPATING IN THE ILLUSION:
PRACTICE MAKES PERFECT

The most efficient oppressor is he who persuades his underlings to love, desire and identify with his power and any practice of political emancipation thus involves that most difficult of all forms of liberation, freeing ourselves from ourselves. Terry Eagleton.

Blinding oneself to the visual messages in one's physical surroundings by simply ignoring them is easier than ignoring physical (tactile) rules of conduct. Belief is not fostered solely through visuals and slogans. As I began to demonstrate in the previous chapter, to make people believe in the Islamic republic is to make them physically part of the republic and to make them act out: women wearing hejabs acting Islamic in the public sphere. Therefore, by a curious circularity, the ability to make people act out, to write and to discipline bodies (through public laws, for example), is precisely what is said to make people believe. So, while teenagers may be adept at circumventing the dominant Islamic message, such an act is more difficult when that message is inscribed in one's actions and on one's body (the ultimate Islamic space).

Following on the discussion of tactility in the previous chapter, in this chapter I will delve deeper into the role that enforced habitual practice plays in formulating belief in an ideology in the public sphere; in short, the idea that action creates believers. According to Louis Althusser, ideology and ideological state apparatuses (visual materials and religious holidays and practices) form the subject—they exist prior to the subject and yet neither can be thought of separately.[2] The subject is formed in the reproduction of social relations and skills. Learning and reproducing rules in the form of ritual actions, through performance, supposedly spurns belief. Therefore the state's potential successfully to form Islamic subjects is greatest in the complex maze of rules and regulations (and less so in the visual aesthetics of Islamic space). We are reminded here of Mohammad Avini who says the best place to "practice" one's faith and religion is at the war front. And it was, as we saw, the best place to "be" Islamic.

While the project to produce Islamic subjects out of a generation that has been exposed to nothing but the Islamic republic may not have been completely successful, twenty years of sustained efforts by the government, aimed especially at children and young adults in public schools, strongly affected the worldview of many urban Iranians. Despite attempts to ignore the project of Islamification on the part of many secular youth, it would be naive and simplistic to say that the Islamic republic did not succeed in penetrating their lives and worldviews, or that Islam is not or will not be an important component of their value system.

21. A small child learns to mourn Husayn. (Photo by Roxanne Varzi, 2000)

DIARY ENTRY, TEHRAN 1993 *The creaking, dilapidated cage-type eleva-*
tor is the tarnishing skeleton of colonialism that we climb inside to see our
future. We walk into an apartment on the first floor, remove our shoes, and
sit beside two other young women who are also waiting.

The curtains are pulled and the room is small and dark. Shiva is a young
woman in an older woman's body. Her frizzy hair is hennaed auburn and tied
back with a rubber band. Dark bags under her eyes suggest that she spends
too many hours awake, probably taking care of her three-year-old son, who is
presently zooming his toy truck around the living room. But not even he can
cut her concentration.

"Cards, coffee grounds, or tarot?" Shiva turns to ask us between sittings.

"Aren't you a palm reader?" asks Leila, turning from the wall where she is
still hanging her Islamic gear. Her russari slips out of her hands like a person
in shock. Her disappointment surprises me. Fortune-telling is fortune-telling,
I think, what's the difference—especially to someone who considers it super-
stitious.

"Cards or coffee," Shiva repeats her offer, ignoring Leila's comment. The
other women are silent, pretending not to hear.

"Coffee," Leila answers.

"You too?" asks Shiva, wiping her brow with the back of her hand before reaching for a cigarette. She stands and walks toward the kitchen—cigarette in one hand, the other hand gently resting on the small of her back, palm facing in.

"Yes, please," I call after her.

Leila bends over to pick up her russari, catching the eye of the woman sitting across from us as she raises her head.

"Wasn't she once a palm reader?" Leila whispers. The young woman looks over her shoulder to check that Shiva is still in the kitchen before telling us that Shiva stopped reading palms a few years ago. "There were rumors," the woman begins, but she is unable to finish her thought as Shiva returns with a tray of four cups of Turkish coffee, mostly grounds, that she places on the table and instructs us to drink. She has left the tray in the middle of the room so that each of us has to rise, walk over, and collect our own cup.

"Do not drink it all, leave some at the bottom, then turn your cups over. If you're single, turn the cup with your left hand, nearest your heart," Shiva tells us as she takes her place at her table, stubs her cigarette out, and turns to ask who is next. We watch the two other women place the saucer over the cup and tightly hold it there as they turn the cup upside down and toward the heart. One woman closes her eyes and silently moves her lips as she asks her question or makes a wish. Leila hands me a mint, "I hate the taste of Turkish coffee."

"A cross, the sign of a miracle." Shiva points to a muddy-looking cross, a smudge of coffee grounds and water. I look at her intently, she's an Armenian, would a Muslim have interpreted a cross for a miracle?

"You have a trip, to the other side of the ocean," she tells me, interpreting my accent as easily as the cup.

For Leila's coffee, she interprets, "You're being deceived, a cat, see. . . ." She points to a cat figure in the cup, "a cat is clawing you from behind . . . a woman is standing in the way of a love affair."

She reads the cup contents with speed, interpreting symbols and dishing out definitions. Magic begins when you stop looking for meaning.

"Who told you Shiva was a palm reader?" I ask Leila later.

"I should have just stuck with Hafiz's writings. It's just that if I ask my father, who is the best interpreter of Hafiz that I know, he'll tell me what he wants me to hear—that I should go to a technical college, marry some boring businessman, that type of thing. I want the truth."

"You really think the truth is in your palm?"

FIELD NOTES, TEHRAN, 2000 Two Muslim girls take off their Islamic coverings and wait their turn to consult the Armenian fortune-teller. One girl is crying. They thank the fortune-teller for seeing them on such short notice; it was an "emergency." The Armenian fortune-teller ends her session by telling the girls to pray to the Imam Ali.

FIELD NOTES, TEHRAN, 2000 The hallway of the Kamkar Music Institute in central Tehran is crowded with young men and women tuning their instruments and awaiting their ten-minute meetings with masters of Persian classical music. The bearded, long-haired boys holding tambours and dafs project the image of Sufis, who traditionally were the only ones allowed to play these instruments. These instruments were taught in the khanehqhas, Sufi lodges, where the dervishes lived, removed from society, seeking oblivion. These boys whirl within the mass and mess of Tehran, far from the khanehqhas, far from religion, but close to the mystical poetry that they read nightly by candlelight in their self-made lodges.

A group of Iranian youths sits silently in awe as their hero, Paulo Kheulo (the top-selling author in Iran), lectures to them on the great poet and seeker Mawlana.

A woman lies on a long thin mat in a dark room where a hypnotist's hand circles the air above her head, moving energy, removing blocks, moving her to cry. She is taking part in a self-help class that teaches transcendental meditation, a class that began with a parable from Mawlana.

The Imam Ali, Hafiz, instruments of dervishes, sitars, dafs, Sufi poetry, and Mawlana are all signifiers of Islam. The youths who embrace these signifiers attempt to travel outside the conventions of the Islamic world in which they were raised, and yet their flight never leaves the confines of Islam. As long as they remain within the cultural confines of Iran, public and private, they cannot escape the Islamic sphere.

Two young boys in the museum of martyrdom walk among glass cases containing the slippers, last will and testaments, pictures, and dog tags of the boys who at their age died in the war.

A theater lays fallow and empty waiting for the actors who will play out the horrors of the war and the audience who will validate and mourn their rendition. Television monitors play Avini's documentary serial on a never-ending loop. A relief image on the wall depicts a 16mm camera mounted on a splatter of blood—it is dedicated to Avini.

"We were unaware. We're too young to remember the war and the government projected too much propaganda about it. They should have just let us hear directly from the martyrs through their writings. We understand and feel for them, but we think the government has done them a disservice with all the propaganda."

"What made you think this?"

"Going to the front on a school trip and seeing for ourselves. It changed how we feel. We come here often now." They are the only two visitors to the martyr museum in the past three months.

A theater director, also too young to remember the war, enters a play in the war commemoration festival. It is a vivid account of martyrdom with all the components of any war production: the good Muslim fighter and the unbelievers.

"Did you do a lot of research? How did you know how to create your piece?"

"I just know," he laughs.

"You must have watched a lot of war films and television programs."

"I was not inspired by anything in particular, I just came up with it. I've never watched a war film or documentary—at least not that I'm aware of," he says nonchalantly, sweeping his hand as if to say the material can be found in the very air that surrounds him. (Iranian television is constantly replaying war footage like Avini's documentary series.) He leans back against the wall and takes a drag on his cigarette—there's really nothing more to be said. Most young directors detest this material but choose to participate in the war commemoration festival because it is one of the few opportunities they have to show their work on stage.

A girl dresses for school. She is careful not to wear any makeup and to ensure that her hair and neck are completely covered so that she can pass the main *university entrance with ease. "Is there an illustration or did they teach you how to be Islamically dressed?"*

"What? No, of course not, we just know."

How does one "just know" and claim not to watch, not to have been told, not to pay attention? These examples illustrate the ways that public policy appears to have succeeded in penetrating the surface and ingraining Islamic revolutionary images, if not ideals, against the conscious will of its subjects. Because of lived experience within this strong public social sphere, the citizens of Iran know how to act Islamic and how they should represent themselves and their world.[3] They represent themselves dutifully as the model Islamic citizen, and yet almost all the youths that I questioned claim that no media material—Western or Iranian, especially propaganda—has adequately described them. At the same time, when asked how they would describe themselves almost everyone answered: plain, normal, like everyone else.[4]

Again, this attempt to form monolithic Islamic subjects was carried out on already-consenting secular (but Muslim) subjects. Iran was a Muslim country before the revolution. Islam was and is bound to be a major component of an Iranian's identity, regardless of whether or not there ever was an Islamic republic. Many Iranians lived, and would continue to live, by the main pillars and principles of Islam regardless of whether they were enforced by the state.

THE RULES

In a religious state, rules or cultural values and morals are displayed by behavior. When an individual enters the public realm in Iran she or he is conscious of "being Islamic." The Islamic republic is counting on Islamic ritual to produce Islamic subjects. The government propagates Islamic ideology in every possible daily ritual and rule—for example, in elementary school physical exercise where students are instructed to shout out numbers, followed by "Allah," after each move: a side bend, "one Allah," touch toes, "two Allah." The repeated practice of Islamic acts is vital to building an Islamic

22–23. School-text images from before and after the revolution. (P. J. Chelkowski and Hamid Dabashi, *Staging a Revolution*)

citizenry. Blaise Pascal writes that practice generates and fosters belief; like the act of kneeling in church. Do exercises or the act of covering for women create good Islamic citizens? Other theorists would answer no, because there must first be a consenting subject (prima materia) present in the psychic space before it evolves onto the material realm. For ritual to be effective a seed of belief must first exist. Ideology must presume a consenting subject prior to the performance of the ritual; a volitional subject must already be in place to give an account of motivation.

How does this consenting subject come to be? Does it precede entrance into the symbolic (material) world and hence becoming subject? The majority of Iranians were Muslims before the revolution and continued to raise their children as Muslims, which provides the state with what could be considered preexisting consent, at least as far as acting out ritual is concerned.[5] However, the Islamic persona formed at home and the persona formed by the state are not necessarily consistent. This inconsistency is leading ultimately to a situation of social crisis.

RULES: PLAYING IN THE PUBLIC SPHERE

During my time as an outsider struggling to live in Tehran, my main concern was learning how to "be" Islamic. For the first few weeks that I lived in my uncle's home, my thirteen-year-old cousin was allowed to leave the house alone but I was not; according to my uncle, my cousin knew the "rules." The "rules" followed by my cousin, as I was to learn, were not written Islamic law but rather the unwritten rules or ways in which teenagers have learned to operate in a potentially dangerous Islamic sphere (should one not follow the rules), where a simple slip of the hejab can land a girl in jail.[6] These unwritten rules are also the ways in which teenagers avoid or defy state-imposed restrictions, often working within the system to defy it.

It is every Islamic citizen's responsibility not only to obey the law but also to ensure that fellow citizens strictly adhere to all moral rules and regulations. Paranoia and the ever-present watchful eye define public space in the Islamic republic. The custom of *amr-e be ma'rouf* and *nay as monkar*, encouraging good behavior and discouraging bad behavior, advocates that Islamic citizens give moral guidance where they see fit. For example, when a young man sees a young woman whose hair has slipped from her hejab, he has the social responsibility to tell her she is in the wrong and to suggest how she might correct herself. The required training in Islamic morals gives young people the ammunition to counter "advice" within the context of Islam. For example, a female student, after being told to correct her hejab by a younger man, countered his admonition by suggesting that his act of looking at an improperly covered woman was also immoral. Of course, if a man is true in his heart, then he has a shield of protection and can handle this sight—an easy out. And so the struggle goes.

Many secular Tehran teenagers enter a strict Islamic public sphere (be it that of class, the workplace, or the streets) knowing that what they do or see at home contradicts what they are forced to ritually adhere to in public. These teenagers go home and mock their school exercises (I learned of these exercises by watching my cousin act them out for her mother). Can habitual school exercises and enforced behavior foster belief in Islam in Iranian youths, especially if these exercises are mocked or contradicted at home? Those children whose parents are ideologically aligned with the Islamic republic most likely encourage their children to take seriously these rituals and rules. In turn, these youth may "benefit" from the practice and become stronger believers. But what of secular teenagers whose parents are not aligned with the state?

At schools, in the care of the state, youths appear to be prime examples of perfect Islamic citizens, while at home other "knowledge regimes" contradict the state's efforts to create an all-encompassing Islamic reality. Many northern Tehran youths come from households where parents engage in or condone illegal activities like drinking alcohol, smoking opium, gambling, and watching satellite TV and black-market videos. Due to opposing ideas about what is deemed proper or moral in the two different public and private spheres, these youths develop an ability to participate in both worlds despite the ensuing confusion and contradictions. For example, teenagers know that they can get away with keeping Western music in the car by also keeping a religious tape (recitations of the Quran) on hand to slip into the deck in case of a search. By adorning their cars with plastic stickers with quotations from the Quran they decrease their chances of randomly being pulled over by the komiteh. (Some boys even go so far as to grow a beard before visiting a government office or going to court.) These contradictions are not conscious transgressions but rather the ways in which youths have come to counter the state-produced "real" by participating in a double existence.

As a result, Islamic moral law was not effective with a majority of the Iranian young people because they did not take the laws seriously (when and if the law was ever followed). With so many rules and contradictory advice on which rules to follow, it was impossible not to break rules constantly. Teenagers were often applauded (by their parents and peers) for breaking rules as a show of strength and revolt. Eventually they begin to see themselves as above the law, not part of it.[7]

NOT AN ALTHUSSERIAN SUBJECT[8]

In the mountains above Tehran a teenager skis away as a komiteh officer calls after her, demanding that she turn around and acknowledge his call. Although aware of the call, she refuses to turn around—should she turn and look she would be subjecting herself to Islamic authority; she would become an Islamic subject. By not answering, or by turning and ignoring the voice of authority, she remains free. As another tactic some secular teenagers "appear" to obey: when stopped by the komiteh, they say "Yes, sir, never again"—but five minutes later the same teenagers will turn and curse the officer and run. Thus while they "show" respect they do not actually respect the authority behind the "law."[9] Is the cursing a form of resistance? Or is it redirected anger at oneself for willingly submitting to the law and becoming or acting like an Islamic subject? A turn to the law is a denial of oneself, and yet teenagers in Iran "turn" to the law, show face, and then turn around and do what they please.[10]

According to Louis Althusser, the subject comes into being when she or he is called or hailed (interpellation). Thus, through narration—a demand to align oneself with the law—the subject is formed in guilt.

Surkeh bazaar is a stout two-story mall where hip northern Iranian teenagers buy their overpriced Italian shoes, Levis, and Gap cotton wear, and it is where they go to be "seen." It is also home to a pre-revolution café decorated with bright yellow and blue Iranian ceramic tiles and with antique Singer sewing cabinets used for tables. The second floor of the café is the perfect perch from which to view the entertaining mating habits of teenage Tehran on the sidewalk below.

It is almost evening and the traffic outside is heavy, men on scooters, students walking. There are fresh flower stands on nearly every corner. My friend Yasmine lights another cigarette and takes a long deep breath of smoke.

There's a sudden flurry in the café. The women around us pull their head scarves down farther on their foreheads and nonchalantly wipe off their lipstick with their napkins. Yasmine sits still and stares, making no move to correct her russari. The komiteh clunk around the café in their combat boots for a few minutes, and when they cannot find a reason for any arrests or bribes, they leave. The café is aflutter again; a few curses are heard here and there.

"How disappointing for them. You know, revolutions need disobedient citizens in order to collect bribes," Yasmine says, freshening up her lipstick.

Khomeini emphasized the moral obligation in Islam to submit, because submission is the ideal trait of an Islamic subject. While the world looks on and asks why so many people who are not aligned with the government submit to its practices, it is easy to see how merely going through the motions is easier than producing a second revolution or spending a night in jail. Given this view, if one acts while thinking defiantly then action will not produce believers.[11]

People leave religion, they change ideologies—they are born again. A religious subject (or any other for that matter) is not a fixed subject. Althusser says that the subject's existence cannot be linguistically guaranteed without passionate attachment to the law. This limits the critique of the law: for one cannot criticize the terms by which one's existence is secured. But, again, can acting Islamic while keeping up the surface (zaher) without intention, especially once it becomes habit, actually foster belief (baten)? Perhaps what it does is create the appearance of belief, and things are not always as they appear.

SEEING IS BELIEVING

Complicating the divide between visibility and belief, intention and appearance, is the notion of riya. As noted in chapter 3, riya, which literally means deceit, is acting like a good Muslim (for show) without truly believing in what is being practiced. An example of this would be a man who is not a devout Muslim but who wears a beard, carries prayer beads, and mutters prayers loudly so as to display piety. Riya allows for appearance to exist without belief. An Islamic morals professor at Sharif Technical University in Tehran lectures that riya is a sin in Islam. In a country where Islamic behavior is enforced, does every nonbeliever then become a sinner? If riya is a sin then why does public policy encourage people to sin? Am I performing riya by wearing a hejab as a nonbeliever? Do religious minorities in Iran who do not believe in these rules, but who are forced to follow them under Islamic law, commit riya? According to the professor at Sharif University, in my case as well as that of religious minorities in Iran, we are respecting cultural values by keeping up appearances. We are not sinning because we are not part of the belief system. As non-Muslims we are not expected to illustrate false belief, but we are expected to comply with Islamic law. As a non-Muslim woman I am not expected to cover myself in order to protect or display my own beliefs but rather so that Muslim men are not tempted to sin. According to Ayatollah Khameini (Khomeini's successor), the act of tabarruj (wearing makeup and showing one's hair; the act of making oneself beautiful to attract men) encourages disturbances, fitnah, which is why women must wear cover.[12]

Thus by covering my hair as a non-Muslim woman I am neither participating in riya nor practicing Islam, but respecting Muslim men. A good Muslim, however, should practice his or her faith with good intentions, unconsciously, and not to show off his or her piety by merely keeping up appearances. Covering my hair is obeying the law, I am not required to pray or to follow the other pillars of Islam. The law can only enforce ritualistic behavior that is seen on the surface in public. What is done or not done behind closed doors is impossible to monitor unless one is caught in the act (like a komiteh raid on a party). Of course, one cannot be caught in the act of not participating (praying, for example) unless they are on school grounds where they are monitored all day and where prayer is enforced, or on school fieldtrips like one I attended where all the women went to pray (it appeared to be voluntary, yet some girls told me that the Islamic chaperone would mark their absence had they not gone).

So, are nonpracticing secular Muslim students who are required to pray and wear hejab in the university not being forced into riya? According to a professor at Sharif University, because the secular students are also following enforced regulations and not actively choosing to display their belief they are not committing riya. The idea is that practice will eventually produce believers. According to Ayatollah Khameini, if a person continuously repeats proper acts until they become habit, these acts will eventually lead to faith. His idea is akin to Pascal's example of kneeling in church. As noted above, the Islamic republic used the idea of conversion through repetition in acts as common as school exercise programs. My cousin mocked her school exercises, but did they affect her worldview? Can one's habits, even when they contradict one's true belief, instill faith? Public policy has not been concerned with faith, but with religious practice and creating practicing believers. Belief is based on certain laws of conduct and certain facts whereas faith is blind; it is invisible and not every believer can be faithful.[13] Religion is a habit—faith is not. According to a Tehran university student, religion is like brushing your teeth—no one thinks about it consciously, it is just there; you just do it.

The aim of the revolution was not to create faithful Muslims but to create good Islamic citizens. The difference is that instead of concentrating on faith (which was expected to exist a priori in Iranian Muslims or *prima materia*) and intention, the regime concentrated on appearance and ideology. Practice was emphasized over inner faith, which is exactly why an Islamic concept like riya can coexist in a nation of forced "believers" or practicing Muslims and not be considered a sin.[14] Iran was and is still predominantly Muslim (pre-consenting subjects), thus making it initially easy for the clerics to establish a political ideology based on Islamic principles. In a totalitarian state, power is not found in the depth of an individual citizen's belief but in the ability of the state to control the outward behavior and appearance of the individual. The legitimacy of an Islamic republic rests in Islamic ideology and people's show of belief. Citizens are expected to dress the part, act the part, and know their lines. It was enough for the revolutionary government that the masses accepted this authority by acting out their role as good Islamic citizens. Concentrating solely on surfaces and practice (forced prayer, dress codes, propaganda) might bolster an Islamic ideology, but it will not necessarily touch the core of an individual's faith in Islam. This is especially true of Iranians who historically were forced publicly to show belief (in Islam) that contradicted their true faith (in Zoroastrianism).

KEEPING UP APPEARANCES

Throughout history Iranians have created different personas to appease various invaders. During the Arab invasion Iranians faithfully "converted" to Islam while they continued to privately practice Zoroastrian customs.[15] Later, due to persecution as Shiites in the Muslim world, they developed the practice of takiyya, dissimulation, which allowed followers to lie (without being considered unfaithful) about their Shiite identity.[16] This was especially useful when they traveled to Sunni lands—for example, to Mecca for the hajj.

In the past twenty years Iranians have again cultivated a culture of sameness at the surface in order to appease the ruling clergy. Strict Islamic uniform dress is the regulation for all citizens at all times in the public sphere. This surface created a world where nothing was really as it appeared, and yet the sameness had a meaning that was understood by all. While outsiders look at Iran and see one thing—law-abiding Islamic citizens—Iranians have always been able to discern political sympathies, class, and even religious belief based on small indicators that are added to or subtracted from the uniform required by law (examples of which are in the varying degrees to which women may choose to pull their hejab over their foreheads, the choice of a traditional chador over an overcoat, whether a man chooses to tuck his shirt inside his pants or leave it out, and so on). Sameness created a feeling of security: undercover, one could be whomever one pleased to be, while everything, at least on the surface, was clearly defined. The government, having been satisfied with appearances, was also less likely to interfere in private life (though it often did). At play in Iran's understanding of its own world is the notion of a public secret.[17] Everyone in Iran knows that religion does not exist on the level or in the form that it appears to exist on the surface. Even Islamic policy makers know this, which is why it is crucial that the surface remain untouched and unquestioned and the secret never voiced.[18]

The ease in which secular-minded Iranians were able to escape to the private sector is what rendered Islamic public policy mostly ineffectual. Like the duality of zaher and baten, surface and soul, there also exists in Iran's architectural and spatial history a duality of *andaruni* and *biruni* (private space and public space). This duality makes it impossible for the public sphere to solely define or inform one's identity. This division intensified after the revolution when public space became defined in terms of prohibition.

REEL LIFE: PUBLIC LAW, PRIVATE LIVES

The physical and psychical tension caused by the movement between public and private and the metaphysical struggle of the *zaher* and *baten* in urban Tehran is best illustrated in Rakshan Bani-

Etemad's film *The May Lady*. Of all the contemporary Iranian movies claiming to be a barometer of the "reality" of Iranian life, this film comes closest to portraying the struggles and contradictions of public and private life for the secular middle class in Tehran. The film illustrates the problematic relationship between secular families and the Islamic state, secular individuals and the Basij, mothers and their children, and ultimately the pre- and post-revolution generations as well as interpersonal relations outside of the institution of marriage.

The May Lady is about a middle-aged, divorced documentary maker, Furugh, who lives alone with her teenage son, Ramin, in northern Tehran. The story revolves around Furugh's daily life, which involves juggling a career as a filmmaker, a budding love relationship, and raising her son. At the center of the story is Furugh's film project, which documents her search for exemplary mothers. The movie moves in and out of documentary footage as Furugh interviews a variety of mothers in Tehran (ranging from those who have given their sons to the state as martyrs to those whose sons are in prison on drug charges) who have done something extraordinary for their children or society or both.[19]

At the same time that Furugh is searching for the exemplary mother, she is struggling with her own guilt and her son's anger that results from her romance with an executive producer, Dr. Rahbar. She struggles with the feelings, needs, and desires that she does not feel are compatible with being a good mother. In short, her sexual and romantic feelings lead her to believe that she is anything but an exemplary mother. Due to the cinematic difficulties in Iran of showing on-screen romances, Furugh's romance is played out through an exchange of romantic letters and phone calls.[20] Her lover becomes the disembodied voice of her other self who battles with basic human desires and needs (of sexual needs and companionship: things, she tells Ramin, that he has yet to experience or understand).

When speaking frankly with Ramin about these things Furugh alludes to the fact that the state is as much a hindrance to Ramin's sexuality as he is to hers—something he cannot understand now, but will one day. In dealing with Ramin's sexuality and development into manhood, Furugh's challenge is to instill a sense of values through teachings that are outside the dominant value system.[21] How can a parent teach his or her child values that differ from those deemed important by the state without being hypocritical, without belittling laws/rules of conduct? How can one be modern and also adhere to outdated religious morals? Furugh asks this question of a parliament member who is the daughter of the former president, Faiseh Hashemi (Rafsanjani), who tells her that the problem is not the law per se but the enforcement of the law. "We are not enforcing the law," says Hashemi.

The next scene indicates that this is not the case, and that the law is indeed being upheld, but at what expense? Furugh drops Ramin off at a birthday party, where it is obvious from the children who are gathered at the door that boys and girls will be mixing (contrary to Islamic law, but condoned by these parents). After the children go inside the apartment, Furugh gets out of the car and buzzes the door, to speak with the parents and make sure they will be at home chaperoning the party (according to her own principles and rules for her son). They assure her that they will be home all night, and they invite her in. She declines and drives off.

Before the party is over, and well before she is scheduled to retrieve Ramin, the komiteh arrive on the scene to arrest the children and cart them off in a large school bus to the komiteh station where they are to await trial for being caught at a mixed-gender party.[22] The event portrayed is rather a common one in northern Tehran on a weekend, and it is a crucial (as well as controversial) scene for Bani-Etemad to show on film. The scene illustrates the frustrations of living between opposing belief systems, not only for teenagers who bare the brunt of the system's wrath but for parents who grapple with circumventing the system without condoning a total disrespect for moral codes.

Parents gather outside the komiteh station to negotiate the release of their children.[23] Many of the women who would not ordinarily wear a chador have put on such dress in the hope that it will help her son or daughter's case. As new parents come on the scene we hear them ask each other how much they are expected to pay in bribes to release their children, yet given the late hour they are unable to see anyone to negotiate the release of the thirty-odd teenagers who will now have to spend the rest of the birthday party in jail.[24]

In the morning each parent is seen privately to discuss his or her child's behavior. The komiteh general is harsher with Furugh because she is a single mother.

"What's his offense?" she asks.

"Why do you ask, are you not his mother?" he asks.

"Of course I'm his mother."

"If you as a mother do not know the law of our country, and that going to such parties is illegal, what can we expect of our children?"

"I do not want to get in the way of my son and the law. But do you have any idea what is befalling this generation? The habit of lawlessness. Why? Because their natural needs are not being taken into consideration."

"I have a lot of work and no time to sit here and debate this with you until you leave this room a law-abiding citizen."

"Yet you want to try my son?"

"He's at the age where he can be tried. He must be accountable for his deeds. You parents need to think of these things before it reaches this stage."

"I'm a little confused as to what stage you are talking about."

"Apparently you do not understand what I'm saying. Where's his father?"

"Not here."

"Are you divorced?"

"Yes."

"Why?"

"Does it have anything to do with this?"

"The issue is not entirely separate. The absence of a guardian leads to this."

"My son is not without a guardian. Every single one of these kids arrested last night has two parents."

Furugh then goes on to point out that the other children who have fathers are in the same predicament as her son, and that lack of a husband does not make her any less of a mother. Like many secular middle-class women in Tehran, Furugh defends her child's right to go to parties — even at the expense of talking back to authority, and often in front of her child.[25] During the revolution, criminal acts became nationalist acts in a moment of suspension when criminality and nationalism became blurred. After the revolution criminal acts became opportunities to mock the state.[26] A favorite pastime among secular youth is to tell komiteh stories — for example, a boy who spent a night at the komiteh station was told to change his attitude (in Persian, literally "reverse your position"), so in response he stood on his head. The point is to give the komiteh as much grief as possible; to entertain oneself and one's friends and parents with stories; and, according to this boy, to bother the komiteh enough that they would want to release him sooner. This is also a way for youth to save face and not be completely demoralized by the law every time they are arrested.[27]

Between the strictly Islamic education system, Islamic public sphere, and secular parenting, that may or may not condone Islamic law as it is interpreted in Khomeini's *Velayat Faqih*, there is not only little encouragement to obey "laws" but also more validation for outright mockery and disrespect of the law. This leads to the problematic situation of parents who disrespect and distrust the law within the framework of the state (public laws), and yet who at the same time are trying to teach moral values within the family structure.[28]

Bani-Etemad's film paints the picture of a smooth family life where Ramin's friends gather on occasion, and where Furugh takes calls from her lover (mostly when Ramin is asleep or in the shower). But brewing below the surface is the frustration of a generation whose members do not have an outlet for their anger, and who are not practiced in speaking with their peers or mentors about their problems.[29] It is not until Furugh's birthday, when her lover appears at her door (which we learn when Ramin answers the doorbell), that personal lives and the public sphere intersect and the true restrictions on teenagers and the inability of parents to discipline their children, let alone control their fates, come to the fore.

After Ramin answers the door and learns that Dr. Rahbar has come to join Furugh's birthday celebration (which until now was just for mother and son) Ramin grabs the car keys and makes for the street.[30] Sometimes the frustration can be overwhelming to the point where one will either implode or explode, and Ramin needs to get out, perhaps of his own skin, but there is nowhere to go. And thus Ramin, like so many Tehrani boys, uses his car to speed off when he is angry. A young, angry, energized boy, speeding through the night alone behind the wheel, is a familiar scene on northern Tehran streets where teenagers drive their cars the way they would their bodies if they were allowed to go dancing. They race and pulse to the beat of techno music on the car stereo, pounding and vibrating through the ton of moving metal.

Ramin, who is angry and at wit's end, makes the grave mistake of speeding right through a Basij barricade, which lands him in prison. We only see a short chase scene between Ramin's car and the Basij vehicle before the next scene cuts to the following day and we find that Ramin has punched a Basij officer.[31] What follows is the ultimate intertwining of the state and private secular citizens (or the Basij and their secular peers) when Furugh goes to the house of the mother of the Basij who put Ramin in prison (she is also the mother of a martyr, which is apparent from the sign on the house welcoming the visitor to the house of the martyr) and begs her to show compassion toward her son.

"You're a mother," Furugh appeals to the older woman. The woman tells Furugh to look for the Basij at the mosque. At the mosque Furugh appeals to the Basij by saying, "I'm a mother. My son is a youth like you. The difference in your outlooks should not make you stand against one another in the place of understanding each other. Do not make my son spend the night in prison with a bunch of drug addicts and thieves. He's a good boy."

"When your son was playing with rattles, I was playing with bombs at the front," he tells Furugh.

"Everyone shares your values, but I'm a mother; you kids have to try to understand each other . . . please do not leave my son in prison," Furugh appeals tearfully.

The next morning Furugh waits outside as Ramin comes down the main stairs of the jailhouse, side by side with the Basij.

The boys shake hands and Ramin joins Furugh. On the way home she tells him that she wants to speak with him seriously.

"No, let me out, I cannot handle hearing anything," Ramin pleads.

"My mistake was not speaking with you honestly. You are going to have to listen now. No one is more to blame than I. I was so worried about you that I put myself between you and reality as a buffer. I did not allow you to experience life for yourself, I was afraid you would get hurt. That was a mistake. Every generation is a world in and of itself. Mine was more serious."

This film only begins to hint at the volcanic energy seething and ready to erupt beneath the thick skin of Tehran youth.

REAL LIFE

Youth is a category constructed within the theme of potential danger. Being young and especially male in Islamic Iran is potentially dangerous. Young boys are frequently stopped by the komiteh, and often they are questioned, searched, and taken in, even when no charge has been made against them. In the eyes of the law, youth present the potential for subversion and thus must be contained and controlled, especially young men.[32]

One night my cousin, who is tall and noticeably secular (baseball cap, leather jacket, jeans), disappeared. My aunt and I frantically searched the streets, even going to the nearby komiteh to give them my cousin's description (my aunt knew he'd never ask them to call his mom). When we returned home my cousin was sitting safely at home in front of the television eating dinner. He had gone out to get French fries at the deli next door. My aunt yelled at him about how worried she was.

"I'm supposed to never go out because of them (the komiteh)?" he yells back.

"You're tall, you insist on wearing those baseball caps, I just want you to be careful."

"I refuse to dress differently or not be allowed to go out for take-out for the sake of the komiteh."

My aunt sighs and kisses him on his forehead, "No, of course not," she says.

Unlike in the United States where a parent would be angry with a child for being arrested or talking back to authority, the child in Iran is instead pitied and given a little extra free reign to cool off. Parents speak of the stress that this generation suffers as a result of always having to look over their shoulders, be on their best behavior, and fear arrest for doing nothing wrong.

FIELD NOTES, PARK BENCH, PARK SAII, TEHRAN, 2000 *"Have you heard about the crow?" he asks me.*

"The crow?"

"Yeah, my generation is like the crow story . . . The crow watches a human walk and decides that he wants to walk that way, so he practices and practices, but cannot seem to get it, but in the process he forgets to walk like a crow. We're like that when we try to follow the West; we're like that when we're forced to follow Islamic rules. Have you heard what Ali Shariati said about taqlid (emulating a religious teacher through imitation)? He said something to the effect of having a country full of monkeys imitating one man . . . that it is a form of riya."

In the end the idea of an Islamic moral character became not only an exercise in riya, as youth complied on the outside while disobeying that morality in private, but also it became a vehicle for utter confusion. By acting like proper Islamic citizens in public and thus denying the existence of their true selves, Iranian youth began to feel a sense of confusion that led to the lack of identity that is bi-khodi, the not so sure-footed walk of a crow.

CHAPTER SIX

Majnun's Mask

Sex, Suicide, and Semiotic Malfunctioning

DIARY ENTRY, VALI ASR STREET, TEHRAN, 1993 A small crowd has gathered on the corner near Vanak Square to watch a woman on the other side of the street wave her russari to flag down a cab. Her gray hair is neatly woven into a bun on the back of her round head—she could be anyone's grandmother. Her chador is wrapped around her waist, as if she were at home. Her layers of heavy sweaters and big plastic shoes accentuate her plump, unseductive torso. What does the komiteh do with an unseductive body? With an aging body? With a protesting mind? With an unveiled woman? The only desire of a regime that is out to control desire is to watch this woman in the brief moment of a fleeting taboo, of the forbidden, hoping she might disappear before they have to make a decision. They know they should arrest her—even if hers is a less-desired form, these are formalities. The komiteh thus stand watch a safe distance down the street, keeping an eye on her, not quite sure what to do.

A few young women and a man have stopped to watch. People smile at each other, knowingly. The women wear lipstick; their black bangs are sprayed stiffly to sit just above the top of their designer russaris in silk leopard prints, Gucci signatures, and the latest winter colors. They follow the rules precisely, and yet they are more seductive and un-Islamic than this older woman without a hejab. Indeed, beneath the back of one russari, just above the shoulders is even a little protesting tip of chestnut colored ponytail. Their lack of effort suggests that these girls would not cover if they did not have to. The brown eyes dart back and forth between the helpless komiteh and the woman that no taxi driver will take.

"She's insane," mouths a pair of full red lips. Even the komiteh signed it off as temporary insanity: to protect their indecisiveness and lack of action; to save themselves from having to make a decision; or perhaps to admit the undesirability of an old, unveiled woman?

The act of branding a woman insane disarms her attempt at making a statement. The label of insanity neutralizes politics. A crazy woman is not out to make a political statement. But here, in Tehran, madness becomes an excuse, a way to live freely—a way to break down boundaries and walls. It is a label that can disempower at the same time that it empowers. Only the insane would not obey the law. Only the insane would not be forced to. That was 1993. Now madness has a new mask.

Islamic revolutionary public policy has led to a serious crisis in identity, governmentality, and belief. A fissure between what is seen and unseen, belief and disbelief, and signs and meaning that leads to an overall disconnection to the language of the public realm has created an atmosphere of suspicion and distrust. While ethereal notions of identity are debated for political purposes, below the political surface festers a real crisis among the youths who were born and raised exclusively under this regime. As policymakers struggle to find ways of resurrecting belief in Islamic ideology, they overlook youth's loss of faith, not only in Islam but in the world at large.[1] As I illustrated in the previous chapter, one reason that the rigid policy of the Islamic republic failed to create a state of faithful revolutionary subjects was its inability to transcend the already strict divide between public and private space in Iranian culture and to stop the infiltration of foreign media (which now includes the Internet) or create a culture that could realistically compete against outside medias.

The desperate and drastic attempt to compete with the interior world of youth by sending strong messages against their private lifestyles resulted not in strong monolithically Islamic identities but in what parents claim is a generation that is *bi-hoviyat* (without identity), or what filmmaker and father of four, Mohsen Makmalbaf, calls "*do shakhsiyat*" (schizophrenic).[2] Even young people themselves define as schizophrenic the generation raised under the Islamic republic.

FIELD NOTES, CAB RIDE THROUGH NORTHERN TEHRAN, WINTER 2000 *Winding down the hill toward downtown, the twenty-seven-year-old cab driver tells me that he is studying psychology.*

"*My thesis is on the schizophrenia of youth. I've been observing my young niece,*" *he tells me.*

"*How old is she?*"

"*Seventeen.*"

"*What do you do?*" *he asks me.*

"*Research on schizophrenia of youth,*" *I think to myself. "I'm an anthropologist.*"

"*Who are you observing?*"

"*You,*" *I want to say, "twenty-somethings." Instead I tell him, "My generation."*[3]

What are the implications for children who are endlessly juggling two opposing worlds? When these two worlds are morally diametrically opposed, to the degree that what is condoned in one world is forbidden in the other (and vice versa), shame comes to play. And with this shame is a denial or a split of self in order to survive. This happens when a youth spends his or her life watching something happening in one world—a parent smoking opium, drinking, not praying, or cursing the regime—and then has to hide this way of being from the outside world. At home, children are told that what they hear in school is all lies. At school, teachers ask students to report parents who are not abiding by Islamic law. School children are shown empty bottles of alcohol and asked if they have these bottles in their homes. In order to protect their parents they are thus forced to lie at an early age. At school and when applying for jobs they are asked "morality questions," such as "Do you wear a hejab when your uncle visits?"

A girl knows that the answer to the question is supposed to be *yes*, and that a truthful *no* could be potentially dangerous. So, she answers yes even if she wears a miniskirt in front of her uncle. (In most instances a public secret is at play: the teacher knows the child is lying, the child knows that the teacher knows she is lying.) Needless to say, in the course of this process these children not only learn to lie but to distrust: "Do not tell anyone anything about yourself or your family or your views: never let anyone know what you are thinking," their parents tell them.

To live in both worlds and not be ashamed means disassociating oneself from that shame by becoming two different people or personas. Children of alcoholics present an interesting parallel here as they are exposed to a certain world at home that they are unable to speak of or are ashamed to mention, and thus they grow up either in continual denial or in a split world where what is acceptable and normal in one world may not be in the other. Further, their worlds are so strongly differentiated that only when the two worlds begin to blend slightly and behavior becomes confused do these issues become problematic (as has increasingly become the case as Iranian society begins to look less Islamic). Children of substance abusers suffer symptoms of shame, depression, anger, and guilt.[4] They often spend their lives hiding their parents' addiction from society and sometimes from the law (which is always the case in Iran). In response, many children become placaters, which is a characteristic that an administrative official I spoke with attributes to Iran's youth. In some ways these symptoms are more pronounced in a place like Iran where what is socially condoned and what is not are strictly separated. Children who come from secular families are, by virtue of a normal life (which may mean avoiding prayer, watching satellite TV, or drinking), transgressing the state's definition of acceptable social norms and laws. Unlike children of alcoholics, however, who feel alone and ashamed in their isolation, a majority of northern Tehran participates in this double existence, which in

creating a community makes living separate private lives less iso-
lating and more socially acceptable.[5] What children of substance
abusers and those from secular families in Tehran both share is a
sense of hypervigilance that keeps them hyperaware of their surroundings in order to protect the discovery of behavior that is not
condoned. In so doing it also leads to an early practice of deception.

One young woman I met has a religious friend who wants her
to accompany her during prayer time at the university. This woman
was not taught to pray at home, and she tells me that she does not
know how to pray. She could never tell her friend this, however, so
she makes excuses. Even if she wanted to pray at home, she is afraid
that her parents might think that she has become religious, which
is cause for concern in some secular families. Due to such opposing
ideological forces and wanting to be accepted by both sides, she is
scared not to pray at school and scared to pray at home.

Many families became and still are divided ideologically. There
are sons who martyred themselves for the state against the will
of their parents, and conservative parents who support the state
and liberal children who do not. Siblings who grew up in the same
house were often influenced differently, which shows that both private secular culture as well as public state ideologies were strong
enough to counter each other once the individual, for whatever reason, chose one or the other. Early on the state demanded people
to choose it over family, and family members were encouraged to
turn in other members who were not abiding by revolutionary law.

JOURNAL ENTRY, TEHRAN COLLEGE STUDENT, 2000 *Psychologists
have started telling us on the radio that it is better to speak than to hold things
in, when they know we are in a place that speaking the truth has worse reper-
cussions than social stigma—it could mean imprisonment, lashes. But, the
deliveries by the black-market thugs at midnight, the stuff in the house, the
stuff I do not touch—the poison—is not just his problem. They could kick
me out of college; they could do much worse. But he's my dad. No, you never
think you are living a lie or that you are lying, because it is different when it
is about protection.*

Drugs (like martyrdom) form an expressway to self-obliteration (bi-khodi). Many modern "mystics" use drugs as ways to reach other planes. It is not surprising that as an aftermath of the war, even the most religious of war veterans have become opium and heroin addicts. Too frustrated, depressed, and angry, and not strong enough to take the correct mystical path to self-obliteration, they now opt for drugs. These same men once attempted to move to a higher spiritual plane and failed. The goal now is to survive, when before the goal was to live meaningfully. What remains, under a new guise, is the same mentality that existed before the war (the very one that led these men to the front in the first place): if one cannot live with meaning it is better to die.

TEHRAN 1995 *The flicker of the gas pilot on the stove as it struggles to become a flame, and the long shaky first note of the azan from the masjed as it struggles to become prayer, mark the sunset hour when evening lightly rests on Tehran, like an opium smoker with one elbow on the ground and one in the air holding a pipe.*

Most evenings for the past seventy years Mr. Rezai prepares a large silver tray-type box full of coals, which he places in front of him for the duration of the evening. He fans the coals until they turn white, at which time he arranges them in a heap and covers them with what looks like a small tin megaphone that retains the heat while it provides oxygen for the fire. While the coals heat, he takes out a long, thin velvet-lined box and removes two long pipe ends—one end is a bulging bubble while the other tapers off into a small hole. He screws the two pieces together and places the pipe at his feet. He then pulls a little silver pillbox from his pajama pocket and removes a small piece of clay-like stuff, which he rolls in his hands and warms, softens, and then forms into a little roll. With a small antique silver knife that he inherited from his father, who inherited it from his father (and thus probably retains traces of the stuff from Marco Polo's time), he cuts off an end piece and places it on the pipe, smoothing it over a tiny hole in the big bubble.

After he is finished applying the material over the opening, he takes a set of silver prongs and lifts a hot coal over the clay on the little hole. He takes a long drag from the pipe, causing the clay to fizzle and emit a sweet smell. He has never suggested or offered that she smoke. Nor has he felt the least bit self-conscious when she is there. When he is through with his first puff, Mr. Rezai turns to the samovar and pours a tiny teacup of strong black tea before lodging a sugar cube between his teeth to suck the tea through.

"Hmmm . . ." Mr. Rezai raises his little teacup to his lips and immediately pulls it away. "Hot," he says as he pours a little tea into his saucer, swirls it about and pours it back into his cup.

Each day the papers report the tonnage of opium seized at the border of Afghanistan and Iran. The drug war is one of only two international political areas where Iran and the United States are in cooperation (the other area is the Afghan refugee situation). Opium, which once was part of the very air of an earlier Tehran—the smell of everyday life, the bitter taste placed under a crying infant's tongue to calm—has never officially been legal in Iran, but until the revolution it was more or less tolerated (under the shah, addicts were given a daily dose). Opium has been in use in Iran for hundreds and hundreds of years, but now heroin (the poor man's opium) and other varieties of drugs have left a mark that is no longer private: men sleeping on park benches, drugged soldiers swaying their way through a public park, women beggars slumped over on the sidewalk with their children either doped and slugged across their shoulders or out selling cigarettes and gum in the streets. The picture of an Islamic paradise thus begins to shift. The scenes of drugged individuals may be shocking to the outside world, but for those who have lived in Tehran it is not particularly surprising to see that what already existed is merely seeping into the public sphere.

SCENE FROM THE FILM ETERAZ (PROTEST), SCREENED IN TEH-RAN IN 2000 *The boy sits on the floor of his comfortable denlike room in the garden of his parents' home in northern Tehran. The house is so large, the garden so deep, that no one ever bothers him or even seems to notice what is happening to him. His college buddy comes to check on him, however, because he has not come to class in months, and their conversation implies that per-*

haps he has dropped out of school. The friend's face shows concern as the next shot shows the reclusive boy slide opium paraphernalia under the bed (too late) from his friend's sight.

He speaks of the archeology of death, pointing to the video that plays on his television screen depicting excavations of bodies at the former war front— the unnamed burial sites.[6]

"I cannot stop watching."

Behind the facade of an Islamic social sphere there has continued to exist a complex cultural world permeated by black-market foreign video rentals, illegal satellite dishes, and the latest Western popular music. For years, Islamists turned a blind eye to any evidence of cultural invasion by the West and by pre-revolution culture, and they persisted in suggesting that the population of Iran was exposed solely to Islam. In the recent past, an increase in drug use, premarital sexual relations, HIV, suicide, prostitution, and what many call an identity crisis among youth suggest that this is not the case.

The intensely puritanical world developed through public policy to purposely contradict the values fostered in private space has resulted in a fissure defined by a lack of trust, unclear values, a lack of faith, and disrespect for elders, for life, for oneself, and especially for the law. A (self-proclaimed) fragmented identity has become the norm among Iranian youth who simultaneously inhabit two worlds. Instead of providing a consistent image of reality, in most cases the public world (which condemns anything un-Islamic) and the private world (where there might be an opium-addicted parent, satellite TV, or political dissidents in hiding) have directly contradicted one another in terms of rules, beliefs, ideas, and dress.

The Islamic republic no longer denies that Iran is experiencing a drug-use crisis. The government's concern with the drug problem has lessened restrictions on filmmakers by allowing them to show drug users and the problems that surround them in hopes that such images might deter anyone who finds drug use romantic. In the 2000 Fajr Film Festival there were at least four films depicting older opium addicts. The biggest box-office hit for the

2000–2001 season was *Shokaran* (Hemlock), which tells the story of a young nurse who has an affair (temporary marriage) with a married man. The protagonist is a young unmarried, clean-cut nurse from the lower, educated middle class who supports her father and his opium addiction. The film was surprisingly uncensored, even in its portrayal of a well-known Tehran square where hard-to-find prescription drugs as well as illegal recreational drugs like opium and heroin are sold. In another film, *Scent of Jasmine, Smell of Camphor*, we are introduced to a successful upper-class middle-aged lawyer who is an opium smoker. In *Eteraz* (Protest), a young upper-middle-class boy is ruined by his addiction to opium and heroin. Elsewhere, even a middle-class, educated do-good social worker appears as a protagonist in a film about a children's rehab center, where many of the children have addicted parents and come from the poor sections of Tehran. Addiction and its tragedies do not discriminate, and surprisingly, neither has the government in what they now allow the media to show. In the past, Iranian television only showed drug-use among the *tagoot* classes (decadent upper-class secular Tehran) as a warning that wealth and a lack of religion lead to drug abuse and death. While such images mainly point to opium addiction and use among middle-class and upper-class Tehranis, evidence in documentaries like Bani-Etemad's *Underneath the Skin of the City* and television shows on drug abuse show that behavior contradictory to Islamic law (such as drug use and criminal activity) has also affected the lower classes (traditionally the backbone of support for the government). This situation was much more prevalent after the war as the country's economic problems forced many to turn to criminal activity, the black market, and other places for money and or escape.

POOCH

The results of a questionnaire I distributed in Tehran in 2000 contain more than statistics. Conveyed within the answers to my questions is a tone, an expression in the writing that is usually lost in standard replies meant for data entry. There is sarcasm, bitterness, a dark humor—in short, a Persian word I remember from a Furugh Farokzad poem: pooch.[7]

I was sitting on the veranda in the garden reading poetry when I encountered the term pooch. Three simple letters: peh, vav, and che. Pooch is hard to define because essentially it is an existential term meaning nothingness, darkness: the space wherein one feels most heavy and yet less tangible. Further, is not an easy word to translate, especially in English. The feeling of the word, however, might be described as depression, alienation, heartbreak, and loneliness. Pooch somehow describes the tone or the theme of most of my returned questionnaires, which is not surprising given that the suicide rate in Iran in 1998–1999 exceeded the previous record by 109 percent.[8] For example, in answer to the question, "where would you like to travel to?" one student answered, "To a world reachable only through death."

Not long after learning the word pooch, I learned the term khod-koshi from a friend.

JOURNAL NOTES, A FRIEND'S STUDIO APARTMENT, TEHRAN, 1993 I look down at the books and struggle to read and understand the titles.

"Islamic ideology," he tells me, "It's a required course for all students in every major and every university in Iran."

"Are you learning anything interesting?"

"The difference between coup d'etat and revolution—what do I care?"

"So what are the differences?"

"Hell if I know; let's talk about something more interesting."

"You promised to help with my Farsi. This is important vocabulary."

"For a revolutionary. Are you becoming a revolutionary?"

"Are you kidding? I cannot even leave the house without a chaperone. Life is bi khod, meaningless," I sigh, using a new term, one I hear often.

"There's always khod-koshi," he jokes.

"What's that?"

"Figure it out, what does khod mean?"

"Self."

"And kosh?"

"To kill; so, suicide?"

He concentrates on the apple he is slicing while a moment of uncomfortable silence passes before he laughs. He offers me the plate of fruit. "Death is not the end. Life is not just physical existence. For all we know, we may already be dead.

Seven years later things have only gotten worse.

DARAKEH, TEHRAN, SPRING 2000 It is barely noon and already another unidentified body rests on the shoulders of a hiker who carries the dead weight down the mountain where the sun casts the shadow of a funeral procession. The bodies are found hanging from a tree, bleeding at the wrists, passed out from an overdose. A dead body is a heavy, empty body. Climbers ascend these mountains for exercise or for escape, only to descend prematurely, carrying a body, or being carried like dead weight: a vessel from which the substance has escaped, and yet strangely heavier and harder to hold without the soul flitting about. Some go to the mountains to escape the city for a while; others go to the mountains for the kind of escape from which there is no return. The mountains are a higher plane: a geography of death, ascension and transcendence. Even pollution finds a place, hovering dead air, like a lover with bad breath, threatening to come closer, threatening never to return. The struggling stops and life is superseded from earth to the higher plane of death. The geography of suicide is never horizontal.[9]

Field notes, TALAR RUDAKI IN DOWNTOWN TEHRAN, SUMMER, 2000 (4 PM, AND HOT, HOT, HOT) Juliet floats about the stage, her movements are carefully choreographed so as not to touch a male character. Long light-brown yarn woven into braids are attached to the sides of her headscarf. Her dress is long and shapeless like a rupush. She is not allowed to sing.

The house lights are dim, but the face of the young man sitting next to me is visible and expressionless. I'm trying not to look or show my concern, or let my gaze fall on his hands, neatly folded and resting on his lap. His long-sleeved shirt covers his wrists anyway (compliance with Islamic law, even though the temperature is over one hundred degrees). It's hard to imagine that a story about two lovers who kill themselves is the best reintroduction to society for a young man who spent the last ten days in the hospital under twenty-four-hour surveillance and on heavy antidepressant drugs and drips.

"Maybe it was just a plea for help." I comment to his cousin.

"No, he took pills then slit his wrists, he was not planning on failing."

This is the story of two star-crossed lovers.

"Did he ever mention why?"

"Why not? What does this generation have to live for?"

"Not all of them opt for suicide. I sometimes wonder why some do and some do not. Is it a personality thing? Or something one opts for like the decision whether or not to go to college?"

"I think it had something to do with a girlfriend."

Romeo, Romeo wherefore art thou? Romeo?

"Maybe it's a good thing, then, that boys and girls are not allowed to meet."

"They have to meet eventually and when they do they are not prepared for intimate relations. They spend years segregated and then, boom, one day they're in a classroom full of girls. It's not easy."

Relative to youths in many other societal sectors, for those in the secular middle class it is much easier to meet members of the opposite sex; opportunities to do so come from private parties and other forms of visiting that are condoned and often chaperoned by parents. For people from the provinces and from more traditional households, however, the issue of coming face to face with the opposite sex in a classroom is a lot more threatening. These youth have been censored all their lives and thus are conditioned to communicate indirectly (especially with the opposite sex). After years of encouraging just this, the government has changed its stance: "The main problem facing the younger generation is an inability to communicate with one another. Young people do not suffer from the lack of a good educational background. There are different ways of conveying messages. Young people should try to verbally communicate what they actually mean." [10]

JOURNAL ENTRY, TEHRAN COLLEGE STUDENT, SPRING 2000 *I have a problem. An old friend of the family, a professor, even older than my father, has come to teach at Tehran University. Do I greet him when I see him? To not greet him would be rude, but to greet him will elicit questions from my teachers as to how I know him, why I am greeting an older man, etc. It* makes me sick to think that my father is one of these men who think of sexual thoughts when he sees my friends. They teach us that men are like this, and this is why we have to behave this way and to cover. I just cannot accept that my dad is like this. Perhaps I'll ask my father to call his friend and explain why I cannot greet him. He should know, but older men forget the nuances of these issues women my age face. The boys who are my age know. We grew up like this, we're used to it: being at school and seeing a male friend, someone you see at parties, go out with to restaurants, talk with on the phone, but at school you have to pretend that you do not know him . . . why? because he's a boy.

You do not say hello to a boy your own age, he walks by flanked by two friends, you're sitting on the school garden bench trying to read, pretending to read, he whispers something silly, you try hard not to laugh, to control yourself, to show no emotion as he passes. He smiles at you, but angles his face so an onlooker might think he's smiling at what his friend is telling him. But you know, and in a few hours you'll be able to talk to him, take off your covering, relax.

Some days I feel like everyone is spying on me . . . I have not done anything, I do not deserve to have a guilty conscience. When everything is forbidden you are bound to break a rule at some point. And once a rule is broken, it's easy to break another . . . once someone tells you you're guilty for doing nothing wrong, then you can do anything. When no one expects anything of you, why bother?

While everyone changes slightly within different contexts (with a different persona for work, friends, teachers), Iranian youths are forced to consciously create a new persona for every situation.[11] They have a system comprised of a set of rules by which they present their identity in different contexts. Needless to say, this inability to form a consistent persona creates a host of psychological problems. Not surprisingly, psychology has become a popular topic on radio and TV programs, as a school subject, and as a medical treatment due to the unfortunate rise in suicide attempts and depression. In the past, problems of the soul were solved by religion.

In a cab headed downtown, the radio is tuned to a psychologist's call-in advice show. I ask the cab driver why psychology is so popular. "When the nation goes crazy the government is forced to throw some psychology our way," he replies.

But for a generation accustomed to hiding everything, can the idea of talk therapy ever work? Is it not too late? These young people spent twenty years misinformed and uninformed about certain things such as premarital sex, because the government did not want to suggest that such a thing might even exist. What happens when there are no mentors? What happens when the soul is lost in a geography of war and darkness, with signals that point in opposite directions? What happens when nature continues to run its course even when humans try to defy it?[12]

UNIFORMLY UNINFORMED, WINTER 2003 *He had sent her home to die. But she returned.*

"Five hundred tomans." What some families live on in a year. Her boyfriend hands the doctor the money and instinctively reaches for her hand, but then pulls it back, remembering that he is in public. This doctor with his metal magnifying instruments of exploration and torture is allowed to look into the most intimate part of his girlfriend's being and he is not even allowed to hold her hand.

"No men allowed. This office plays by the rules."

"The rules?" The boyfriend wants to say, "This is illegal." But he says nothing.

The hejab, the body covering, the reason why women sit behind and not in front of men — the absence of women altogether from certain public and private places — all to protect men from temptation.

The doctor walks to the other side of the room and opens a drawer that does not contain the usual hospital-tray variety of scalpel sizes and types. This drawer is more universal, like a kitchen cutlery drawer, though most kitchen drawers are a bit more diverse. This drawer contains one knife and a wad of tissue.

"I am going to make a small incision after which you will return home. You will abort slowly (and painfully) for the next few days (should it even last that long)."

He takes his knife, spreads her legs and pulls her closer.

He feels around inside her with thick hands and calluses that she can feel through the latex gloves. She is sweating and gritting her teeth, but she remains silent. The tension, the tightness of her muscles, will cause her more pain—but he does not tell her to relax. She has forgotten to breathe—he does not remind her.

"It will be over in a minute," he says, wiping the knife on a wad of tissue.

Beneath an edifice of stillness, a partial ballast of calm is rush hour on a highway of neurons honking anger, treading over fear, skidding on anxiety, attempting to take a short-cut past regret, remorse, and disgust. Imagine the noise of neurons. She tries to quiet all the inner traffic and remind herself that no one else would do this for her. She has no choice.

He tightens her scarf around her chin, careful not to get any blood on it, pulls her up, slaps her to partial consciousness and sends her out to her boyfriend.

"Three days of heavy bleeding and unbearable pain," the doctor tells him, "and she'll be ok. Do not be alarmed by the blood or pain—she'll be ok." She planned to tell her family that she had the flu. How do I explain the blood? What about the blood?

Blood slowly escapes the new stitches and collects beneath the car seat. They turn up the main road that takes them out of the southern Tehran slums directly north and toward a real hospital. The drips become a puddle that will stream out the door onto the fresh snow and paint it red when they arrive at the hospital where they wheel her straight into surgery.

Her body turns dark red as blood bubbles right out of her skin. Her sheets crumple beneath her like wet, red tissue.

Those who could gave blood, though it was not worth the effort, for as soon as the blood went in through the IV she would sweat it out through a million tiny pores working overtime to purge any attempt to save her. They're still waiting for her to die. She is already a ghost—as good as dead. She's untouchable.[13]

It is a double-edged sword: most parents do not speak with their children about sex, and the state does not provide sexual education training in school.[14] (Classes for marriage preparation come too late, especially in a generation that cannot afford to get married.)

Young people thus have no one to talk to about condoms and no one to help them out when they find out the hard way why condoms were invented; these are taboo subjects. Because of the high cost of marriage (apartment rents have skyrocketed along with the unemployment rate), many young girls are opting for abortions, which, though illegal, are readily available for a high price.[15] Because of the stigma associated with condoms (women believe that men who insist on using condoms are suggesting that they are dirty or that the woman has a disease) few youth use them, which has led to unwanted pregnancies and the spread of HIV (which like other topics is kept under wraps).[16]

Western satellite television and other media forms spark curiosity but also only show the surface romance of wine, flowers, candlelight, and drama, and nothing about protection and the consequences of not using it. And not just the kind of protection needed in sexual acts but also yearly check-ups and learning about possible problems. One group of young secular college women I interviewed believed that they are sexually liberated compared to their parents, and yet at the ages of twenty-three and twenty-four they avoid yearly gynecological exams in order to keep their hymens intact (or not to risk discovery that it is broken).[17] One young woman I interviewed belongs to a family of Western-trained doctors, and still she was never told that having a gynecological check-up was imperative for women her age, especially if they have not had sex.

This is reinforced in the ways in which young men think about a woman's sexuality. Young men claim that their attitude toward premarital relationships is different from that of their parents' generation because they do not think any less of girlfriends who agree to have sex with them. And yet, such men still want to marry a woman whose hymen is intact (unless they deflowered the girl in the first place). The young men say that this practice is dated and wrong, but they insist that it's ingrained (a fact that they are consciously aware of).

"But this is your girlfriend, the woman you love, and the minute you sleep together she's dirty and unmarriable?"

"More or less. It changes everything." A girl is considered kharab, ruined, if she sleeps with a boy, but a boy is considered experienced.

A car full of young boys slows down along the side of the road. They wait a few minutes to see if I acknowledge them.

With the increase in prostitution among middle-class average-looking girls, any young woman on the street could be "working." According to my neighbor's son, it is hard even for the boys to differentiate between prostitutes looking for customers and women merely out walking.

"How can you tell whether a girl walking on the side of the road is prostituting herself?"

"We cannot. My friends (not I, he's quick to point out) slow down, and if she runs over and jumps in the car then that's it. We know."

"Where do you find these women?"

"Everywhere, there is no red-light district, which makes it easier . . . it is everywhere." But, officially, nowhere (of course).[18]

TEHRAN, SUMMER 2000 It's the noontime rush hour and I need to get to my uncle's house in time for lunch, so I flag down a cream-colored Peykan and jump in the backseat.

"Where to?"

"Ghandi."

"Why there?"

"That's where I'm headed."

"I know a better place."

"Excuse me?"

"We can go to . . ."

"Aren't you a taxi?"

"Lady, this is a new Peykan and I have a master's degree, what did you think?"

"What do I owe you, I'm getting out."

"We're not there yet, honey, I have a master's, what an insult, I'm not a cabbie."

The minute the traffic slows to a halt I throw a 500-toman note at him and jump out.

Against the will of those in power, the surface is beginning to break and a real crisis in appearance has come about where nothing is at all what it appears. Metaphors are beginning to shift and the semiotics of physical space needs a new code in order for meaning to be deciphered. Contradictions and misuses of symbols have led to semiotic chaos. Even the masses can no longer read their own world.[19]

An afternoon walk in Tehran, through the park and back home, reveals the eerie uncanniness of a society in conflict. A young, unmarried woman in a black chador, wearing heavy makeup and allowing her hair to fall out of the corners of her hejab, sits on a park bench with her hip boyfriend. She smiles coyly, mocking my look of disbelief. Who is she? She cannot possibly be religious, with heavy makeup and hair flowing out of her hejab, and yet she wears a chador? (The chador is a traditional covering that is not required, but is chosen by women who support the revolution.)

When the meaning of sacred symbols shifts, power structures are renegotiated, as well as trust in one's own vision. An example is the Arab *qafiyeh* (scarf): a symbol of Palestinian resistance. The qafiyeh was first donned by Islamic revolutionaries to show support for Palestine and resistance to Westernization. Later, it became a symbol of the volunteer soldiers fighting for Islam in the Iran-Iraq war.

The qafiyeh is still worn by Ayatollah Khameini. Just before the Iranian New Year in spring 2000, a hit man in the assassination attempt on the reformist Said Hajjarian was described as wearing a beard and a qafiyeh. Suddenly the symbol sacred to Islamic revolutionaries became descriptive of a suspect against reform. Hatamikia, a well-known war film director, wrote an editorial reminding the nation that the qafiyeh is not the symbol of an assassin or murderer; and he added that it was disrespectful to emphasize this characteristic in the description of Hajjarian's would-be assassin.

The sudden inability to read one's world, even an illusory world based on appearance, creates a feeling of unrest and distrust: nothing is as it seems or is supposed to appear. Meaning is confused and a semiotic malfunctioning occurs among people who are usually adept at thinking through layers (of clothing and meaning).

While youths feel a need for more information about the modern world, the conservative clergy claim that heavy infiltration from the outside has already done too much harm. The clergy use the example of corrupt U.S. society infected with HIV, prostitution, drug use, premarital sex, and suicide as an example of what will happen should Iran abandon Islamic law and allow the "pornographic culture of the West to infiltrate."[20] And yet, HIV, drugs, prostitution, abortions, and suicide are on the rise in Iranian society despite twenty years of Islamic moral guidance from kindergarten through college, as well as on television, radio, and billboards. Reform-minded individuals have come to see that choice and religious domination cannot peacefully coexist in society.

Kierkegaard is a favorite of the reformists, who consider him a religious existentialist because he posits that choice coexists with faith.[21] The reformists have warned the clergy that any more pressure caused by the disillusionment, feelings of hopelessness, and anger inherent in Iranian youth will force the entire Islamic system to collapse.

When the surface changes it does not necessarily change what it covers. Baseball caps do not attest to a "Westernized identity" any more than a hejab points to an Islamic one; rather, such forms of Western clothing show a certain degree of rebellion and attest to the infiltration of Western culture through the pores of the strong surface of Islam. This has complicated further an already complex cultural identity—for example, many youth with access to satellite dishes claim they are not affected by or interested in foreign culture, but this goes against everything, such as dress forms, seen in the streets.[22] Journalists like Christiane Amanpour and Western policymakers with an eye on Iran are both determined to show Iranian youth as monolithically Western and secular, and in doing so they emphasize the surface: baseball caps, pushing back the hejab a bit further, listening to rap music, or painting graffiti all over Tehran.[23]

The attempt to isolate and affect the identity of an entire generation of Iranians at the end of the twentieth century and at the beginning of the twenty-first is proving to be a failed project. On the surface, Iranian youth appear merely to want Western freedoms, economic stability, and a relaxation of rules; below the surface, however, exists a crisis of morals, a lack of belief and faith, a strong distrust of authority (including of parents), an inability to make decisions, and no preparation for a sexual identity. A strong separation of public and private spaces; modern media technologies like the satellite, the Internet, faxes, and radio; and strong ties to a large expatriate community in the West make it impossible to stop the non-Islamic world from infiltrating the clergy's project—and what the clergy blame, correctly, for a failure in policy.

CHAPTER SEVEN

The Ghost in the Machine

(Just War?) Remainders and Reminders of War

In spring 2000, the following cartoon appeared in an Iranian newspaper: *Frame one*: Reformist (and former Basij) Said Hajjarian lies immobile in a retractor in a Tehran hospital after an assassination attempt on his life. He awaits vital medicine from Germany. *Frame Two*: A crew disembarks from a helicopter at Mehrabad airport. They unload a small ice cooler with a label that reads "antimartyr medicines." This cartoon is a poignant reminder of postwar Iran, where the atmosphere is not one of martyrdom but of its antithesis: survival. Hajjarian, a member of the city council, a former Basij, and a key player in the new reform movement (as close advisor to President Khatami) chose not to be martyred for the cause—he wanted to live.

In previous chapters I have shown how martyrdom was the driving force behind nation-state formation in Iran during the war years. The emotions that surrounded the war helped foster an unbreakable bond among citizens of the Islamic republic. But has its excessiveness worked counter to its original purpose? What remains of the war? A strong silence shrouds the topic of war among youth in Tehran. The continued exchange of POWs encourages further reminiscence, more welcoming parades, and even more murals and banners. What effect has this had, and still has, on public life in Tehran? In the end, did this space of death strengthen belief in an Islamic republic? Today, for the most part, the repetitive reminder of the war has worked against the regime. The cathartic qualities of these reminders that are meant to inspire nationalism have instead given rise to emotions of anger and disillusionment with the regime. A general consensus believes the war was fought in vain. Now, films that were produced uncensored by the government as memories of martyrdom have instead conjured the violent and empty effort that caused the country to lose a large segment of its future generation.

As with the war, the area that has been most revolutionary in dealing with its aftermath has been the cinema. While the government's war film project moved to appropriate critique by portraying images of the war in a specifically religious and pious manner, it also opened a new arena—that of post-revolution Iranian cinema—where historic and contemporary social issues that previously were never addressed could be brought to the surface.[1] In war films, the history of martyrology and practice of mourning in Shiism and the appropriation of this history by the cultural producers in the war work both together and in conflict. Cinema was used as a device for mourning at the same time that it attempted to cover the injustices of the war; yet cinema can only maneuver the reality of a bloody eight-year war to a degree, because what eventually comes to the fore is the sense of the injustice of war and the production of martyrs who are mourned and lost. As I show in my discussion of the cinema of Ebrahim Hatamikia, injustice plays out in the space of mourning, which becomes a space of haunting. Iranian cinema was both aided and burdened by the ghosts of Shiite history. What is compelling about postwar films is that the same filmmakers who trained and fought in the war, as well as worked to promote it, are now its foremost critics.[2] As I note in chapter 3 in my discussion of Avini, just as time spent at the war front in the line of duty gave the Basij a unique authority to represent the war, it also gave them the authority to criticize both the war and the role of the administration years later.[3] Thus their voices can be the only legitimate ones for change. Those who once worked on projects like *Revayat-e Fath* are now grappling with disillusionment regarding the ideology they worked so hard to promote (and perhaps with the failure of instilling faith where only a surface remains). If any single individual exemplifies the existential struggle of the postwar generation to change in the face of adversary, it is Ebrahim Hatamikia.[4]

At the age of eighteen Hatamikia was a faithful revolutionary volunteer at Jahad-i Sazandigi working on the TV series *Revayat-e Fath*. His experience as a Basij filmmaker under Avini's tutelage left an indelible mark on his films, which in his words exemplified "the physical and metaphysical planes that a soldier and a mystic novice experiences on the spiritual path—even after the war."[5] Hatamikia is one of the first Basij filmmakers to take a critical look at postwar Iran by portraying the disillusionment of war veterans and their treatment by both secular society and the government that reneged on its promises. While his Basij credentials once kept him above reproach in the view of his fellow revolutionaries, being Basji does not preclude him from being immensely and surprisingly well received by secular audiences. His films delicately tread the thin line between what many secular Iranians define as typical Basij government propaganda and the secular antigovernment sentiment, and thus they appeal to a broad audience. In so doing, his films have allowed a space for Iranians to begin to think about and debate the war.[6]

In some instances, Hatamikia's films have encouraged a generation of young Iranians to rethink the war and revolutionary values in general.

REVAYAT-E FATH OFFICES, TEHRAN, SUMMER 2000 *My meeting with a documentary maker at the production offices of* Revayat-e Fath *is interrupted by two young, clean-cut boys (that is, without the usual Islamic facial hair most men have in this office); one is thin, short, and wears all-black, the other is taller, with a larger build. The boys sheepishly nod to me and mutter their apologies before shyly approaching the filmmaker's desk.*

"We heard you were in, sorry to disturb you. We are only in town for the

day," says the younger, smaller boy, giving a polite but short pause before abruptly asking, "Did you receive my second letter? I was surprised by your previous reply and a bit confused. I am anxious to speak with you."

The documentary maker smiles at him and motions for him to sit, "Everything will be alright. We will find time to talk. This is Ms. Varzi, she's an anthropologist." Then he turns to me, "These boys are in the age group you're interested in. Have a chat with them until I return," he says, "I'm just going to find a tape for you."

We exchange pleasantries for a few minutes before the boys muster the courage to ask a personal question.

"What are you doing in a Basij place?" the smaller one blurts out.

"I'm interested in war films," I tell them.

"You must know Hatamikia's work then? He's my idol, he's the whole reason I want to be a Basij."

"You want to be a Basij?" I ask him, "But the war is over."

"The work of a Basij is not finished. My name is Mehdi, this is my cousin, and we're visiting from Shiraz. If you come to Shiraz I can introduce you to all sorts of people who can help with your war film research." Mehdi gives me an earnest and intense expression.

"You're too young to be a Basij," I comment, "You must have been seven years old when the war ended."

"The Basij still take members. I aspire to be a Basij, but I do not always agree with them."

"How does one become a Basij?"

He gives me a surprised look, no one has ever asked him this question. He looks nothing like a Basij in his black Levis and black T-shirt, clean-cut haircut, and shaven face (he does not look like he has even reached puberty).

"You fill out a form at the mosque and take a test."

"Did you do that?"

"No. There are not any real Basij, just hypocrites, at my mosque. They go out and arrest people wearing Titanic T-shirts and then brag to me about all the times they have seen Titanic. I ask them why they watched it if it's illegal, and they say they need to know what it is in order to judge it. Sure, but five times?"

When the two boys leave, I am told that Mehdi spent his summer vacation without pay on Kish Island working on Hatamikia's last film.

"He aspires to be a Basij, and recently he fell in love with his distant cousin and so he wrote to me for advice. He is afraid it is against Islam to be in love. He thinks that any decent Basij would not think of such things." The film-maker laughs before continuing, "I told him that it is perfectly natural and one must perfect human love as a mirror to God's love [a view that is very Sufi]. Mehdi sees it like an illness and a sin. No, I told him earthly love is a vehicle to God's love."[7]

"Do you have many young men coming in for relationship advice?" I laugh.

"It's a hard age. They do not have role models or mentors. He has alienated himself from his family by wanting to become a Basij. He decided not to go to college. I told him, 'Get your degree and you'll be a more useful Basij.'"

Two months later I visit Mehdi in his hometown of Shiraz, city of Sufis, poetry, and wine (before the revolution).

"I'm sick of the Basij my age; sorry, I cannot introduce you to any. They are no longer my friends. They waste my time asking me why I choose to wear jeans and not wear a beard? It's a problem, a mistake."[8]

"And yet you still aspire to be a Basij?"

"I like the older Basij; the real Basij. My uncle was a shahid, a Basij. I was one year old at the beginning of war when he died, and yet, still when I see his picture, I feel connected even though I have no memories of him. I cry at his grave, I do not tell anyone else. There are only a few people who think like me in my family."

Mehdi feels alienated and has no one to talk to, hence the letters to the television producer and his diary.

"I write in a diary when I am upset. But my family found it and they be-came upset. I speak to my shahid uncle in there, even though I've never seen him; he's different. I heard he was a good boy. I'd have gone to the war, if there were a war now, I'd go.[9] They have misrepresented the war in our society as one fought by poor, illiterate people. That's not the way it was at all. Both of my uncles were shahids: one was a painter and became a captain, and the other was a pilot and an engineer. The Glass Agency shows how no one wants the Basij in society. When he [the main character in the film] went to war he had character and he gave it in the war and came back emptyhanded. The Ansar-eh Hezbollah—I feel sorry for them. They want to be at the front, they live for the front, they have no idea about how to live in the world going on out-side of the front, they think of the world as an ocean, where a boat takes us away.[10] The values that existed during the war no longer exist. It's like when you're used to sitting and eating on the floor for twenty years and suddenly someone comes and tells you to sit at a table, or vice versa; your legs cannot handle the floor, scrunched up, your body protests (eteraz). This is the Hezbollah, it's hard for them to reenter society; one that is nothing like what they are used to [or fought for]. Society could not retain those values and it's hard for them now."[11]

At lunch in Shiraz, Mehdi meets my young secular cousin from Tehran who is already a college student but close in age to Mehdi.

"So what's the problem with society," she asks Mehdi.

"This society has become too competitive."

"Competition is what takes people forward; society will only move forward if there's competition, there must be competition," she tells him.

"You must have the world, humans, and yourself to move forward. The Right wants God, they will not let go, the Left have humans, and will not let go, and as a result everything falls apart. This is the first time I've spoken of politics. I hate it. I get upset when things turn to politics; Hatamikia did not speak for two years after The Glass Agency because people automatically decided whatever he said was political."

They remain in silence for the rest of the meal. But a few months later Mehdi visits Tehran and asks if I'll invite my cousin out for lunch with us.

Not until his film The Glass Agency did Hatamikia provoke the government, which then took him to court over the film and barred its release.

The Glass Agency is a metaphor for the glass house that Iran became after the war, where internal conflicts have been more salient than international ones. The film is a controversial portrayal of a war veteran who enters a travel agency and takes customers hostage in demand for a plane ticket for his friend, a wounded war veteran, who must go abroad for surgery. The veteran, a quiet family man, initially has no intention of taking hostages; he does so only on impulse after making multiple trips to the agency to wait for a plane ticket, all the while observing wealthier Iranians secure the impossible-to-obtain tickets (it is the Iranian new year and tickets are in short supply). At the same time, he has also been denied help from government institutions dealing with war veterans' affairs. Ironically, it is not the government that he takes hostage but the secular Iranians who have the money to buy their way out of the country.

The conservative Iranian newspaper *Resalat* appropriated the film's critique of the government by describing *The Glass Agency* as an artistic miracle likely to be targeted by the Western media and those in Iran who desire a Western-style civil society. The conflict, they claim, comes from the Basij's inability to reconcile their extreme idealism marked by 'martyrdom' to postwar materialism, calling it a story of victimized Basij at odds with Westoxification, capitalism and aggressive liberals."[12] Thus, what could easily have been read (and was by many audiences—both secular and religious), as a critique of a government that forced the country to fight a bloody eight-year war, only to turn its back on those who fought it, is appropriated by the government as a critique against the reforms of the new president, Mohamed Khatami, whose first summer in office was just getting underway when the film was released. Even directors like Hatamikia who never had problems with the government felt more freedom to express themselves post-Khatami and it is no coincidence that Hatamikia's first attempt to outwardly critique the postwar regime would occur after a reformist president is elected to office. *The Glass Agency* ostensibly was banned and defended in court due to Hatamikia's unauthorized portrayal of the Islamic police (who end up in a compromising position that shows little support for the Basij). Despite its shaky start and cold reception in the West, at the sixteenth annual International Fajr Film Festival *The Glass Agency* managed to receive awards for best film, director, leading actor, supporting actor, and supporting actress as well as script, editing, and musical score in competition with twenty-one other movies.[13]

In *The Scent of Yusef's Shirt*, Hatamikia tries to traverse the division between feelings and thoughts, facts and love. In his films we see a move away from a space of what might be termed martyrology to one of Derrida's hauntology, and this is especially the case in the popular work *The Scent of Yusef's Shirt*.[14] When in the film the number of dead began to outnumber those still fighting at the end of the war, ghosts became an important part of the landscape. At this point, certain soldiers begin to exhibit the ability to tap into the world of ghosts, which provided them with a following of men who counted on them to communicate with the world of the dead. A former soldier told me that during the war ghosts were called on to help out with little things like moving ambulances that were caught in ditches. Later these soldiers became cultlike figures in Tehran where they led zekrs[15] promising help to those who attended.[16]

MARTYROLOGY AND HAUNTOLOGY:
THE SCENT OF YUSEF'S SHIRT

Hands tie together loose wires on a row of colored lightbulbs. Eerie music plays as the camera pans below the festive rows of wedding lights to the figure of Daii who is tying ribbons and flowers to his car. A man dressed in a brown robe (like the grim reaper) walks by. For a second he turns; he looks like the same actor who plays Daii. Then he asks: "You are preparing for the return of a POW?" *He is referring to the festive lights and decorated car. Daii is visibly surprised; shaken, he replies, "A wedding."*

"*Do you have a* POW?" *The man asks.*

Daii nods his head yes. "Do you?" He calls after the man, "Is he on the Red Cross lists?" Daii starts to cough, he cannot finish his sentence: "Be assured he will re——," Daii tries to say. But the man is gone.

The bride sits alone in the middle of a circle of family and friends. She is dressed in white. The traditional wedding mirror, the Quran, and sweets surround her. Nearby is a framed picture of the absent groom. The phone rings, but no one is on the line. The long drone of a cut phone line suggests an absence; it also presents a ghostly presence or a sign that someone or something is trying to speak.

The phone rings again; this time it is the groom calling from abroad. A man with a camcorder moves in toward the mother of the groom who is speaking with her son, "I have become a foreigner to you," she says. The camcorder spans the room, recording the wedding, while the camera closes in on another framed picture on the wall of another young man, Yusef, whom the bride would have married had he returned from the war. The framed pictures mark a double absence created by Yusef's flight into war and the groom's flight away from war. The pictures are of exiles and POWs waiting to return: being waited for.

The phone is handed to the bride. After a few minutes, a woman comes over with the picture of the groom and places it in front of the bride and nonchalantly hits the speakerphone button. The groom is now present in image and voice. He is far away, but locatable. The bride continues to keep the receiver to her cheek, as though she were having a private conversation and is unaware of the crowd of people who listen as if this was the exchange of vows they all came to hear. The groom's voice asks her: "Are you still in love with Yusef? Are you marrying me because you want to, or because Yusef's father, Daii, wants you to?" She does not answer, the line is cut, the electricity goes off, and everyone claps as if the vows had been exchanged. The camera moves to Daii's face where it rests for a moment on his sad expression before moving behind him toward the dark night. It is unusual to have the exchange of wedding vows at night; they waited all day for the call. Outside, the festive, brightly colored wedding lights blow in an increasingly gusty breeze — as if a ghost is moving through them. A lightbulb pops. Inside, everyone waits silently in the dark. There is the sense that something outside human perception is at play and that the empty night is charged with invisible energy. Ghosts: khyal, feelings, ruh, spirit, Shabi-eh, similar: like a shadow of one that was.

The next scene is at the airport where the bride is about to walk through the departing gates to go abroad to meet her groom. She turns back for a final glance at Daii to catch him mesmerized by the evening news, which shows images of the busloads of returning POWs. The bride comes to his side and asks: "What are you after? When the dog tags were returned to us, I got my answer from Yusef," she says.

"Do you love your new groom?" asks Daii.

"Why?"

"Do you love him, I have to know."

"Yes."

"Well, then give me the tags," he says pointing to the dog tags she is holding in her hands.

"You never wanted them, please do not take them from me," she says. "Give them," he says. She puts the tags in his hands and before walking through the gate, she says, "I too believe in miracles, but only ones my size."

Hatamikia's *The Scent of Yusef's Shirt* depicts the social aftermath of the Iran/Iraq war for Iranians in Iran and abroad. The film documents Daii's friendship with a young expatriate Iranian woman, Shireen, whom Daii picks up as a passenger in his taxi from the airport, the same night that he sees off his son's bride. Shireen has returned from Paris after a fifteen-year absence to look for her brother, Khusrow, whom she believes will be among the POWs to be released by Iraq. The story of Shireen and Daii relays the different yet similar way each deals with mourning, faith, and the ambiguity that surrounds MIAs: bodies that are missing, but not positively dead. The film plays on the complexities of a death that may not be a physical death: the problematic of mourning a missing person who may or may not be dead. The trope of return is played out in the return of exiles, POWs, and the many ghosts who have come to haunt the Tehran landscape.

Before moving to the haunted landscape of postwar civilian life, I will take a detour through a war film that sets the scene for the haunting after the war. The battle film *The Horizon* strongly anticipates the problematic of mourning and the remains of war that later haunt POW films. The relationship of Nusrat, a head diver in an underwater military operation, to the partners he loses anticipates the ghosts of war and the agony caused by missing bodies—both of which are pronounced in postwar films. The story here is not just one of an elite underwater military operation but of a diver's inability to deal with the death of his partners. As Paul Virilio says, "Rest never comes for those transfigured in war. Their ghosts continue to haunt the screens or, more frequently find reincarnation in an engine of war—usually a ship." [17] The Iraqi ship thus becomes the repository of unidentifiable Iranian bodies—ghosts that haunt the surrounding waters and feed Nusrat's nightmares.

The movie begins with the surreal sounds of bubbles underwater as the camera swims among the brightly colored fish of the Gulf. Suddenly the anticipation of death experienced through the sounds of heavy underwater breathing is realized as a dead diver, unidentifiable because his oxygen mask is pulled over his head. Before the audience can register the scene, they are back in a bedroom where Nusrat has just woken from this nightmare.

The next time that Nusrat goes to the water, he insists on going out alone. He is forever searching for the missing body of his dead partner, Hamid (who was killed aboard the Iraqi ship). As he powers the motorboat at top speed, alone, through the windy river out to the open water, we hear a voice telling us about the soldiers: "They are without name or glory, but they have not given up." When Nusrat reaches a certain point he gears up and dives in. His new partner, Ahmad, follows him out just in time to save him from drowning during a traumatic flashback to his old partner's death.

"You yourself told me never to go alone," Ahmad reprimands Nusrat, "You're becoming a war machine." In this way the ghosts of past partners, through traumatic memory, interfere with the wiring of the spiritual machine that is supposed to be as strong as a war machine without becoming that machine. Right after reprimanding Nusrat, Ahmad dives in with the camera to finish the surveillance alone.

He swims out to a certain point and comes up for pictures. As he watches through the camera lens, the Iraqis on the ship catch sight of him. The moment he is seen, he is as good as dead. "Once you see a target you can expect to destroy it," as Virilio quotes colonel Perry.[18] In the same way cinema destroys the ghosts of war by presenting them. Ahmad is shot at and wounded. Nusrat tries to save him, but Ahmad insists that he swim away before the Iraqis come for the bodies. Both know that Ahmad is dying; Nusrat says: "With what ruh (face) do I return if I do not take you with me?" It is better to return with a dead body than a ghost. If Nusrat leaves before Ahmad dies, then the ambiguity of his status, dead or alive, will forever haunt him.

In Hatamikia's *The Scent of Yusef's Shirt*, Daii suffers from an inability to mourn without proof of death—a dead body or face. In his dreams Nusrat lifts the mask of the dead diver and makes a positive identification. While Shireen's brother is most likely dead, and Ahmad is most definitely dead, both Daii and Nusrat suffer from the ambiguity of their own losses and cannot voice the reality of another possible death.

Waiting for the return of a lost person or soul is the condition in which many Iranian audience members view their country. The stories are of POWs and their families, of exiles abroad and being exiled abroad.[19] This world of lost souls replaces the earlier cinema by moving the battleground from the Iraqi border and the body to Tehran and the soul. No longer is there a replaying of emotional scenes of battle or mystical scenes of trance, so often given in scenes of the Iranian war front. Instead, battle and trance are incorporated in the search for bodies, for POWs, and for meaning after the war. The nation is entranced and in mourning; going off to battle ghosts in the same manner that the now missing soldiers went to war.

In *The Scent of Yusef's Shirt*, Shireen and Daii move away from Tehran toward the battlefront in search of Shireen's brother, Khusrow, and in so doing the possibility of another psychic space is opened. In the car ride to the front, Shireen sits in the back seat, alone, where she stares at the dog tags that sway to and fro in the rearview mirror. She pulls down the window and yells Khusrow's name. As they go into a tunnel the lights along the wall, like tracks or halos above the dog tags, move to the rhythm of the incoming sound of the dafs drums. The sound of a daf plays with the rhythm of the moving car, the dog tags sway from the rearview mirror and Shireen slowly begins to sway with them until she's in a full state of trance. A flashback of the video montage that Daii showed her in Tehran of the men returning from the water with Yusef's bloody dog tags that now sway from the rearview mirror brings her out of the trance. She cries. She knows that Khusrow is dead.

The Scent of Yusef's Shirt plays with the ambiguity that surrounds the question of death in relation to the MIAs. Is he dead or alive? The question of presence and the need to have bodily proof form a major problematic for mourning in postwar Iran where so many soldiers became MIAs or POWs. What is at stake is visibility or its inverse, invisibility: lacking physical proof of death. A ghost is only present after death. Even if a particular POW is not identified as dead, there are enough ghosts in Iran to haunt the waiting family. With so many unidentified dead, the whole nation is easily haunted. The POW films, unlike those of battle, are more about absence and disappearance than death. The Iranian revolution played on the absence or exile of Khomeini in relation to the Shiite expectation of the hidden Imam and on the Shiite concept of Entizar. An abstract link between these concepts was created so as to suggest that Khomeini could embody the returned Mehdi who disappeared in the twelfth century. Khomeini says, "The Islamic ruler is a shadow of God, what is meant by a shadow is something that has no motion of itself. Islam recognizes a person as the 'shadow of God' who abandons all individual volition in the sense that he acts only in accordance with the ordinances of Islam, so that his motion is dependent, not independent."[20] The same ambiguity that is based on the theme of disappearance, invisibility, and waiting comes to pass in the POW scenarios. The POWs are more than just hidden saints; they are the leftovers or the excesses of war.[21] The ones that are most disturbing are those that leave only a trace—for whom there can be no real burial and no bodily evidence of death, only anonymous ghosts. These nameless ghosts that do not speak or identify themselves haunt the scenes of The Scent of Yusef's Shirt.

The inability to identify the subject of one's haunting complicates the process of waiting for someone or viewing unidentifiable remains. This invisibility, or inability to locate a body or identify a body, makes mourning that much harder: As Derrida notes, "Nothing could be worse for the work of mourning than the confusion of doubt: one has to know who is buried where and it is necessary (to know—to make certain) that, in what remains of him, he remains there, let him stay there and move no more."[22] Mourning begins when remains are made present, by localizing the dead.

Daii's daughters attempt to solve the problem of locating the spirit or body at a site by buying a grave and symbolically burying flowers in memory of Yusef. But, as replayed in the video of the memorial service, Daii is aloof and unwilling to participate, refusing to allow that site to be a place where he could locate Yusef and bury him for good. Yusef will inhabit Daii's mind, where he will continue to haunt Daii until his body is found, dead or alive. This refusal to believe that Yusef is dead is also fueled by a doubt, which keeps him partially alive. It is doubt that haunts, in some cases, not an actual spirit. In a spiritual state, there is no room for doubt, haunting is not supposed to occur. Doubt is so unjust, so unsettling in postwar Iran: it is the injustice that will continue to haunt the scene.

Justice is a ghost that haunts every bloody conflict or crime. It haunts as a collective of unnamed souls. There is no justice without a crime. And yet, not every attempt to recenter the logos ends in a system of justice. When Shireen becomes upset with Daii for not telling her the news of her brother's possible death, he goes to Yusef's grave where he yells: "See what you did to me Yusef?" As if Yusef, in his disappearance, in his haunting, has disturbed the order of things, in the Greek tragic sense, and made Daii perform an injustice. Daii stands over the grave in the night and cries out: "Show yourself to me. Is this justice? Who do I cry to? Show yourself." He waits for a sign before hitting the grave and continuing: "I know you're not there, are you in the stomach of a whale? What do I do with this heart? Tell me Yusef." Mourning music comes in slowly as he yells: "Yusef." [23]

Injustice is a veil that covers the truth as to whether one's loved one is dead or alive. Injustice resides in an unmarked grave, an empty grave, an unidentified body, and the space of an absent body. Shireen hangs lights for the return of her brother. Daii helps her, though he knows that her brother is dead. When the man from the POW camp comes to tell Shireen the truth, he sees the lights and lies to her. After he leaves, a storm comes and the lights start to pop, as if a ghost has arrived to point to the injustice of concealment; just as a ghost came at the beginning of the film on the eve of the bride's departure. There can be no justice without illuminating the truth. We make sure that what we would like to see dead is dead. We mourn so that the dead will not return as ghosts; and yet they do return as ghosts because the body is not available to be mourned: and thus is Derrida's hauntology.[24] Iranian war cinema does this work. The images on screen come to stand for the dead; they make present what is absent. Like the video within the film, the ghost in the machine comes to stand for the body and becomes an object to be mourned. The cinematic images help to mourn the dead. The cinematic images cannot bring back or bury the dead, and can only point to the impossibility of return.

Like a manifesto, a proclamation of death, cinema provides an image to be mourned, a ghostly presence. It provides a cathartic space: a manifesto of martyrs, a martyrology. The martyrology of the earlier war cinema is replaced by a hauntology of the postwar films that are created in the wake of now-dead martyrs. Media, neither living nor dead, absent nor present, spectralizes.[25]

While Iranian war cinema consciously provides a visual image for the mourning theater audience, within the film video unconsciously creates a ghostly image of the missing person. In both of Hatamikia's POW films, *The Scent of Yusef's Shirt* and *From Kharke to Rhine*, video comes to represent a place of visual ambiguity. This is done brilliantly and quite controversially in *From Kharke to Rhine*, when the POW in Germany gains back his eyesight and sees for the first time a video recording of the funeral of Khomeini. He grabs at the screen and begins to cry. The image of Khomeini on the screen thus replaces the actual body as the soldier tries desperately to grab at the screen, in the same manner that other hands in the crowd infamously grabbed at the body of their imam and pulled it out of the casket. The sequence ends with a shot of the POW's fleshy hand over that of the video hands reaching toward the casket.

In *The Scent of Yusef's Shirt*, Yusef is only present as a video and photo image. Even the moments of pure mourning, when Daii cannot hide his sadness and lack of faith, are captured on video. It is the video montage that brings Shireen back out of her trance and into the realization that her brother is dead. It is only through video that she even knows Yusef; as she watches the video sequences of Yusef and others at training camp, listening to trance music as they put on their fins;[26] watching the sun set with them as they descend into the water but unable to follow them where the video turns blank and becomes a ghost. The next shot is of Yusef's bloody dog tags—the remains found in a shark's belly. Daii says: "I should have named him Yunis, and not Yusef.²⁷ Daii never believed that Yusef was dead. Unlike Majnun, who incorporated the image of Leili to the point where it replaced her, Daii did not watch the videos nor did he allow them to replace Yusef in his imagination. Thus in life after the war we see that for some people, like Daii, the image is no longer an acceptable substitute, the path and the journey have been abandoned, people want to live in the realm of the real and not in the imagined realm espoused by Ibn Arabi, not in the place of trance and otherworldliness created just before and during the war, where Shireen retreats during the trance sequence.²⁸ Here, zekr is no longer performed by soldiers going off to war but by a woman, a secular, French-raised woman who is looking for her brother. In a different context, in an empty realm that is not fully understood, the zekr lacks the necessary faith to bring forth that which she hopes to achieve: knowledge of her brother's location. Daii says: "If you do not believe, who will?" When we see that Khusrow will not return, it is clear just how impotent the imaginary realm has become—it has become the realm of death.

Yusef was never a ghost for Daii; he never spoke to him nor appeared at his own grave. Daii's faith keeps Yusef alive, as we see in the end when Yusef returns. The space of faith, baten, becomes stronger than that of the surface, zaher. Daii's own faith is stronger than that of those who give into an image (Majnun, Yusef's fiancé, Shireen—all of whom lose the one they love with the loss of their faith).

When someone is missing, along with so many dead, confusion ensues and it becomes hard to identify individual ghosts, to claim the right spirit, just as it is difficult to claim the right mutilated body. War confuses identity. The irony is that these video ghosts, these re-creations of images are what help to find many POWs later, by identifying them in the camps. And still there are other ghosts: those of the photographers who took the tapes and pictures, who witnessed without being hurt because they were practically invisible.

When the soldiers return they are confronted with ghostly images of their battalion, as half-grieving, half-hopeful family members of the disappeared appear with now ghostly images as large framed pictures. In *The Scent of Yusef's Shirt*, Shireen and Daii visit the home of a returned member of Khusrow's battalion. A group of older villagers sits in a circle holding their large framed pictures; they drink tea and eat halva (traditionally a sweet for mourning holidays). They ask the man if he's seen their sons or witnessed their deaths. The returnee, having the horrible task of bringing the news of death, asks: "Well, has he written to you?" But these villagers are most likely illiterate and have not received a letter. When Shireen asks about her brother, the returnee cannot bring himself to tell her of her brother's death. He takes Daii aside on the way out and says: "He was captured and killed."

Daii asks: "Did you see him being killed."

"No, that is what happens, they kill them."

"If you did not see it, how do you know?"

Without proof, without having seen the death, it cannot be officially established, officially mourned. We know in the film that wayward ghosts are present, and yet these presences in the film are never named as ghosts. They are alluded to through cinematic devices—the gusty wind, the popped lightbulbs, storms, eerie music —that create an effect without ever solving the problem of presence or of answering the question that drives the movie: Is Yusef still alive? Is Khusrow still alive? Which one of them is haunting the movie, as more than just a missing person, but a returned death? Which one will return alive?

The remainders of even a just war, however, present a problem of excess. It is exactly that which is made visible in these films, the ghosts that point to the crime, that some want to keep hidden. It is this problematic of missing bodies and returnees that are the remainder, the mark of failure of martyrdom: a martyr is not meant to return except as a dead body. Yet, it is these ghosts that haunt

the cinema. Obviously, the return of men sent off to war to be martyred marks the failure of martyrdom; POWs present the return of
something that should have remained buried. The injustice of war
is written on their fragmented bodies, in the space of a lost limb
(Yusef returns with one arm amputated). What is at stake is visibility. What cinema does is reappropriate possibly critical images
and memories and places them in a space of controlled mourning,
where the correct effect and proper ghostly nuances are at hand.
But even ghosts permeate celluloid. Ghosts of the dead point to
a failure, they remain invisible but also come through the way a
spirit would, to point toward a place of injustice. Here we see a partial failure of the task of concealment, because mourning becomes
critical. What is finally at stake is one's own survival and ability to
move on.

Hatamikia's films brilliantly deal with the different and unex-
pected types of returns: the video tapes recovered from the front,
dog tags, ghosts, and most interesting, exiles from abroad. Shireen, the sister in *From Kharke to Rhine*, an English passenger in Daii's
cab, all represent exile—the other form of return. They illustrate
just how large an area the war encompassed, an area that reaches
beyond the Gulf and into the rest of the world. Through the image
of exiles we come to understand the international scope of the war,
and that what binds a nation is so much more than land. Not one
Iranian, by virtue of association, could escape the mark of war.
Every Iranian takes part in the act of mourning. As Deleuze notes,
"We have ours [ghosts], but memories no longer realize such borders by definition, they pass through walls, these remnants, day and
night, they trick consciousness and skip generations." [29] Eventually
all ghosts return home.

In presenting the nation with its death in a beautiful and artistic way, Hatamikia's films open a new, and safe, realm for mourning. The task of these particular postwar films becomes the task
of mourning itself. It is a many-layered project that strives to use
images as supplements that beautify and spiritualize a war-torn
environment. It is a project in making the invisible, the missing
bodies, visible without naming ghosts, without pointing to a pos-

sible injustice or crime on the part of the government. It is a project in returning from the imaginary realm, the one created by Avini, ironically through the very visual realm that made that journey possible. At the same time that these films reinstate the importance of faith, they stress the importance of remaining in the realm of the real, with those who are still with us, the returnees, instead of continuing to move on the path of self-loss that is now marked by drugs and alcohol, delusions and disillusionment. These films point to the very important role of the former Basij (especially those like Hatamikia who once worked on *Revayat-e Fath*) in paving the way toward social change; toward redefining the nation after war—the ultimate place of return, dead or alive.

CHAPTER EIGHT

Reforming Religious Identity in Post-Khatami Iran

JOURNAL ENTRY, FEMALE TEHRAN COLLEGE STUDENT, SPRING 2000 *Recently I haven't been too concerned about making sure my hejab is ok at school (rayat nemeekunam). I want them to throw me out. I heard that if you're thrown out of the university in Iran, the United States will give you a visa. Once I have graduated I'll be like a donkey lost in the valley, so why not get kicked out?*

We told everyone about our relations with boys. I thought shit, whatever happens, fuck it. Everyone talks about us behind our backs, as if we were sluts, but when a girl wearing a chador speaks with a boy it's no big deal. Why is what we (who do not wear chadors) do is so much more important? Lately no one bothers with the hejab. People are more concerned with sandals and socks and light colors. Everyone shakes hands—boys and girls, which is great. One day we went to a restaurant and a man played all the songs from before the revolution on a violin and someone sang. It was great. My dad says everyone has gone crazy and no one can be normal and you see things that are shocking. In Africa they dance and stuff, in the twenty-first century, why can't we? No wonder everyone is crazy. I have decided to go abroad to continue my studies.[1]

With President Khatami's election in 1997, and the subsequent re-laxing of social rules that resulted in a more open social atmo-sphere, came a battle of surfaces. Khatami's policies shifted the emphasis from religious national identity to an Iranian national identity, thereby spurring an ongoing conflict with the spiritual leader of the Islamic revolution, Ayatollah Khameini.[2] In a speech in summer 2000, President Khatami reassured the country that a shift in physical appearance did not signify a move away from Islam.[3] "Just because someone shaves his beard does not mean that he is not a practicing Muslim," he stated.[4] And yet the ongoing anxiety at the time that centered on changing the surface points to the level of investment held by the conservative clergy in keeping that surface, and thus in turn points to the power that resides in the image of an Islamic nation.

As the Islamic surface fades, efforts are being made to shift the emphasis back to the true nature of belief and identity. The baten has taken on a more powerful role than the zaher. But, as I noted earlier, that space may or may not include Islam. For a majority of Iranian youth, revolutionary ideology dampened a faith in the reli-gion it used as a vehicle. Indeed, one former revolutionary told me that had revolutionary policy aimed at creating faithful Muslims and had it been less concerned with converting revolutionaries it would have been more successful. As he noted, "If a woman really has faith in Islam, covering would not be illogical or oppressive."[5]

This shift came about as youth raised under revolutionary dic-tate began to mature and question their surroundings. It also came about as a group of key revolutionaries known as *eslah talaban*, students of reform (who were supporters of President Khatami), began to question their own ideology and identities. Many eslah talaban remain practicing Muslims who no longer accept the domi-nant revolutionary ideology. They believe that religion should not mix with politics and that ideology is not the same thing as faith. In short, when mixed with politics, religion loses its core and be-comes an ideology. This is especially true when riya comes into play, as politics is public and a public religion has the potential of be-coming a deceptive act.

Many reformists were among the main cultural producers under the Islamic regime.[6] The key to understanding reform can be found in the fact that the major players (like Said Hajjarian) were once Basij and heavily active in the construction, propagation, or administration of the Islamic republic. This fact is important for two reasons: reform in the Islamic republic can only come from within, and there can be no reforms without addressing the legacy of the failure and the tragedy of the war and the culture of martyrdom that was born of it. Those who fought the war, who gave family members to martyrdom, and who expected to be taken care of by the government and the Islamic society they created have the most to lose should the Islamic republic dissolve. Among the veterans that I interviewed, some said in retrospect that they were thankful that they were not martyred and that God saved them from dying during a moment of insanity. Some, as we are increasingly seeing portrayed in contemporary cinema, would rather be dead or just numb.[7] The important shift in identity came not just in youth per se but also in the reform generation, who demonstrated for revolution, fought the war, and now have children who are part of a new and different generation. One reformist I interviewed during Ashura, also a former Basij, could no longer bear to observe the rituals surrounding Muharram. He remembered the days when he was immersed in these activities, and he not only regrets those days but also can no longer participate in the activities as a faithful Muslim because for him they hold only an ideology that he has left behind: "In the end, none of this mourning ritual kills the pain."

This particular refomist began to have marital problems when he lost faith in both Islam and the ideology of revolutionary Islam. He regretted wasting his youth fighting for Islam, especially at the front line of the war. His wife, although disillusioned with the ideology, remained a faithful believer. He hated what her outward practices, such as wearing Islamic covering, represented to him and he began to lose respect for her. In turn, she lost respect for him the further he moved away from Islam. However, as the political battle between the reformists and conservatives intensified, she found it harder to negotiate her faith in Islam and her dislike of the revolutionary ideology. And even though she still believed in the faith, she stopped covering because the hejab became inseparable from the ideology that she believes to be marring the name of Islam. For many, it is no longer necessary to show their belief or to propagate it by joining in the masses, and thus religion has left the public sphere and become privatized. Ideology, including ideological religion, however, thrives in the public sphere and cannot exist without a public show of support. According to one reformist, "Religion has not disappeared, it's merely slipped into the private sphere."[8] Further, as young people demand more autonomy, the survival of clerical rule will depend on the importance that youths place on the Islamic component of their identity. The idea of an Islamic democracy works when one is both Islamic and secular (and when a secular identity incorporates Islam, but the Islam component does not dominate that identity).[9]

One of the critical issues among politicians in Iran is whether the revolutionary government was successful in creating Islamic subjects. What institutions, practices, ideologies, and values from the revolution retain their legitimacy and remain useful for policy purposes? Both reformists and conservative politicians in Iran are vying for power by subtly debating the way in which an "Islamic citizen" is defined. The main concern of social planners and cultural producers in Iran, both in the government and outside of it, is how to continue implementing policy and producing culture for a nonresponsive mystery generation. While over 60 percent of Iran's population matured strictly under revolutionary Islamic law, there is no assurance that revolutionary Islamic values succeeded in affecting the identity of Iran's youth. There is overwhelming evidence that the twenty-seven-year effort to create Islamic citizens worked against itself and instead made the country more secular.

One cultural producer that I interviewed believed that objects of the familiar world—cars, trees, parks, and Iranian citizens—are Islamic by virtue of the fact that they exist inside an Islamic nation. Thus are these modern, self-certain subjects, by participating in an Islamic nation, also Islamic subjects?

Abdul Karim Soroush, a leading reformist philosopher and

former revolutionary, claims that the experience of the past twenty years as an Islamic republic created a shift from a "modern" Cartesian subject to a "modern" Islamic one.[10] This might suggest that the government's attempt to form a monolithic Islamic identity was somewhat successful. But was it? What is interesting is the extent to which Western theories of the subject have permeated the Islamic intellectual scene. New notions of subjectivity and agency that support transmutable definitions of identity have supported the shift in contemporary Islamic thought from the realm of conservative Islamic politics based on a clerical government back to the early, more liberal, philosophy of the revolution that called for a democratic Islamic government. These philosophical debates question the notion of a singular Islamic subject (created by the Islamic republic's public policy) and in turn have allowed space for new versions of a secular Islamic citizen to emerge. The idea of a transmutable identity threatens the legitimacy of the conservative clergy for whom there can only exist a monolithic Islamic identity.[11] The reformists support the claim that Islam will remain a strong component of identity even after a shift toward secularism. The conservative clergy claims that a religious identity cannot be maintained in a secular state—that is, that one cannot simultaneously hold true to Islamic values and be secular. This is true if the notion of Islamic values functions as an ideology and not as a belief. (The ideology of political Islam runs counter to that of secularism, but the belief in Islam does not.)

Can killing the Islamic character of the nation change the true nature of Islamic identity? True Sufis do not identify themselves as Sufi. To be Sufi is to be pure of heart, something that is practiced privately and not announced as an identity or political or religious affiliation (and thus is akin to riya). Sufism is about the baten and not the zaher. This principle brings us back to the notion of riya and the belief in mystical Islam. As noted in Avini's project, the attempt to film or visually capture the essence of Islam is problematic and points to Islam as an invisible entity that resides not in the appearance of things, zaher, but in the essence of one's being, baten. One should not use personal practice to announce religiosity or morality, because when one does so Islam ceases to exist solely for the purpose of faith. Given the notion of riya, one should ultimately be more concerned with the space of inner faith rather than the surface of things, zaher.

Because of the strong illusion that revolutionary policy created, it is impossible for policymakers to claim any empirical evidence as to the true identity of Iranian youth. In order to continue their program and formulate policy, they need to look below the surface without shattering it or voicing the "public secret" (once the secret is voiced, it loses its power). As Khatami said, "This country needs calm now and real research (not slander). Instead of asking whether reforms are killing Islam, we need to ask ourselves what is Islam? How can we make it livable?"[12]

Revolutionary artists, philosophers, and other cultural producers realized that the culture they were working so hard to produce was not being consumed. For example, Iranian cinema was not popular in Iran until after Kiarostami won the Palm d'Or—international recognition gave Iranian cinema legitimacy as an art form where formerly it was dismissed as propaganda. These cultural producers thus became disillusioned, knowing that in forcing Islamization the youngest generations would turn away from it entirely.

Policymakers have begun to channel their efforts into sociological research (mainly polls) in order to discern what the masses need to remain happy Islamic subjects.[13] While I was doing my own research on secular youth in northern Tehran, the government was doing very similar research across the entire socioeconomic spectrum of the country, but using very different research methods (primarily polls, especially door-to-door types).

THE FOUNDATION FOR YOUTH AFFAIRS, TEHRAN, SUMMER 2000 *The unbearable heat and humidity cause my rupushe to stick to my shirt and pants and thus outline my body, which defeats the whole purpose of wearing it. As usual I've been called at the very last minute, and I only have a short time to make it to a "casual" interview with the head of the Government Research Center on Youth.*

At the center, the director of a provincial youth center is in town to discuss his budget and education programming. My host, a former Basij and an engineer, suggests that a toy missile-building kit might serve as an effective education tool: "It's a lot of fun and it teaches them engineering skills."

"Is there something else that is less violent and teaches them engineering?" I ask.

"They do not actually have explosives, they're just wood."

After spending the morning discussing popsicle-stick projects (my idea, because they are cheap, accessible, etc.) it's time for prayers and lunch. On the way to the lunchroom my host states: "Well, we have not discussed much about your research and there is not much to say about ours except that our general concern is that Iranian youth are under a great deal of stress primarily due to the economic situation, and if this stress is not kept inside it seeps out and spoils family life and public culture, and the government then has to step in.[14] We're looking for the most effective ways to help youth with their stress, we have found that television shows on psychology help a great deal."

I'm about to mention that many youth I know never watch Iranian television, when we abruptly turn the corner into a large lunchroom with two floors.

"I'm sorry, Ms. Varzi, the office abides by Islamic law, you'll have to eat upstairs with the women."

The men excuse themselves and leave me to pick at my sandwich and curse my social science skills and inability to have learned even a single thing about the government's research on youth after three uncomfortable hours in the president's office drinking tea and making sure my hejab was not falling off.

"Are you a sociologist?" asks one of the young women.

"I'm an anthropologist."

She smiles, "We're all studying sociology at Tehran University, this is our part-time job."

"Oh?" I perk up, "Are you learning a lot of sociological skills at this job?"

"Not really, we were hoping to do more practical training, like polling, or research, but we're only doing data entry."

"Really? Are you at least learning how sociologists do their work?"

"We enter all the data for the polls that the office is in charge of taking."

"Well, learning to ask the right question is one of the most important skills as a social scientist. What do you think of the types of questions being asked on the polls, are you able to at least offer feedback and suggestions? It's good to learn the reasons why certain questions are asked and what the answers might indicate in terms of larger social import."

"The questions center around satisfaction, the quality of life, feelings of security, financial and physical security in the city, general feelings about the future, employment prospects, and whether youth think the state can provide these basic human necessities," the women tell me.

The polls appear to center around the question as to whether youth feel that the state can or do meet their needs, whether they feel safe and feel that the state provides that safety. This is what the Hegelian state promises and this Islamic state is struggling to deliver.

"Most people do not fill in the polls, or turn the pollster away when they come to their doors. People never know if the government is trying to corner them. Iranians do not like to give personal information."

"What if the polls were anonymous and not given at a person's house where they can later be found?"

"I do not know if they have tried that. They are anonymous, we type in location just for class markers."

On the way back upstairs I ask to use a washroom.

"You'll have to use the men's room. Until recently they did not employ women." I thank them and head home.

On another occasion I am introduced to a more open study.

TEHRAN UNIVERSITY, CENTER FOR SOCIOLOGICAL STUDIES OF YOUTH, 2000 "I'm worried about this generation. We have nothing in common with them. This generation does not choose, they placate, they allow things to be done then they react or reject, but they never initiate anything. They have a notion that whatever evolves comes from the government and not the people, so why bother?"

Mr. Daneshgu, a young Ph.D. student who is conducting a study on contemporary youth culture for Vezarat Irshad (the Islamic Guidance Ministry) is genuinely concerned about the young generation. He continues, "When I was in my late teens I was at the front, leading a battalion. I had responsibilities—heavy life-or-death responsibilities. There was camaraderie in our group. War gave responsibility to youth and confidence.[15] Being in charge of a battalion at the age of twenty gave youth something to protect and nurture, these youth are given nothing to protect, nurture, or be in charge of.[16] There was equality; we had uniforms, uniformity—a common cause. But this generation has no higher goals or purpose.[17] They are not interested in religion. Religion moves against pluralism, whereas choice gives one rules."

"Why do you think that is?"

"You know, religion had a function for my generation, we were thirsty for it. We needed it to bring the country together. We were thirsty for change, for higher awareness of spirituality and purpose. This generation does not see any function for religion in their lives.[18] This generation wants choice. They are a capitalist generation, they want the things they see on satellite TV. They have different desires and interests. The problem is we are their cultural producers and yet they do not consume anything that we produce. At the same time, neither do they attempt to produce anything of their own, they are extremely passive. We are the ones who are tired and they are the ones taking a break."

"Are you saying religion is done for? I think they retain a respect for religion and are still somewhat religious."

"There is a big age gap in this society. This generation does not care about morals. We want to know why. How do we turn this around? Our movement is trying to figure out where morality has gone and why good is replaced by evil and how to bring good back. This is the theme of our ten-volume study.[19] We are very concerned about this generation and morals. If our enemies [the West] give us the time and space to work with this generation we could save it."

Among conservatives the attitude remains that it is outside infiltration in the form of satellite dishes and black-market videos, and now ongoing communication via Web blogs, that is the cause for the failure of Islamic values. The blame is always directed to the outside. At the same time Daneshgu's research is somewhat self-reflexive in its attempts to discern where government policy may have taken a wrong turn with youth. In fact, the Tehran University study went to the heart of the matter. The poll on which the study is based was conducted with over fourteen hundred youths between the ages of eighteen and thirty. The general data on religion found that youths do not believe that a religious leader needs to rule a religious state, and that a religious state could just as easily be run by a religious intellectual who is not a trained cleric. The study further found that youths today have very little knowledge of Khomeini's life or any notion of Velayat-e Faqih (which is surprising given the education system which stresses this history), and that youths attend religious hey'ats (ceremonies) but do not pray. The polls also found that the religious section of the newspaper is the least read, though people have a positive view of religion. Only 3 percent of youth are against Namaz Jumeh.[20] They do not agree that the reformists' papers were opened to steal youth away from religion. Most youth do not buy the paper, but do read it when their parents buy it (most youths get the news from the Internet or from satellite). They also believe that society is becoming less religious and more criminal, which they blame on economics and the clergy: "All the bad things clerics do is done in the name of religion." Their favorite pastimes are, in order of popularity, cinema, music, painting, and theater (cruising must not have been an option on the form, because from what I have seen that would be the first pick).[21]

When a reformist newspaper published the results of a poll indicating that 75 percent of the general public and 90 percent of schoolchildren do not pray, the clergy reacted by passing a law allowing women to become prayer leaders in segregated situations in order to encourage praying. Two additional laws passed as a result of the polls include one allowing bright colors to be worn in school, and another allowing young girls in segregated schools to go without the hejab in all-female classes. These came as a direct result of medical and psychological findings that point to overall depression on the part of young adults.

In my own research I found a very similar disregard for organized religion, but I also found that most youth at the college level knew a lot about Islam, Islamic law (including Velayat-e Faqih) and were well-versed enough in it to use it to their advantage (as noted in chapter 6). I also found that youth attend hey'ats for their own purposes (as demonstrated in the discussion about Jordan Street in chapter 6), but they do not pray unless made to do so. I do believe that there is a major shift both in knowledge and worldview between those secular youths whom I worked with in the university and the generation below them in high school and in middle school. Indeed, the generation in high school is culturally completely different, in large part because they missed most of the war.

The most interesting part of the poll was aimed at determining the effectiveness of public discipline (amr be maruf).[22] Among the questions asked were, "Who should have the authority to tell you what to do?" and "Who would you listen to?" Students do not think that those who demand that youth act a certain way are practicing what they preach; both Basij and secular youth agreed that many clerics and their family members do not uphold the same moral standards for themselves.[23] When asked what they think about the type of person who does not respond positively to moral instruction on the street, most youths reasoned that such a person gets his or her morality from within and has his or her own inner structure and values (again, the emphasis is being shifted to the baten).[24]

JOURNAL ENTRY, FEMALE TEHRAN COLLEGE STUDENT, SPRING 2000 I think I lack something others have. I am stupid and do not know a thing, and I'm writing all this stupid stuff in this journal. The big words of my life are behind most people, I will be twenty-two in a month and I know these words are stupid . . . I feel like life is just a dream, a dream without value . . . it cannot have meaning with all this depression. In elementary school they made us believe we should be intellectuals. I do not have the patience. I feel empty one minute and the next I feel just normal like everyone else. My thoughts are all mixed up and I forget everything (my father tells me that he feels the same way, it's normal).

I have so much to do and I'm depressed and do nothing. One says write a list, so I write it. I have things I want to do but do not know where to start. I think things were better before the revolution, wish I lived then, when there was good music, dance, and a nice atmosphere. I said this to someone once and they said "You're imagining Paris at that time, not Tehran."

Time flies. I feel like it's too late to start anything and that I've lived a hundred years. I feel like I'm on a dark road or dark valley looking for a light to show me the way, but the light is also lost, sometimes from afar I see flashes. Furugh [Farokhzad] says such light can as easily be the light of a wolf's eyes.

They just shut down all the newspapers, but that's fine. Now my father has more time to talk to me without all his damn papers to read. Besides, even if they kill Khatami, all the young people are leaving the country behind, who's left to construct this place? I could care less. Descartes says that if a person imagines something exists then it comes into existence. Makmalbaf says that truth is right in front of us, but it's not. That's too easy.

My thoughts are heavy, busy. I'm going crazy, two more terms and my studies will be over and I'm not sure what to do with myself. My college friends say go for the master's concourse. I don't know. I wish someone would tell me what to do. I need to find someone to give me advice. I feel like a roach whose foot and hands are caught in a tree and cannot move. I do not feel like doing anything. Even breathing is hard. God, I've filled this notebook with so much garbage.

I am friends with three boys from the university; we're very good friends, but at school I have to pretend that I do not know them. Imagine everyday you see someone you are friends with but you pretend not to know each other. This play acting was hard at first but now I'm used to it. I am a doruhi person (two-faced), hesabi (for sure). If we had important things to say to each other at school we would write letters . . . there is a place at school where we put our personal things, during lunch and prayer when no one is around we would put notes in each other's bags. [Prayer is a moment of suspension when the authorities are unavailable.] Still other psychological things remain. We sometimes put letters in those plastic eggs that hold chocolate and hide them in the university garden. I wonder what would happen if we were able to be normal around each other. The younger poru kids speak with each other. It's just my generation that is scared all of the time, we remember the days before Khatami.

Time is running out of my hands like water and I cannot contain it. I love the end of winter, life seems more valuable, and I love going to Tajrish, to the bazaar there, to shop. I love the new year, Nowruz, and all of its rituals . . . I feel like I've been born again and everything is lovely. Greenery, newness, branches budding, rain that's new and fresh, tea, saffron candy, all these good things make me happy. This tree in front of our house has seen a few different Nowruz's, maybe even lovers under its branches from the old days. One day when I'm dead and gone this tree will be here and the river in Tajrish will *also be here. [Will lovers gather then?] With all this breath I've taken and all the food I've eaten, all the happiness and unhappiness, how small I am. Our existence is a mystery, a puzzle.*

While Khatami appears to have made a difference as gauged in the inches taken off of the hems of rupushes and the decrease in the number of martyr billboards, these surface differences do not make the ultimate difference necessary for real social change to occur. My research shows that as long as change remains concerned with the surface of things, zaher, there can be little change in inner identity, worldview, baten—the place where real change occurs. In many ways it will be up to the next generation to make a difference, but they have learned from their parents' mistakes that it does not pay to be political. Even the landslide vote for Khatami was not an overwhelming decision on their part to make a political difference. Perhaps the first election in 1997 gave them hope and a space to voice their concerns, but that changed by 2000. In the 2005 presidential election most reform-minded individuals did not bother to vote because they felt the outcome was inevitable.

JOURNAL ENTRY, TEHRAN COLLEGE STUDENT, WINTER 2000 *A few days ago we went to vote. People were talking loudly about whom they planned to vote for. A Hezbollah guy was dictating his vote loudly to his daughter. He mentioned all the conservatives, foremost Hashemi-Rafsanjani. For some reason I took great pleasure in walking past him with my hair falling out of my russari. We all voted together for Khatami.*

I did not want to vote for Khatami; he is no assurance for the future security of this country. I do not really care what happens to the future of this country. I voted for Faizeh Hashemi last time, and look at what happened. The only reason I voted at all was because we had to have a stamp on our student ID cards indicating that we voted in order to take the college entrance exam, and now we need one in order to stay in school. No one in my family has voted since the revolution.

The registration line was full of people like my family who had not voted since the revolution. Our neighbors who were shah people even voted for the first time. The line was full of women wearing makeup and men in ties! Those against the regime were surrounded by clouds of perfume that mixed with the Hezbollah's clouds of rose water. Again the same group went and voted for city council members and I remember a lot of people in our group voting for a candidate just because he wore a tie.

For youth, public politics are not the proper platform for change. For them, change is something that has to come gradually from within the individual. This change might occur in much the same way Shariati espoused—as a return to self—only this self will not be obliterated but rather reconstructed through a phase of khodsazi. We see evidence of this in the self-help groups, the turn toward psychology and the twelve-step programs, but also in the choices of many youths to become teachers, psychologists, social workers, and lawyers.

The selflessness and martyrdom of bi-khodi has proven to be deadly. The political aspects have played out and proven to be empty; it is time to seek out a new kind of leader, not through elections or revolutions but from within. While it appears as though Iranian youth is on the verge of moving in this direction, of looking inward and concentrating on baten as opposed to zaher, there is much evidence that many young people continue to be concerned with appearances and the surface of things.[25] These youth make their statements by presenting themselves as differently as possible from what is deemed Islamic—rebelling without concern about inward self-awareness or change.

There is, however, a contingent of youth (as well as former Basij reformers) whose members are trying to see beyond the many-layered surface in order to find a truth that they can live by. But even these youths are lost when it comes to the notion of a strong individual that is self-certain and autonomous. As illustrated in these pages, the movement of a strong Islamic public policy grinding against a strong private sphere has left most youths confused and alone.[26] While there has occurred a shift in the political landscape that lends validity to public opinion and locates the seat of political change within the individual and inner reality of baten as opposed to the revolutionary policy that concentrated on the surface of things, zaher, this shift is occurring gradually and with difficulty. Iranian youth are moving toward a stronger notion of self, even in the midst of bi-khodi and hopelessness, but they have yet to reach the peak. They are still on the long journey toward the peak, moving their way up the mountain toward the Simurgh. Not all of them will make it, and many will fly away to foreign lands like the generation before them, but the majority remain caught in a web of shifting and foggy visionary terrains in which they battle to see and be seen.

Mehdi's Climb

It's too early in the morning to tell whether the gray sky is an indication of bad weather to come or just the start of another polluted morning, already marked by honking horns and the regular downtown hustle and bustle. Because it is the weekend the bus and shared taxi hub is teeming with people trying to get out of the city on day trips. I look around, trying to locate the southwest corner of the traffic square, expecting to see the small group of college students who have invited me on this day trip. Instead I find what looks like the makings of a sit-in: a crowd of young people, weighed down with backpacks and walking sticks, are making absolutely no effort to look inconspicuous as they yell out to the minibus drivers and tea vendors.

"There's a bit of a delay," my friend tells me as she ushers me over to the crowd, "Mehdi needs to hire a second minibus, we will not all fit."

"Who are all these people?"

"Well, it was supposed to be only serious hikers, but it looks like everyone invited at least one cousin or friend. There are almost one hundred people."

"Will the komiteh give us any problems?"

"No, see that guy over there?" she points to an older man with a walking stick, "He's a professor and we have a letter saying we belong to the university hiking club, so they should let us pass."

Finding an extra minibus to accommodate the overwhelming response to

24. A view of 2000 Jungle, Caspian Region, Iran. (Photo by Roxanne Varzi, 2000)

this last-minute excursion is proving to be somewhat difficult, but Mehdi pulls it off. Ten years ago when Rafsanjani was president, a group of college-aged unmarried boys and girls would never dare to take a trip alone together. Today, the fact that the buses are "public" transport, and the number of youths in the group is so large, makes it hard for the Islamic police to find fault. If asked, most of the boys and girls will feign ignorance and pretend they have never met the members of the other sex before today on the bus. Even so, drivers do not like the idea of transporting a group of mixed teens. There are minibus services during ski season, but they are organized ahead of time through ski shops and girls ride in one minibus and boys in another (no matter that they all end up skiing the same slopes, supposedly segregated, but not everything is always controlled, especially given the impact of the sheer force of number).[1]

The minibus winds its way up the mountain, passing tiny villages and the remains of a castle before reaching a small and crowded traffic circle where the buses leave after agreeing to return for us at five. It is barely eight when we start making our way up the mountain.

By the second creek crossing, via the makeshift bridge of a suspended log, it becomes obvious that this is not a beginner's trail. Some of the girls have already handed their packs to their boyfriends while others have merely dropped out and are now sitting along the side peeling oranges and gossiping. Mehdi makes his way up and down the line of hikers encouraging those who have dropped out to keep going, as the weather is beginning to look increasingly ominous.

Hikers pass us on their way down the mountain; they warn of an impending storm and tell us that the area is prone to mudslides. There are areas in northwestern Iran where hundreds of people are killed yearly due to mudslides. Just two weeks ago a tour bus fell into a ravine in a Caspian village and was buried in sludge. No one survived.

"Shouldn't we think about heading down?" I ask Mehdi.

"Why? The weather? No, it will blow over."

My friend gives me a doubtful look. People are starting to complain about the cold. The temperature feels like it has dropped ten degrees, and there is a light drizzle and none of us has umbrellas or gloves. My hands are numb. It's becoming increasingly foggy, and Mehdi, who was just at my side, is no longer in sight.

"We should go back down," suggest a few members of the group.

"I'm cold," says another boy.

"Let's build a fire."

"I'm hungry."

"This is stupid."

"Why are we still climbing upward if no one thinks it's a good idea?" I ask the group of young people nearest me.

"Well, Mehdi is up there, still leading. We cannot let him lead without following, he'd be alone."

"He is alone." We are the closest group to him and he has barely looked back to check if we're still following. His faith that we are following him is strong; as well it should be, given that no one is prepared to stray from the path he leads. We finally catch up with him and he asks me how I am doing.

"Fine, a bit cold though, and worried about possible mudslides." He laughs and tells me that this is normal for this part of the country. I tell him that the others are also worried and they want to turn around. He tells me that they are looking for excuses, "Everyone wants to sit around and peel oranges, slice cucumbers, and chit chat. They're not serious hikers; they should not have come. But, since they're here, I need to look after them, so we are going a bit slower. Sorry," he apologizes to me, brushing the rain out of his eyes.

"Do not apologize to me. I am willing to turn around at any minute."

"Roksana, you just climbed Sahand and hiked through the 2000 jungle.[2] This cannot possibly worry you?" He laughs. But I am worried and so is everyone else.

On both the trip that Mehdi mentioned, through the valley of the assassins to the Caspian and on another trip in northern Tabriz we had chosen a leader before setting out. Both trips had been with the mountain climbing federation of Tehran, a group of climbers that meet twice a week to climb in the Tehran mountains and make trips out to other mountain ranges on long weekends or holidays. On both trips I attended with the group we had politely acknowledged as leader the eldest member of the group (a retired military general who had been hiking for over forty years). The group was made up mostly of people from my generation (in their formative years at the beginning of the revolution) and older. So, I assumed choosing a group leader was a generational practice. My interviews with members of Mehdi's group indicated that they considered themselves to be more independent and less traditional or group oriented than those of their parents' generation, and yet my experiences with them and with my own generation, who had made similar claims, had proven to be the opposite.[3] For group events ranging from ski trips to private parties there was nothing that was done spontaneously or from individual initiative. The group was always consulted; everyone participated once the activity was decided on; and there was always somehow a de facto leader (chosen usually for age and experience) whom everyone deferred to.[4]

Later I saw what Mehdi meant when I went to the Tehran Museum of Modern Art for a roundtable discussion with Swiss video artists who were there to work on a group project. Almost every question from the youthful Tehran audience members was in reference to how the group made decisions. No one believed that there could be harmony without a leader to make the final decisions. The concept of majority rule (or voting) was not so far off, but in the end everything came down to having a leader in order to stop disagreements, break ties, and make the important decisions: voting simply could not replace this function.

On the mountaintop with Mehdi's group, things became increasingly ominous and cold. Mehdi's friends began to complain more and more, and many were physically shaking from the cold. I wore hiking boots and yet I could barely feel my toes, while some of the hikers were wearing soaking-wet canvas tennis shoes. I could not believe that we were still hiking toward the top when we should be making a run for cover.

"Let's return," I suggested, as yet another group of hikers passed us on a mad dash back down the mountain.

"No, it will blow over," Mehdi promised.

Some of the boys went to find dry wood for a fire but it was already raining too hard and everything was soaked, including us. I noticed that the boy next to me was particularly disgruntled. He was the little brother of one of the students in my dowreh, and I knew that he was a strong-willed individual — a member of the next generation, still in high school. I began to work at convincing him to convince the others that we should leave. A few of the students, including a girl with particularly blue lips, shot me disapproving glances as they overheard me attempting to unite against Mehdi and abandon the idea of hiking to the peak. But I was not about to be martyred to prove my loyalty to Mehdi, and eventually the young high school student and I left the group. We walked for two hours before finding a small traffic circle where we caught a bus back to Tehran.

Later that evening I called Mehdi, who told me that those who stayed ended up going to his uncle's villa on the other side of the mountain where they warmed themselves by a fire, played cards, and listened to music for the rest of the afternoon.

"Roksana, if you had just been a little more patient." I could not appreciate the beauty of having an afternoon completely free of the komiteh, or of being in a place where I could listen to whatever music I desired and be with my friends despite gender differences. I had grown up without these restrictions and took it for granted. Anyway, he had been right — just as we hit the village on our mad rush down the mountain the sun began to come out.

I

Finally we arrive at the mythical mountain where we have gone in search of the Simurgh, only to find dead bodies, obliterated minds, fallout from the journey and what remains: the metaphoric thirty birds, *simirgh*. The journey suggested that we look beyond the historic event of the revolution to understand it not only as a phenomenon in space and time but also as a mind-set lived on another plane or a reality activated from the alam-al mithal, from hyperspace, clicked into being through the full force of mass-majority belief, if only for a moment. The integral elements remain: Islam, Hafiz's poetry, activated and deactivated. They are part of the archeology of Iranian social history. But instead of archaically looking at history and its physical space as layers buried under dirt, we begin to see it as hypertexts, ghosts, the alam-al mithal—as a dimension outside of the physical dimension of daily life; as a mind-set that exists in a different realm and that has the possibility to inhabit our space. Empty space is a place that is always already filled—by ghosts, by the possibility of our next move, and by the excesses of history.

At the end of *The Conference of the Birds* we see that power is not outside the individual, in the zaher, but rather within the self, in the baten. The surface, zaher, is just that, and the inner dimensions of the individual, baten, is where power lies. The image has lost its aura and its power (as we saw in Hatamikia's films, especially with the character of Daii). This is increasingly apparent in Iran as a majority of the population (mostly under thirty) begins to look inward. Young Iranians have thus begun to see the need for individuals to come together without the mediation of a leader to form a just society that is spiritual (but not necessarily religious), democratic, and reformed, and that moves from within to the outer reaches.[1] This society will not need to manipulate images or create a surface in order to control the inner reaches, for as we have seen on this journey the outward appearance of things can be deceptive (thereby bringing us back to the notion of riya, which already anticipates such deception in religious practice). As our tour of the visionary terrain of post-revolution Iran is complete, the story returns to Attar who reminds us that it is not the arrival but the journey that should concern us.

THE SIMURGH, IRAN, 1993 *The windshield wipers click methodically as the village of Damavand begins to appear on the horizon. The landscape is gray and wet and not at all like my sunny childhood memories of tulips and wild poppies blanketing Mount Damavand. I look back at my book and stay quiet while my uncle concentrates on the complicated turns that take us higher into the mountains.*

"What are you reading?" he asks.

"I'm reading Ibn Arabi, about absence—being one's own master," I say self-consciously. What a dilettante. My uncle smiles.

Absence. Starring out at the foggy terrain it occurs to me that my life has been defined by absence since the day my family left Iran. It rained that day, much like today. My uncle took us to the airport in a Jeep similar to the one he is now driving. The fog-covered street appeared like a dream and made Iran seem distant even before we were gone. I wonder what my last moments in Iran would have felt like had it been sunny and warm. The fog prepared me in a sense for what was about to happen to an entire section of my life. My childhood is now a strange, static fog, while Iran continues to change seasons.

"Roksana, so deep in thought?"

"It's so dark."

"This isn't dark. It's a different sort of light. Appreciate the light, its shades, its tones."

A prison mate of my uncle's told me how they had been blindfolded for months. I try to imagine my uncle sitting in a cold prison hall, blindfolded, tying knots on a silk string.

"Have you read Attar's The Conference of the Birds?*" he asks.*

"No."

"It is about a group of birds that takes a journey in search of a mystical leader, the Simurgh. It is an allegory for the mystical path, for life. There are times when things get hard for the birds and they want to quit."

My uncle knows how hard it is for me here, but I hadn't realized that he senses my longing to quit and go home.

"Attar's story is composed of the birds' excuses to abandon the journey, as one by one they quit. After losing most of their members along the way, the birds reach the mythical peak of Mt. Qaf (Damavand) to find that there is no Simurgh. They are all alone.

"Roksana, what is si?"

"The number, thirty," I say.

"And murgh?"

"Chicken?"

"Bird. So what is Si-murgh?"

"Thirty birds."

"Right, a phoenix to be exact, the Simurgh. When the remaining group of thirty birds reaches the peak of Mt. Qaf, they find that together they are the Simurgh. The Simurgh is the very group that journeyed toward a mystical leader. All you need to know about mysticism is in Attar. All you really need to know is in you. The mistake everyone makes is to look for life outside of themselves and to seek out a leader or a guide by his or her zaher, surface. This exercise is bi-khod, meaningless. Meaning is within you, baten. The guide you seek is within you." Seven years later, in Shiraz, a former Basij quoted Mawlana to me: "When you reach the place to see the truth you see yourself."

At the end of Attar's The Conference of the Birds, of the thousands of birds that undertake the quest all but thirty have died.

Attar writes: " 'We have come,' they said, 'to acknowledge the Simurgh.' When they were completely at peace and detached from all things they became aware that the Simurgh was there with them. The sun of majesty sent forth his rays, and in the reflection of each other's faces these thirty birds (si-murgh) of the outer world [zaher], contemplated the face of the Simurgh of the inner world [baten]. This so astonished them that they did not know if they were still themselves or if they had become the Simurgh. At last, in a state of contemplation, they realized that they were the Simurgh and that the Simurgh was the thirty birds.

"The Simurgh, also without speaking made this reply: Annihilate yourselves gloriously and joyfully in me, and in me you shall find yourselves.

"Thereupon, the birds at last lost themselves forever in the Simurgh—the shadow was lost in the sun, and that is all.

"When a hundred thousand generations had passed, the mortal birds surrendered themselves spontaneously to total annihilation. No man, neither young nor old, can speak fittingly of death or immortality. Even as these things are far from us so the description of them is beyond all explanation or definition. And now my story is finished, I have nothing more to say."[2]

INTRODUCTION: DIVINATION

1 After the revolution, members of political organizations not in line with the Islamic republic were rounded up and jailed, and many were eventually executed. See Abrahamian's *Tortured Confessions* for a history of political opposition before and after the revolution.

2 The shah fled the country in fall 1978, leaving it in the hands of a prime minister. Khomeini returned in January 1979 and took power a month later. On the events that led up to the revolution, see Fischer, *From Religious Dispute to Revolution*; Mottahedeh, *Mantle of the Prophet*; and Abrahamian, *Iran between Two Revolutions*.

3 For further readings on Khomeini's use of cassette tapes, see Sreberny, *Small Media, Big Revolution*.

4 Khomeini's notion of martyrdom was in line with Shariati's in that it referred back to the martyrdom of Husayn and Ali. It is important to note, as Abrahamian has pointed out in *Iran Between Two Revolutions* that the cult of martyrdom was already in use earlier with the Tudeh Party, which referred to its dead revolutionary heroes as martyrs (although this was done in a secular sense, not in reference to Shiite Islam's famous martyrs).

5 For the purposes of this work I use *bi-khodi* as a general term in reference both to Sufi ideas about self-annihilation (the annihilation of the material ego) and to revolutionary notions of *shahadat*, or martyrdom (notions influenced by the mystical definitions), which indicates a physical self-annihilation (resulting in a physical death) and also is a colloquial term for meaninglessness.

6 I am indebted to Farhad Khosrokhavar for his suggestions on my use of khod-sazi and khod-shenasi. It is important to stress that while Ali Shariati is again popular among young Muslim intellectuals in Iran there is a difference between the idea of khod-sazi or khod-shenasi that he espoused and the one that I write about in terms of Iranian youth today. Ali Shariati was a Muslim intellectual and he refers specifically to a Muslim self, while youth today are moving toward understanding and identifying themselves in terms of secularism. This idea is expanded later in this volume in the chapters on youth in Tehran. Shariati, author of *Marxism and Other Western Fallacies*, is best known for founding an Islamic center in Tehran (Hosseiniyeh Ershad) in the late 1960s and for his critique of Marxism coupled by a radical reworking of traditional Islam that is meant to encourage young intellectuals to think about concepts like martyrdom within the context of modernism. For more on Shariati, see Rahnema, *An Islamic Utopian*.

7 Ahmad, *Gharbzadighi* [*Westoxification*], 27.

8 Amanat, "The Study of History in Post-Revolutionary Iran," 5.

9 Eagleton, *Ideology*.

10 This goes for youth who volunteered as Basij at the frontlines in the 1980s and stopped believing by the late 1990s.

11 For further readings on secularism and nation-state formation, see Asad, "Religion, Nation-State, Secularism."

12 A few years after this fieldwork I read a volume of essays by the late anthropologist and filmmaker Jean Rouch, in which I discovered a very similar methodological approach, which he refers to as "direct anthropology," invented by the documentary maker Robert Flaherty, who engaged the people he filmed in his work process by having them view their appearance in the film and then comment on it. See Rouch, *Cine-Ethnography*.

13 Spying is a serious charge that is punishable by death. It is also easy to make such a charge, as illustrated by the Jewish spy case in summer 2000, when members of the Jewish community in Shiraz were accused of spying for Israel.

14 The *dowreh*, or intellectual salon, is an institution that has been in place in Iran for the better part of the twentieth century. Traditionally these meetings focused on politics and literature (as I pointed out in my uncle's case in the 1950s, literature was political and the two themes mixed effortlessly in dowrehs). After the revolution the dowrehs that had been held in the years before continued in a weaker and more exclusive fashion (as many members had fled the country and many topics were now considered taboo). It was not until Khatami's presidency that youth in Iran began to participate in more-formalized dowrehs than those of their

parents' generation (in that they are produced through capitalist exchange and economic necessity on the part of the people who are running them). These dowrehs are akin to the continuing education classes taught by, and in the homes of, semiqualified teachers of poetry, "film studies," and other topics of interest to young intellectuals.

15 The Iranian university entrance system is based on the French *concourse*, where all high school students take an entrance exam that will not only place them at a particular college but also in a particular field, leaving them with very little choice as to their future occupation.

16 In the end I refrained from collecting the notebooks, and I did not require those who wrote in them to discuss the content if they did not feel comfortable doing so. While as an anthropologist this probably was not the best research move, it seemed in the best interests of the students. The journals that I did receive were astonishingly blunt and revealing.

17 I will discuss this further in chapter 4. Michel de Certeau's *Practice of Everyday Life* influenced the ideas that I discussed with them.

18 The Basij were the original revolutionaries who upheld the jihad (holy war) called by Khomeini in defense of the Islamic republic. They were the first to go to the front and the first to be martyred. The survivors, veterans of the Iran-Iraq war who still believe in the Islamic republic, spend their days policing the streets from their motorcycles, searching for behavior that is out of line with Islam.

19 For further discussion of writing in anthropology, see Marcus and Fischer, *Anthropology as Cultural Critique*; and Marcus and Clifford, *Writing Cultures*.

20 Throughout history there has always been tension between Sufis and the state.

21 For further readings on Ayatollah Khomeini's Sufi love poems, see the appendix by Abedi in Fischer and Abedi, *Debating Muslims*.

22 Often the types of "discussions" that went on during ethnographic interviewing were far more intense than anything I encountered in my oral exams in graduate school.

23 Many of these groups meet in very private spaces—either in the mountains or private gardens in the suburbs—where the *komiteh*, Islamic police, are less likely to appear.

1. THE IMAGE AND THE HIDDEN MASTER

1 Much of this "propaganda" was constructed around images, not just text.

2 Chelkowski, "Ritual and Revolution," 10.

3 "Idolatry is the subordination of the true spiritual image to the false ma-

terial one; something we find in revolutionary art, which, while ostensibly presenting the everyday, really presents an invisible, hidden ideology" (Mitchell, *Iconology*, 37).

4   Khalil, *The Monument*, 41. This is also the case with Syria's Hafiz al-Asad, as demonstrated in Weeden, *Ambiguities of Domination*.

5   Sontag, *On Photography*, 38.

6   Benjamin, *Illuminations*, 243.

7   This was the case in the beginning of the revolution, although it began to change once the war had started in the early 1980s. After Khomeini's death in 1989 there were more pictures of Rafsanjani and Khameini. Once Khatami was elected in 1997 painted movie posters displaying actors were more common. This chapter refers primarily to the Khomeini years, 1979–1989, when the state was first being constructed.

8   After the inception of the war, images of Khameini and Rafsanjani increasingly were seen, although generally as part of a group photo that included Khomeini. When Khatami comes on the scene almost twenty years later, however, we do see his photograph displayed on its own, which also points to his being outside of the real revolutionary fold that included Khomeini and Khameini.

9   This volume was published in both Persian and English translation, and thus obviously was intended for export. The first time I saw this book was at the United Nations mission of Iran to the United States, where the book was neatly laid out on a coffee table in the waiting room, among other photography books about Iran's nature and tourist sites.

10 This shows the presence of Khomeini at the front, while it puts his image into the film as well (*Revayat-e Fath*, tape 1, part 3). *Revayat-e Fath* is discussed in greater detail in chapter 3.

11 My use of mysticism to discuss contemporary Iran does not engage in academic mysticism but rather in the popular usage of mysticism, which is why, for example, I chose to use a scholar like Henri Corbin (whose readings on Ibn Arabi may not be the preferred choice of many scholars). I engage with Corbin because of his social genealogy rather than his intellectual contribution (though I feel that his intellectual contribution is a large one). Corbin was teaching Islamic philosophy at Tehran University at a time (the late 1950s and into the 1960s) when many Iranian revolutionaries were coming of age in the university. His teachings on Islam are greatly informed by his background in Hegel and Kojève (which is why they will come to play in the next chapter as important theorists in understanding martyrdom in the Iranian case). It is his reading of Ibn Arabi that I feel may come closest to what later moves from intellectual practice to social practice.

12 Tawil and tafsir are defined in Bearman et al., *Encyclopedia of Islam*, as follows: "Both the Shiis and Sufis developed their own style of exegesis wherein they emphasized the difference between tafsir and tawil. The foremost principle of Shii tafsir is that the Qur'an has an outer dimension (the zaher) and an inner dimension (Baten); the elucidation of the inner dimension, called ta'wil, is derived directly from the imams, the ultimate authority in matters of the interpretation of the Qur'an, as they are the repositories of special knowledge. (M Ayoub). Taw'il not only plays an important role in the Shii-Isma'ili formulation of a synthesis of reason and revelation based on Neo-Platonism and Shii doctrine, but it is also considered a science par excellence. For the Sufis ta'wil was a kind of spiritual realization of the meaning contained in the Qu'ran and could be achieved through following the disciplines laid down by the Sufi masters. Thus there emerged two distinct approaches to Quranic exegesis known as Tafsir and Tawil; the former could be accomplished by anyone who had the proper qualifications as it concerned the exoteric meaning, while the latter could be performed only by the imams or the Sufi master since it involved knowledge of a special kind to interpret esoteric meaning" (391–92).

13 For further reading on the role of master and disciple in Sufism, see Chittick, *The Sufi Path of Knowledge*. For further readings on Ibn Arabi, see Nettler, *Sufi Metaphysics and Qur'anic Prophets*.

14 Many Sufis believe that one must learn earthly love in preparation for divine love.

15 This is especially obvious in the way that Khomeini's image is omniscient; for example, it acts as a header above photocopied versions of last will and testaments, on the back of grave pictures, pinned to soldiers' uniforms, and positioned alongside martyrs in murals.

16 Schimmel, *I Am Wind, You Are Fire*, 176. Rumi was born at Balkh in the Persian province of Khorasan in 1207, and he is most famous for founding in Anatolia the Mehvlevi order of whirling dervishes. Rumi was said to have been critical of poetry and often called it immoral and un-Islamic. He was thus surprised one day to find himself a poet—the result of a divine madness, like Majnun's, that came on the tails of love. Rumi's poetic inspiration and what moved him to begin the Sama, or whirling dance, was his love for a wise old dervish named Shams al-Din Tabrizi. It was in this love that Rumi lost himself and realized that poetry was a necessary tie to reality; the last cord to earth, "dust on the mirror of the soul" (Schimmel, *I Am Wind, You Are Fire*, 34).

17 *Nafs* refers to the rational and cultured self. It is the goal of a mystic to annihilate the *nafs*. *Shahid* means witness, but it also refers to martyrs

who die in order to directly witness God (similar to the Christian concept of martyrdom). For more on martyrdom in Christianity, see de Certeau, *Mystic Fable*.

18 It is important to note that in speaking of an image in the practical Sufi sense, we are referring to a mental image or a poetic, metaphoric image that is held in the mind through the power of imagination, or what Ibn Arabi calls creative imagination.

19 Ibn Arabi, born in Spain, 1165–1240, was a mystic, writer, and teacher.

20 "The degree of spiritual experience depends on the degree of reality invested in the image, and conversely. It is in this image that the mystic contemplates *in actu* the full perfection of the beloved and that he experiences His presence within himself. Without this 'imaginative union' without the transfiguration it brings about, physical union is a mere delusion, a cause or symptom of mental derangement. Pure imaginative contemplation, on the other hand, can attain such intensity that any material or sensible interest would only draw it down" (Corbin, *Creative Imagination in the Sufism of Ibn Arabi*, 156).

21 Corbin, *Creative Imagination in the Sufism of Ibn Arabi*, 156.

22 Bi-khodi involves moving away from the cultured, rational self in order that God, or the contemplation of God, can take place. When Sufis speak of their love for God, or of the state in which they are in full contemplation of God or full of the love of God, they speak of becoming Majnun, as in *majnun shudam*.

23 Semiotic malfunctioning occurs when meanings and signs no longer correlate.

24 Zekr literally means repetition; here it refers to the Sufi meditation practice of repeating the names of God. This practice is meant to facilitate a state of trance.

25 This exercise is the first step in forgetting or abandoning the nafs. Love, then, is the yearning of the "I" of the lover to be one with the beloved. To abandon one's self is to forget society, the material world, and the self. In chapter 2 I show how this occurs for Iranian volunteer soldiers during the war when mystical practice at the front not only worked to go beyond the soldier's individual identity but also actually fostered a new identity as a member of the Islamic state.

26 Rumi says language cannot adequately express reality; saying nothing is the first and last expression of all meaning. Hence in Sufi poetry, the beloved's mouth is often deflated to nothing, to a dot of infinity, silently purely existing as an object constituted in the imagination of the lover.

27 The war front thus becomes the ultimate manifestation of the Sufi path (or as they interpret it, the Islamic path) for the volunteer soldiers. In

turn, they are marked as irrational for wanting to martyr themselves for the state. They consider themselves martyrs for God's love.

28 Nizami, *Tale of Leili and Majnun*, 68.

29 Majnun means "crazy" in Arabic and Persian, but more explicitly it refers to someone possessed, perhaps by a jinn, someone who has lost themselves. Forgetting is a common move in the transcendence of the self. It is in memory that the constructs of self are contained and by forgetting that they are shattered. It is when Majnun's father visits him, to find his son has forgotten him and his past that memory comes to play. Majnun's father says, "If he could only win her he could find himself again." His son is "a mind, where reason was once" (98). He has become without self, bi-khod.

30 Nizami, *Tale of Leili and Majnun*, 67.

31 Refer again to the image of the young dead with Khomeini's picture super-imposed.

32 The self here embodies all social constructs, such as religion, ideology, and the law. Walter Andrews, in the context of Ottoman studies, describes the Sufi lover as an alienated subject: "Majnun represents the final annihilation with subjectivity, through a reduction of both subject and object to interchangeable signifiers in the semiotic system of love. This latter relation is dramatically portrayed in the story of Majnun, who finally rejects the physical beloved in favor of her image. The beloved as other implies a relation that constitutes a subject and conversely when the subject ceases to be, then the other too ceases to signify. The result is a radical annihilation of the subject/object paradigm" ("Singing the Alienated 'I,' " 207).

33 Attar, *The Conference of the Birds*, 15.

34 This idea is further explored in chapter 3 in the context of Islamic filmmaking.

35 For further reading on this aspect of Islamic Iran, see Abrahamian *Iran between Two Revolutions*; and Chelkowski and Dabashi *Staging a Revolution*.

36 *Ghazal* poetry is lyrical love poetry or medieval court poetry written in iambic pentameter, which was a style common to many mystics. For an example of Khomeini's ghazal poetry, see Fischer and Abedi, *Debating Muslims*, 451.

37 *Tariqa* is defined as mystical path open, in principle, to every Muslim.

38 There is some slippage where the technical Sufi idea of a transcended self or nafs is interchanged with the self, which later plays into the call for martyrs; that is, more than just a transcendence of the self but a total annihilation that results in physical death.

39 Khomeini, *Islam and Revolution*, 385.

40 Ithna-Ashari Shiism is based on the belief that the twelfth imam was taken into occultation by God and has not been seen in the world since the ninth century. He remains alive, however, and the belief is that he will return as the Mehdi—the one guided by God who will usher in the end of time and the judgment of the world. In his absence the Shii community is ruled by the ulama. (Following the concealment of the twelfth imam in the ninth century, authority was centered on the imami ulama.)

41 Quoted in Corbin, *The Sufi Path of Knowledge*, 32.

42 Khomeini was originally exiled by Mohammad Reza Shah's regime on November 4, 1964 (November 4 was also the same day the American hostages were taken in 1979). He stayed in exile in Najaf, Iraq, until 1978 when pressure by the shah on Saddam Hussein forced him to exile Khomeini even further away from Iran, to Paris, where he was welcomed by such liberal intellectuals as Michel Foucault.

43 Shariati's notion of Iranian roots was inherently Islamic while Al-Ahmad was more secular; his call for the removal of Western influence was from a Marxist economic perspective based on economic exploitation and oil rather than on cultural colonialism.

44 Mohammad Mossadegh was a famous Iranian nationalist who tried to nationalize oil; he ran the country for a short period in the 1950s before the United States orchestrated a coup d'etat and replaced him in 1953 with Mohammed Reza Pahlavi (who many saw as a puppet of the U.S. government and the Anglo-American Oil Company).

45 His photograph held a prominent place in Iran before his return. A scene in a winter 2000 broadcast of an Iranian television serial about revolutionary students who prepared the road for Khomeini's return shows the students clandestinely distributing photocopies of Khomeini's photograph in the mosques and universities.

46 Corbin, *Creative Imagination in the Sufism of Ibn Arabi*, 156.

47 *Rhabar* implies both messenger and leader.

48 Despite everything, including ten years of war and a failing economy, there are still many who refer to Ayatollah Khomeini as Imam Khomeini.

49 As I detail in the following section, he comes to stand for the image of the Islamic state.

50 Shariati quoted in Ram, *Myth and Mobilization in Revolutionary Iran*, 163.

51 Corbin and Tabataba'i, "The Imams and the Imamate," 129.

52 Weber, *On Charisma and Institutional Building*, 23.

53 Ibid., 48. In a book about Khomeini's life, his former servants describe the miracles he performs and thereby provide proof of his supernatural powers.

54 Abrahamian, *Iran between Two Revolutions*, 532.

55 It is as if they are providing the *komiteh* with an opportunity to take a bribe. All in the name of Islam.

56 Weber, *On Charisma*, 281.

57 Abrahamian, *Iran between Two Revolutions*, 12.

58 Khomeini qtd. in Algar, *Religion and State in Iran*, 325.

59 Arjomand, "The State and Khomeini's Islamic Order," 155.

60 Ibid., 156.

61 According to Arjomand, "The jump from the viceregency of the body of the religious jurists to that of the jurist is the most dubious from the viewpoint of Shiite jurisprudence. It was not called for in Khomeini's work, and has been found objectionable by the highest ranking grand Ayatollahs" ("The State and Khomeini's Islamic Order," 157).

62 Abrahamian, *Iran between Two Revolutions*, 527.

63 The constitution of the Islamic republic of Iran was ratified on December 2–3, 1979. It placed the judiciary under full control of the clergy, with extensive revision of the legal codes to render them Islamic. Arjomand, "The State and Khomeini's Islamic Order," makes note of the remarkable similarity of the constitution to Shiite sacred law.

64 Midway through my second-grade term our classes were broken up in order to segregate boys and girls. That same year our teachers were required to don proper Islamic dress.

65 This rule includes all females in Iran, including tourists and even foreign heads of state and diplomats.

2. MYSTIC STATES

1 *Namus* means chastity, purity, and honor. In summer 2000, I interviewed a young man painting the side of a wall with Ayatollah Khomeini's sayings. He was the son of a martyr and had received the paint from the martyr's foundation. When asked about the war he used the word *namus* and said it was a sacred defense.

Reza Shah tells his soldiers to think of the gun not as a gun, but as *Namus*. He turns to one of the soldiers named Ahmad and says, "Think of the gun as your mother, your wife, your daughter. You must keep it and protect it." Reza Shah points to a young Turkish officer and asks, "Now what is that gun?" The soldier answers, "It's Ahmad's mother, sister, daughter, wife." The notion of *namus*, much like *mellat* (national), has only changed ideological hands in the revolution, but the reference to honor and nationalism remains the same, be it a monarchy or theocracy. Nowhere in any of the rhetoric is the word "motherland" used, in its place is the term *namus*—chastity, purity; the citizens were called to defend the purity of their nation and that of Islam.

2 All such passages in this chapter are ethno-historic accounts of the war seen through the fictional character of Amir, who is based on my interviews with a former soldier much like him, as well as on my ethnographic and archival research on the Iran-Iraq war. Other than the historic backdrop of the war and the practices at the front (such as writing memoirs, listening to lectures, acts of camaraderie, and fighting), the actual events I describe are fictional.

3 As noted earlier, Basij were the volunteer militia members who went straight to the front to fight for Islam both during the Iran-Iraq war and the revolution.

4 In an interview, a secular Tehrani told me that some of the secular boys who early on volunteered at the front did so in defense of their home country of Iran, not the Islamic nation. However, after arriving at the front only to find it full of "crazy religious fanatics," they found cause to run back home.

5 Shariati, *Marxism and Other Western Fallacies*, 50. Shariati is not the only source I encountered that addresses Western theory in relation to revolutionary Islam. When I went to the *Revayat-e Fath* offices to interview Seyyad Mohamad Avini, a war documentary maker (featured in the next chapter), I was asked to explain my framework for thinking about the war. I mentioned Hegel and Heidegger, at which time Avini told me that Hegel is considered the Rumi of the West and showed me a translation of Heidegger done by his office for the Islamic propagation agency press.

6 Henri Corbin, the famous Iranist whose work on mystical Islamic philosophy has greatly influenced educated modern Iranians, was a student of Kojève and later taught Islamic studies at Tehran University in the 1950s and 1960s. It is through Corbin that we can most likely trace the influence of Hegel, Heidegger, and Kojève on the teachings of Islamic philosophy at Tehran University in the 1950s and 1960s when these revolutionaries were coming of age.

7 Girard, *Violence and the Sacred*, 4.

8 The Mujahidin Al Khalq is an organization of Iranian Islamic revolutionaries who have been trying to oust the Khomeini/Rafsanjani/Khatami and now Ahmadinejad government from power.

9 Girard, *Violence and the Sacred*, 4.

10 Interview with former Basij, Husayniyeh Irshad, Shiraz, 2000. Perhaps, a necessary fiction.

11 Shariati, *Marxism and Other Western Fallacies*, 180.

12 Pinault, *The Shiites*, 6.

13 Canetti, *Crowds and Power*, 146–54.

14 Scholars and other observers have noted that since the 1960s the Muharram ceremonies have moved from being a mournful commemoration of grieving believers to a day of rage (e.g., Ram, *Myth and Mobilization in Revolutionary Iran*, 66).

15 Grief is seen as a passive emotion, where as rage involves an energy that can be channeled into action.

16 Canetti, *Crowds and Power*, 154.

17 Shariati, *Marxism and Other Western Fallacies*, 232.

18 The shah's father first put restrictions on Ta'zieh as early as 1930. He saw the practice as backward (as having no outward political explanation). His restrictions thus caused it to retreat to the countryside.

19 Abrahamian, *Iran between Two Revolutions*, 521. My mother remembers people taking to their roofs at the time. In interviews, secular middle-class adults in Tehran relayed the excitement they felt when they took to their roofs. These same people stopped supporting the revolution after Iran became an Islamic republic in 1980.

20 While Iraq was a Muslim nation, Khomeini made it clear that it was not a proper one and that any Iraqi Muslim who wanted to stand up and fight for an Islamic republic in Iraq could join the Iranians. The Iranians believed that there would be some Iraqi's who would fight on the Iranian side, but this did not happen in significant enough numbers for it to have any real effect.

21 Abedi and Legenhausen, *Jihad and Shahadat*, 10.

22 Iran's best weapon was its large population. Unlike the Iraqis who had modern weaponry, Iran's weapons had fallen into disrepair. Iran also lacked the proper technical expertise to use the weapons that it had (though the former shah spent billions on arms, his military experts had either fled the country or were executed during the revolution).

23 Yazid is a direct reference to the battle of Karbala. Yazid is the one responsible for the murder of the Imam. Saddam Hussein is called Saadam-Yazid at prayer services and rallies for the soldiers (as seen in the documentary series *Revayat-e Fath*).

24 Rafsanjani quoted in Ram, *Myth and Mobilization in Revolutionary Iran*, 75. Hojjat al Islam Hashemi Rafsanjani was president of Iran from 1989 until 1997. During the war he held the important position of Khomeini's liaison to the defense council as well as one of the Friday prayer leaders. The main Friday prayer leader and president of the country during the war was Ali Khameini. Also, in the documentary series *Revayat-e Fath* (discussed in the next chapter) an older man claims that he came to the front because of Rafsanjani's speeches.

25 Rafsanjani quoted in Ram, *Myth and Mobilization in Revolutionary Iran*, 73.

26 Rafsanjani quoted in Ram, 73.

27 Khameini quoted in Ram, 73.

28 The Historical Center of the Revolutionary Guards Corps has in its possession thirty thousand hours of cassette tapes, three hundred thousand pages of documents, thirteen hundred notebooks from various narrators of the war, twenty thousand journals, seven hundred research reports, and four thousand pages of operational maps. The army has also published volumes titled *The Army of the Islamic Republic of Iran in the Eight Years of Holy Defense* and *The Bibliography of Eight Years of Holy Defense*, a collection of sixty pieces of research and military treatises. Notable among other publications is the journal *Defense Policy*, as well as one issue of *Nameh-ye Pajoohesh* that is dedicated to the war. Many of these items can be seen at the various museums of martyrdom (two of which are in Tehran, among other cities in Iran).

29 The chapter on Shahid Avini's documentary series (chapter 3) will address the production of persuasion in greater detail.

30 An editor from a publication that specializes in the memoirs of martyrs informed me during an interview that these books were once required reading at the university, but that now they are read only in an elective called "War Literature" (he also admitted that it was not a very popular elective).

31 Interview with a former Basij, Shiraz, 2000. Notice the mystical notion of death as transcendence to a higher plane and not a final annihilation.

32 Taleghani quoted in Abedi, *Jihad and Shahadat*, 6.

33 The Quran quoted in Abedi, *Jihad and Shahadat*, 3.

34 In this case Amir is the crazy one among the sane. Michel Foucault illustrates in *Madness and Civilization*, that sanity and madness are historical and social constructions that take meaning in specific historic or social contexts.

35 Chelkowski, *Ritual and Revolution*, 10.

36 At the gravesites, if the dead is a martyr or is young then there is almost always a photograph.

37 This is also true for civilians. I was struck by a photograph on the front page of the *New York Times* showing a group of refugees in flight from Kosovo, whose photo was taken despite the fact that they were holding their hands to their faces (to protect the last thing they had left—shame). The photographer took the photo anyway. Another example of the power that photography has to destroy is in Hitchcock's movie *Easy Virtue*, where a divorcee's reputation is ruined by photographs of her divorce trial. She can no longer hide her identity—the image has circulated, and with it

her social self. The movie ends with a photographer aiming to shoot her and she says, "Go ahead—there's nothing left to kill."

38 As recently as a few decades ago, Iranians were still anxious about having passport photos taken because of the potential for the evil eye to strike them. Stefania Pandolfo discusses the evil eye in her ethnography on Morocco, *Impasse of the Angels*, and in so doing she refers to Lacan's observation that the eye has the power to separate. So too has the camera. Today the taboos on representation have more to do with modesty, with covering flesh and women's hair, than they do with religion or the soul.

39 Quran, volume 7, book 72, number 835.

40 The degree to which this is actually true of the Islamic project in Tehran will be explored in later chapters.

41 Quran, volume 7, book 72, number 842.

42 Benjamin, *Illuminations*, 238.

43 My understanding of Kojève is indebted to a seminar led by Mikkel Borch-Jacobsen at the University of Washington in 1997.

44 Families were even encouraged to report anti-revolutionary family members.

45 Kojève, *Introduction to the Reading of Hegel*, 62.

46 Avini, *Revayat-e Fath* (the translation is mine).

47 Kojève, *Introduction to the Reading of Hegel*, 63.

48 Reporters and filmmakers at the front gave an opportunity for boys from villages and from the south of the city, who were never given a chance to speak, to be heard, to be seen in the limelight, to be stars, and to be something other than poor and ignored.

49 Kojève, *Introduction to the Reading of Hegel*, 66.

50 Khomeini quoted in Algar, *Religion and State in Iran*, 242.

51 Ibid., 239.

52 Kojève, *Introduction to the Reading of Hegel*, 66.

53 Ibid., 67.

54 Khomeini quoted in Algar, *Religion and State in Iran*, 227.

55 Kojève, *Introduction to the Reading of Hegel*, 67.

56 Ibid., 67. Iraqi Muslim soldiers who do not come over to the Iranian side to fight for this Islamic republic are therefore not in line with this notion of Islam and are easily constructed as infidels.

57 Kojève takes this directly from Hegel.

58 Kojève, *Introduction to the Reading of Hegel*, 69.

59 In Kamal Tabrizi's film *Leili Is with Me* (the title is an allusion to Leili and Majnun) a photographer must face his worst fears when he is assigned to the front. As a faithful revolutionary he believes it is his duty to go and yet he is frightened. The film is a comic spoof of the photographer

trying to escape his duty, but fate pushes him along toward the front (at one point the sign on the road with an arrow pointing to Karbala gets reversed, so when he thinks he is sneaking back to Tehran he is actually headed right for the front). In the end the photographer is made a hero. Because of the comedic irony I first interpreted this film as a critique, but later, in speaking with the main actor and the director, I was told that it is an illustration of a man who is determined to fight his fated duties but perseveres in the end despite his fear, and is a hero because it was his fate to go to battle and return triumphant.

60 The mystical notion of transcendence, bi-khodi (the ultimate goal of a Sufi practitioner), is a task that begins on earth with the gradual shedding of the ego and earthly ties and thereby freeing one from one's self. Kojève, *Introduction to the Reading of Hegel*, 69 (quoting Hegel).

61 Battaile, *Eroticism*.

62 Girard will be proven right in time, as we see later in this book when excess works its magic. Obliteration is no longer for the state but to escape the state, through suicide and drug use. Is this the ultimate reaction to fear, or is it a total lack of fear?

63 Some soldiers at the front said that men martyred themselves at one point in order to protest the war.

3. SHOOTING SOLDIERS SHOOTING FILM

1 This vignette is based on the stories of war in Avini's writings and from my interviews with his brother, Mohammad Avini, in Tehran in 2000.

2 The series continues to this day by addressing issues dealing with the aftermath of the war: interviewing the mothers of martyrs, soldiers maimed by chemical weapons, and citizens of ruined cities. Avini himself became a martyr when he stepped on a landmine as he was filming the aftermath of war in a southern border city in 1993; he was forty-six at the time of his death.

3 Similar to the Peace Corps program in the United States, Jahad-e Sazandeghi was also akin to a program already established by the shah. According to one member of the group, however, in its idealism it was more concerned with social reform than with making structural improvements. Jahad-e Sazandeghi's film section gradually evolved with the help of a group of men from television and other film arts who created the Jahad-e Sazandeghi Ilhaq, making it a specifically revolutionary organization under the auspices of Kanoon-e Islami Filmsaz (Organization of Islamic Filmmakers). This section of the Jahad-e Sazandegi was neither fully a government organization nor completely independent or

private, but because it did not depend solely on the Islamic Republic of Iran Broadcasting for money, that organization could not control its programs. According to Avini, "We went with faith to the war, not with money" (Avini, *Yek Tajrobeheyh Mondegar*, 12); all translations from this work are my own.

Avini's film career did not start at the war front but rather in the south, where he was sent at the beginning of the revolution to film the floods in Khuzestan. He first specialized in filming earthquakes and other social traumas and "harsh realities." Like the Italian neorealists, his group believed that the documentation of such realities was necessary for social change. His first film involving conflict was in Shiraz Province, where the Qahsghaii tribes, revolting against the new revolutionary government, had attacked the city of Firuzabad. They believed that Khomeini's government had killed a tribal parliament member. From there Avini's film crew traveled to Iraqi Kurdistan where they experienced their first real taste of the war.

4   Avini, *Yek Tajrobeheyh Mondegar*, 29.

5   Eventually Iranians turned to foreign presses and the radio for news (which was still very limited because of restricted access).

6   According to the Iranians whose sons escaped at the time (mainly via the mountains to Turkey or India), the government was literally taking young boys from the streets and sending them to the front.

7   He had no qualms in admitting this, which works against any argument that he was not making propaganda.

8   This is similar to the documentary projects of other wars—for example, Frank Capra's series *Why We Fight* was made to incite and encourage American soldiers. Capra's films became part of regular military training during World War II, and proved to actually change American public opinion about the British. Episodes in the series include titles like "Know Your Enemy" and "Know Your Ally" (Barnouw, *Documentary: A History of the Non-Fiction Film*, 158).

9   The original "truth film" serial told the story of the town of Khoramshahr and the forty-five-day people's militia that took arms against the Iraqis. Eventually television and the Jahad-e Sazandegi produced Avini's group with funding from the Sepah Pasdaran (Revolutionary Guard Corp) and the Farabi Film Foundation (which allocated a generous sum of funding specifically for *Revayat-e Fath*).

10 Interview with Mr. Jalili, office of Revayat-e Fath publications, Tehran 2000. The publications are an off-shoot of the TV series.

11 This resonates with the belief that one must enter into a world of archetypes in order to tap into the hidden mysteries of faith, or the alam al

mithal, of Ibn Arabi. Mohammad Avini explained his brother's notion of reality in an interview with me. Tehran, 2000.

12 When I mentioned Avini's name, almost all of the Iranians I spoke with knew who he was. While the series was made mainly for potential Basij, almost everyone watched it at some point (even those who were ardently antireligious and antiwar). This high level of viewership is due to the lack of other opportunities to see the front (as the foreign press had very limited access on the Iranian side) and because almost everyone, from every sector of society, had a relative there and hoped to see that person come across the screen. Now the series is being watched by young people who missed the war and are curious about it.

13 Interview with Mohammad Avini, Tehran, 2000.

14 For the producers of *Revayat-e Fath*, film was the modern means by which to reach a modern audience.

15 Cf. the discussion in chapter 2 on the hidden master, where Ibn Arabi's work and Khomeini's speeches on the subject shed light on the relationship between mimetic representations and real experiences.

16 Interview with Mohammad Avini, Tehran, 2000. This justifies violence in an odd way by making the argument that it is passion. How does one separate violence and passion and excitement? A mystic might say that passion and excitement should not be used to kill another human being.

17 Interview with Basij at the Ministry of Islamic Guidance, Shiraz, 2000.

18 Interview with Mohammad Avini, Tehran, 2000. This could be a reference to Rumi, who adored his Sufi sheik and friend Shams al-Din Tabrizi. The word shams means sun, and in Rumi's poetry he was often likened to the sun.

19 Interview with Mohammad Avini, Tehran, 2000. He is referring here to Ashura. It is important to note that many of Khomeini's teachings on martyrdom were similar to Ali Shariati's work on the topic, and this group of Basij were heavily exposed to Shariati's writings and speeches.

20 Interview with Mohammad Avini, Tehran, 2000.

21 Avini, *Revayat-e Fath*, volume one (all transcriptions of this work, and the translations thereof, are my own).

22 Ibid.

23 Dead soldiers, in the form of ghosts, had even more powerful qualities: one was rumored to have helped move an ambulance out of a ditch.

24 Interview with Mohammad Avini, Tehran, 2000.

25 Interview with Mohammad Avini, Tehran, 2000.

26 Avini, *Revayat-e Fath*, volume one.

27 Interview, Shiraz, Ministry of Islamic Guidance, 2000. This discourse of an army that is militarily weak but strong in faith dominated the conversations I had with Basij about the war. It also points to the implicit

unfairness of the war—the Iranians were untrained, ill prepared, and physically weak, but they held onto a discourse that never allowed them to be victimized (though many secular civilians expressed pity for the thin, untrained boys sent off unfairly to fight a professional army).

28 Ibid.

29 Interview conducted with Mr. Lashkarpour, editor of Avini's book series and former member of *Revayat-e Fath*, Tehran, 2000.

30 Avini was an architect and a painter and therefore practiced at creating both physical and imaginary spaces.

31 Barnouw, *Documentary: A History of Non-Fiction Film*, 58. This brings to play the important role of editing film, which I discuss below.

32 Interview conducted with Mr. Lashkarpour, editor of Avini's book series and former member of *Revayat-e Fath*, Tehran, 2000.

33 Of course, the culture that was created was constructed on the biggest propaganda film set—that of war—which like any film set is a construction.

34 Avini, *Revayat-e Fath*, volume one.

35 Avini, *Yek Tajrobehyeh Mondegar*, 20.

36 Interview conducted with Mr. Lashkarpour, editor of Avini's book series and former member of *Revayat-e Fath*, Tehran, 2000.

37 Italian neorealism came out of a fascist world replete with propaganda. In the midst of so much misinformation it offered an understanding, an unwritten agreement of sorts between the audience and the director, that the film would honestly explore the lives of everyday people. Neorealism was thus as much a political move as an aesthetic one. Some of the principles of neorealism are as follows: show reality rather than promote a particular aesthetic; show the triumph of the human spirit; shoot scenes on location; use dubbing versus synch sound (which allows actual street life sound modification); mix actors and real people playing themselves; move emphasis from narrative and plot to the contemporary nationalist experience (in order to purge the fascist past); rehabilitate the national reputation; give the illusion of present tense; allow for elements of humanism (free will) and materialism (self-constructed by material social culture). Neorealism was about individual consciousness versus social history. Because of the politicalization of society at the time, the label "real" was an important and determining difference that separated neorealist features from the propaganda produced by the state. In a country like Iran (much like fascist-era Italy) where propaganda and mistrust are the norm, certain expectations arise from the term "realism." For Italians, neorealism represented a move against an onslaught of government propaganda, whereas many Iranians in post-revolution Iran see it merely as more propaganda under a different guise.

For the filmmaker Rossellini, neorealism literally meant a "new reality" created through filmmaking, and film played a crucial role in creating a new (and what some hoped was a better) reality in postwar Europe. Because neorealism defines reality in terms of the social (created by humans) it promotes individual agency in sculpting reality. But neorealism was not always about creating new social realities that celebrated individual agency or existed solely outside the government or the sphere of its propaganda. Vertov viewed experimental documentary genres as opportunities to depict a new Soviet reality. Can these Iranian war documentaries that are neither purely documentary nor fiction but have so much in common with directors like Vertov, Rossellini, and Buñuel be labeled as neorealist? In the United States, where propaganda is relatively subtle, there is less of a demand to define the term "real" when used to promote television shows, especially those branded as "reality TV." There is no agreement between the director and the audience assuring that what the director promotes as "reality" is real and not a construct of sorts. Reality TV is a publicity ploy that suffers no consequences for the producers should they not deliver what they have advertised. Their concern is more with marketing and less with ethics—a fact that I witnessed at a conference at the Museum of Television and Radio in New York City where five panelists (producers and directors of various reality television programs) gathered to discuss reality TV. The first question asked by the moderator (but never answered by any of the panelists) was, "How do you define reality?" In the ensuing discussion the producers defended the trust they develop with their subjects; their attempt to capture every moment on film; and the "exact replication of reality" that they strive for when they stage reproduced scenes that did not quite come out as planned in filming. The panelists and the audience then debated the label of "reality television" versus "documentary," "neorealism," or "cinema verité" (the lines were blurred for them), yet never addressed was the issue as to why the notion of "reality" is even important in marketing their materials. Why does it matter what it is called? Why must it be "real" to work? What is reality? I am using this example to highlight the difference seen in the label "real" as expected by a culture that is censored and saturated with propaganda compared to one that is subliminally censored and programmed and less likely to explore the breach in trust between a television producer and his or her audience. This is the case with the American media, which offers a biased and narrow version of the news, and it is especially true of the news surrounding the present war in Iraq. Many Americans do not expect propaganda from their government, and thus they are not practiced at reading between the lines and tend to believe that what is delivered to them as news is real.

38 Years of propaganda have made Iranians in Iran both savvier and less trustful than American audiences, which is why even "neorealist" cinema has never been given much attention or credence among Iranian audiences. Samira Makmalbaf's last film, *The Blackboards*, never had more than five people at any Tehran screening, and even most of that small audience rarely stayed until the end of the film.

39 Avini, *Yek Tajrobehyeh Mondegar*, 20.

40 The films he refers to by Makmalbaf and Naderi are both fictional works about the war.

41 In his film *Stardust Memories*, Woody Allen states that people do not want reality (the reality Allen refers to is the stark truth or harsh reality experienced by the man in the *Bicycle Thief*).

42 How are American army commercials, such as "Be all that you can be in the army," any different? They do not paint an exact picture of what happens to a soldier on a daily basis, but rather highlight the glory, muscle, and power. The more recent campaign, "An army of one," which points to the individual in the midst of masses, is very much in line with the kind of thinking that memorialized individual soldiers as martyrs.

43 *Riya* will be discussed in greater detail in chapter 5. It is important to note that an Islamic morals professor at Sharif Technical University in Tehran lectures that riya is a sin in Islam. It is a sin even for a devout believer to use religion for the purposes of displaying piety.

44 Avini, *Yek Tajrobehyeh Mondegar*, 20.

45 Ibid., 16.

46 According to Avini, if you ask clichéd questions you get even more clichéd answers, but the crew always ran the risk of making the war and martyrdom into a cliché. (The word cliché is the same word in Persian, and it was used a lot in the course of my conversations with the *Revayat-e Fath* producers.)

47 Avini, *Yek Tajrobehyeh Mondegar*, 14.

48 Ibid., 20.

49 The same argument can be made for the Basij and draftees, neither of which had formal combat training. Are men supposed to just know innately what to do in battle? Men who are drafted are not given proper training because of the lack of time (by the time a draft is instated, its too late), which is why so many Iranians died in the war. The first scene in the film *Saving Private Ryan* attests to this issue. Further, according to David Grossman's work on Vietnam, soldiers must be trained to kill.

50 Avini, *Yek Tajrobehyeh Mondegar*, 11.

51 A rowzeh khan is someone who sings the story of the martyrdoms of Ali and Husayn at religious gatherings called rowzehs where people listen and cry, mourning the imams' deaths. There are also rowzehs for

other religious figures, like Fatima. The rowzeh I attended for Fatima was thrown by northern, secular Tehrani women and featured a female rowzeh khan (which is something I saw only in a more secular setting, as women singers were banned after the revolution).

52 Here the rowzeh khan wears the standard Basij uniform—military fatigues and a red headband with "Ya Husayn" written across it. This well-known rowzeh khan from Shiraz was the host of a very large weekly rowzeh, during which he encouraged young men to go to war.

53 Interview with Mr. Lashkarpour, Tehran, 2000.

54 Avini, *Yek Tajrobehyeh Mondegar*, 21.

55 You can ask soldiers to smile, cry, or ask them to say something religious, endearing, or enticing to potential soldiers. A scene in *Apocalypse Now* shows a camera crew shooting soldiers at war who repeatedly tell the soldiers not to look into the camera in order to "keep it natural," and yet the most natural thing for a soldier to do when confronted with a camera in his face while at combat is to stare at it, to be curious. What is real is that war is a production in the same way that a feature film is a production; and thus to film that production is to participate in the act of constructing that reality.

56 Avini, *Yek Tajrobehyeh Mondegar*, 20.

57 Ibid., 20.

58 Thus sending a message: You, potential martyr, will not just be a number! At the same time this uniqueness is suppose to be selfless.

59 Avini, *Yek Tajrobehyeh Mondegar* (translation mine).

60 One aspect of the crew's technique that separates them from the neorealists is that they used synch sound instead of dubbing. Neorealists let the tape roll in order to get as much footage as possible, then dub sound in later in order to get natural street sounds and the like. The *Revayat-e Fath* producers wanted the sound to match the shot precisely. They do, however, dub drums and voice-overs over the footage. Present throughout most of the film is a constant drumbeat coupled with the sound of overhead missiles, thereby lending it a particular feel and rhythm.

61 Advocacy films in the 1930s and 1940s were shot almost like silent films with a voice-over added to get the point across (like Luis Buñuel's *Land without Bread*). We see this form in Iranian documentaries in the 1960s, especially in the cinematic works of the poet Furugh Farokhzad.

62 Interview with Mohammad Avini, Tehran, 2000. While the language of the voice-over is nearly exclusively in high Persian and thus may not be understood by the audience members it aims to entice, the use of such language gives a sense of loftiness not unlike the use of Latin at an Oxford high table dinner, where the literal meaning is not understood but a sense of grandeur is communicated.

63 For example, music is heard from the *zuhr khaneh* (an old Iranian weight-lifting ritual), as well as from the rowzehs and from Muharram. Familiar religious and cultural sounds are used to make the audience feel that they are participating, because such oral traditions are participatory by nature.

64 Many TV viewers are illiterate and already know the words as active participants in religious services.

65 One long-standing issue in any anthropological endeavor to relay or represent human culture is the question of authority: that of who may speak for whom, and of the manner in which experience affects the way something is represented.

66 Avini, *Yek Tajrobehyeh Mondegar*, 19.

67 They went out in five-person teams, which in the last year of the war grew to include five to six men from the Islamic Republic of Iran Broadcasting; ten to fifteen Pasdar; fifteen Jahad-I Sazandeghi volunteers; and ten to twelve members of the Basij (Avini, *Yek Tajrobehyeh Mondegar*, 10).

68 Avini, *Revayat-e Fath*, volume one.

69 This is similar to the Soviet film project where two hundred cameramen died at war. The project was so important to the war that the Soviet Film Academy added combat photography to its curriculum, and diplomas were earned in part through front-line action (Barnouw, *Documentary: A History of Non-Fiction Film*, 154).

70 Ibrahim Hatamikia was the only one in their group with filmmaking experience. But what mattered was that he was prepared for martyrdom, otherwise, according to the Basij in Shiraz and from Avini's writings: "He could not have taken a place amongst us" (Avini, *Yek Tajrobehyeh Mondegar*, 11).

71 Here we could point to the amazingly architectural feat and quality of the Nazi propaganda films like those of Leni Riefenstahl where the architectural space created is vital to the effect on the viewer.

72 Interview with Mohammad Avini, Tehran, 2000. The imam here refers to Khomeini: anyone who read Khomeini's writings or listened to his lectures and fought in his path was considered a "student of the imam."

73 Avini, *Yek Tajrobehyeh Mondegar*, 29.

74 Ibid., 20.

75 However, the history of ethnographic representation, from Boas to Marcus and Fischer, illustrates the inability to eliminate subjectivity.

76 Avini, *Yek Tajrobehyeh Mondegar*, 20.

77 This also is an important point in keeping with a negation of riya.

78 Avini, *Yek Tajrobehyeh Mondegar*, 22.

79 Interview with Basij, Shiraz, 2000.

80 Avini, *Revayat-e Fath*, volume one.

81 Interview with Basij, Shiraz, 2000.

82 Avini, *Revayat-e Fath*, volume one. There is a polar relationship between faith and fear; one cannot have faith and be fearful, one who is fearful does not have proper faith.

83 The early action-packed war films are obviously based on American war movies (in some instances, shot for shot). *The Eagles*, for example, replicates exactly certain scenes from *Dr. Strangelove*, which results in a spoof of what is suppose to be a serious Iranian war film. In these films it is virtually impossible to differentiate between Iraqi and the Iranian soldiers. (In the use of weapons, however, some viewers will be able to differentiate the Iraqi soldiers who carry Russian guns from the Iranian soldiers with their American-made weaponry.) The soldiers rarely mention Allah or the imams (notably Husayn who has become the emblematic saint of the war given his historic import as the most famous Shiite martyr). The soldiers are clean-cut and freshly shaven, unlike the bearded revolutionaries brandishing the famous Basij bandannas across their foreheads who will later come to mark Iran's war.

84 Interview with Mohammad Avini, Tehran, 2000.

85 According to the Basij I interviewed, *Full Metal Jacket* and *Saving Private Ryan* show the reality of war. Iranian war film directors say that Steven Spielberg's *Saving Private Ryan* is the most realistic fiction film on war and the one that comes closest to representing what the war was like from an Iranian perspective. *Saving Private Ryan* has all the elements of a national war cinema from the first shot of the American flag. The film is immediately framed in the national collective memory with a visit to Arlington National Cemetery where all the elements of mourning, memorialization, and nationalism are wrapped up into the first scene. Like *Revayat-e Fath*, the film personalizes war by following the individual; only here it departs from the Iranian ideal by actually highlighting the value of the individual over the collective. What really marks a familiarity for Iranian war veterans, who commented on the film, is the first scene, which is extremely gory and, according to them, "very real." In this first scene as the soldiers are headed off to war, one comments, "This is all there is between us and the almighty." He makes the sign of the cross before going to meet his death. Another soldier kisses his gold cross. Others are thumbing rosaries; there are priests on the battlefield. Outward appearances might suggest that this is a religious endeavor. War brings soldiers closer to God.

86 It is important to note that almost all stories, films, and representations of the war have come from the government. Mainstream artists and writers have yet to illustrate their views of the war due to censor-

ship or for personal reasons. Many have already commented, "We've had enough." This "enough," or excess, has worked to silence alternative views of the war.

87 Ashura, the day of martyrdom, is the anniversary of the death of the Imam Husayn, the grandson of the prophet Mohammed, who was killed in the seventh century while fighting Caliph Yazid's army at Karbala, in present-day Iraq. For Iranians, this battle, like the Iran-Iraq war, has always been viewed as a battle of the righteous against the infidels. The commemoration of Husayn's death is marked by a month of mourning. Processions of men march in the street while beating their chests with heavy metal chains. In the villages and in quieter parts of the cities the dramatic tradition of Ta'zieh is played out. Ta'zieh is the reenactment of the martyrdom of Husayn and his family at Karbala.

88 We see the importance of Ashura in documentary footage; especially footage produced by Islamic filmmakers. Just as Ashura was the most important theme at the front and in documentary films, it was also a key theme in most of the war films made after 1984.

89 Posters show Imam Husayn riding alongside the troops into battle. During the war Iranians wanted to know how many Imam Husayns Saddam had captured, and if the imam was helping fight the war, why Iran was losing? (Michael Fischer mentioned this joke in an e-mail exchange with me in 1999.)

90 Chelkowski, *Ritual and Drama in Iran*, 90.

91 In downtown Tehran I saw a billboard showing a graphic design of bloody swirls against a black backdrop that read, "The month of Muharram, Ashura, is a month of epic poetry and sacrifice."

92 Virilio, *War and Cinema*, 5.

93 See Varzi, "A Ghost in the Machine."

94 The war film industry in Iran began shortly after the inception of the Iran-Iraq war in fall 1980 with made-for-television documentaries. These documentaries were some of the most in-depth representations of the front and occupied a substantial amount of televised programming both during and after the war.

95 These prewar Ta'zieh players became a theater company that performed to entertain the soldiers, but they never actually performed Ta'zieh.

96 *Revayat-e Fath* has an episode titled "the Night of Ashura."

97 He's referring to the non-Basij Iranians who participate in Ashura on a yearly basis but do not practice its truth beyond those ceremonies (like Catholics who attend mass only at Christmas and Easter).

98 Interview at the Ministry of Islamic Guidance, Shiraz, 2000.

99 Interviews at the Ministry of Islamic Guidance, Shiraz, 2000.

100 Of course, people continued to watch because there was no other place
where they could hope not only to catch a glimpse of a soldier they knew
and loved, but actually to hear him talk (or maybe hear another soldier
mention him). Because of the tight control of war reporting, this left
Revayat-e Fath as the only opportunity to actually find out what was happening at the front. Many claimed not to have seen the series, and yet
they seemed intimate with its content; thus even if they only watched it
to catch a glimpse of a loved one, the message must have seeped in, if
only just a bit.

4. VISIONARY STATES

1 Most Iranian city streets are named after martyrs. During the Iran-Iraq
war some street names were changed two or three times a month with
each new death of a boy soldier. Negotiating the endless urban sprawl of
contemporary Tehran is hard enough without the street names changing every week. While the memory of martyrs was kept constantly alive
in this fashion, the memory of destruction was quickly erased. Immediately after a bomb was dropped the area was cleaned and reconstructed.
There was no opportunity to live the destruction in Tehran (other cities
closer to the front, however, were a complete disaster).

2 Lefebvre suggests that space is a social product: "What we call ideology only achieves consistency by intervening in a social space and its
production" (*The Production of Space*, 44).

3 By "Islamic social space" I refer to the space evoked through war fervor
that thematically lent itself to the visual and spatial formation of Tehran
as an Islamic revolutionary space (see chapter 3).

4 De Certeau makes the claim that power is bound by visibility.

5 This is in 1993 when Rafsanjani was president.

6 Taussig's *The Magic of the State* makes the connection between visuality
and blindness in creating terror. Lefebvre (*The Production of Space*, 112)
says that a nation based on ideology is fictional, which is the irony of
Taussig's "fictional" ethnography.

7 Islamic dress is required the moment that children start school.

8 Taussig, "Physiognomic Aspects of Visual Worlds," 209.

9 This information is taken from a questionnaire I developed for use in
Tehran in 2000. Consisting mainly of essay and short-answer questions
about life in the city, the questionnaire was distributed by students to
other students, friends to other friends, and then passed back to me. In
the questionnaire I ask how the person would describe himself or herself, and the majority of the replies were on the order of, "like everyone

else," "average," "the same as the rest of Tehran," etc. While capitalism and its bland trend toward sameness, fads, etc. is alive and well in Iran, the transgressive act among youths now is a resistance to sameness and an effort to do anything to look or be different. This is not an easy task in the trend-conscience society of upper- and middle-class Tehran where when one person starts something everyone else follows. The "hippy" long-hair, poetry-reading café scene is popular because it is associated with uniqueness and with rebelliousness, but it is a quiet rebelliousness that does not disturb the law so much as it disturbs the thought (which is covered anyway and not easily traced).

10 In referring to dominate space in Iran I mean the actual physical construction and projection of Islamic revolutionary Tehran as constructed by the state.

11 This is Benjamin's phrase. In Istanbul, an art historian friend told me about a conversation she had with a curator of the archeology museum, at the end of which the two discovered that they were having the same dreams when they were children in which Ataturk's bust appeared as a person. Later, my friend discovered that this is a common recurring dream experienced by many young Turkish citizens. In most of these dreams Ataturk appears as an angry father.

12 The feeling of uncanniness in not being able to recognize myself eventually subsided. Young people who were born in Tehran and grew up there, however, have always recognized themselves as part of the public persona of the revolutionary character of the city. They can also recognize other women in spite of their coverings, whereas it took me months before I could, for example, recognize a woman in the park wearing a russari whom I had met without a russari at a private party the night before.

13 Taussig, "Physiognomic Aspects of Visual Worlds," 206.

14 Epistemological thinking is structurally linked to space by setting up an opposition between the status of space and the status of the subject—the thinking "I" and the object being thought about. This keeps with the function of the image in *Leili and Majnun*, where Leili's image allows Majnun to incorporate her.

15 De Certeau, *The Practice of Everyday Life*, 93.

16 Ibid., 101. De Certeau likens *asendentosis*—the suppression of linking words such as conjunctions and adverbs, either within a sentence or between sentences—with walking.

17 De Certeau, *The Practice of Everyday Life*, 93.

18 As Benjamin notes, "Once we begin to find our way about, the earliest picture can never be restored" (*Reflections*, 83).

19 An anthropologist has the luxury of being a newcomer as well as someone who eventually makes the strange familiar; which relegates it to the realm of the unconscious.

20 See Varzi, "The Caravan."

21 This vignette is based on my experience of Jordan Street traffic on many different nights, fictionalized into one typical night.

22 Poru is a term that literally means full of oneself. Selfishness is a way to counter the culture that these children grew up in at school, which propagated the opposite of poru—a less-developed sense of individuality.

23 In Iran anyone can make a citizen's arrest and either take the person to the komiteh themselves or call for the komiteh to come and take away the guilty party.

24 This is not a post-revolution phenomenon but one that has occurred alongside these rituals in conservative areas of Iran in both the past and present. (There is a great scene of two young people flirting during these rituals in the popular pre-revolution television series My Uncle Napoleon.) In such places, religious ritual has often been the only opportunity for youths to meet one another in socially sanctioned arenas. This was not the case, however, for the parents of the youth found on Jordan Street today. This generation of secular youth who frequent Jordan Street have plenty of opportunity to fraternize privately, unlike their village peers or their parents' generation.

25 No'heh (religious music) and black flags are used to mourn Imam Husayn.

26 It is precisely this kind of behavior that allows Tehrani youths to conclude that religious people in Tehran today are hypocritical. Often in interviews when asked why they do not choose to practice, they say everything that is done politically in the name of religion is corrupt.

27 Of course, once nonclergy caught on to the freedom of extending or leaving through cyberspace, there was a crack down on such activity, and in summer 2000 the Iranian government shut down all Internet cafés (yet only to reopen them a few weeks later). Today one can find thousands of Web blogs kept by youth in Iran.

28 Lefebvre, The Production of Space, 23.

29 This sketch originally appeared in American Magazine, 1999. Things have changed drastically since 2000—now women and men listen openly to walkmans—or iPods.

30 While a woman's uniform was more overtly "Islamic," at the beginning of the revolution (after Khatami much of this changed) there were also strict rules for boys to follow in their self-presentation that did not always agree with how they might want to represent themselves if given

a choice. For boys, hair had to be kept short and neat, shirt sleeves and pant legs had to be long, and anything that appeared too Western, like rock T-shirts or baseball caps, had to be avoided. Now almost anything is acceptable — even for women Islamic wear is barely more than an oversized Oxford shirt and a wispy veil.

31 Because most komiteh officers are men, women often do not get thoroughly checked because it would mean having to be touched by a non-related man, which is illegal in Islam. Due to strict Islamic law, however, there are many women employed by the state as body checkers in segregated entrances to various public buildings, including universities and theater halls. Most of these women, known as the sisters of Zahra (the ultimate Islamic woman and daughter of the prophet), are wives or mothers of martyrs.

32 De Certeau, *The Practice of Everyday Life*, xvii. He is referring here to the ways in which colonials make creative use of colonizers' commodities. The way that a product is consumed is not manifested through the product's makers, but actually is imposed by the dominant economic order.

33 As noted earlier, this is also the case with women who have altered their Islamic wear in specific and determined ways.

34 In my research I found that even secular middle-class youths who disregard government-produced culture are very defensive and proud of Tehran. While there are many problems with Tehran, most youths told me that they would never leave the city because it is a vital part of who they are, just as they are a vital part of what the city is. Most of these youths do not see Tehran as a product of a revolutionary regime, but rather as a type of soul mate that, like them, has been unwillingly covered with propaganda.

35 Hypervigilance is a symptom of post-traumatic stress disorder.

36 Most of the secular middle-class youths about whom I write have access to computers and have experienced this notion.

37 This is the reverse of what happened to me in Istanbul when I was so immersed in war propaganda that every picture of a young man seemed to be that of a dead soldier.

38 This is not to say that these two realities do not overlap and exist simultaneously in an individual's mind, they do.

39 Jordan Street is one of the older streets of Tehran that well before the revolution was a famous north-south thoroughfare. Jordan runs parallel to one of the oldest north-south streets, Vali Asr Street, formally Pahlavi Street.

40 New technologies also redefine a "sphere," which no longer can be just physical but must involve metaphysical space that can be located every-

where and nowhere. This kind of space comes to life at the touch of a computer switch and dissolves just as easily. Highways are no longer concrete but cyber, and God only knows where they lead.

41 The critique of modernity and call for an Islamic/Persian response was first voiced in the writing of Jalal Al-Ahmad in the 1960s. The idea of a commodity fetish is apparent in his work. Al-Ahmad, like Shariati, was influenced by Marxist thinkers like Frantz Fanon.

42 I am referring to the cityscape that is covered with visuals from the war but is devoid of all the other tactics that were used as vehicles for excitement and were successful in soliciting martyrs.

43 Repeated exposure to the same images and ideas eventually causes desensitization. As I describe in later chapters, Iranian youth today is in some ways less Islamic than the generations raised before the revolution—perhaps as a result of this overwhelming visual and ideological excess in the public sphere.

5. SHIFTING SUBJECTS

1 That is, it becomes second nature. Fluency in language means not thinking about the grammatical rules, just as when one has faith in something they do not question the rules or foundation of that faith (i.e., the existence of God). They do not ask for proof. Belief, on the other hand, is about the rules, and these rules become habit, which does not necessarily lead to faith.

2 Subjectivity is derived from the material rituals by which the subjects are constituted: rituals and ideological recognition. Althusser divides the symbolic (social/speech) and the psychic (as ontologically distinct from the social, it is the remainder that the social cannot take into account).

3 And this suggests that tactility is most at play in relaying ideology through physical space and discipline.

4 Such responses came from the questionnaires and interviews I undertook in Iran in 2000. These questionnaires were composed of essay questions about media and public space and were distributed anonymously to college students and other twenty year olds (originally they were passed out by students in my dowreh and by my cousins). Such questionnaires are not uncommon: many college students answer questionnaires and polls for their friends who use them for psychology or sociology courses.

5 And this is precisely why the Islamic revolution was successful.

6 This was in 1993 when Rafsanjani was president and the laws were much more strict and more rigorously enforced.

7 They say that the problem with this generation is fearlessness. However, even though these youths do not fear God, authority, or death, they do

fear a future without the freedom to choose, because they live trapped in a system that has a monopoly on truth.

8 We cannot discern how deeply effective ideology really is, or what it means to "believe." I am interested in the attempts of the Islamic government to foster an Islamic subject, and to this degree I will engage in discussions on subject formation in the context of domestic debates (such as the ones surrounding Abdul Karim Suroush's philosophy). Otherwise, I do not find subject formation to be a useful framework for understanding individuals.

9 The fact that such law enforcement officers will take bribes and pay-offs further complicates the matter.

10 Of course, youth in most parts of the world also behave as such. This is not to point out that young people in Iran treat authority any differently than elsewhere, but that this authoritarian public sphere is precisely no more effective than any other form of authority.

11 Or at least not any more than what would have resulted from this a priori material prima, Muslim citizen. Iran was, is, and will remain a predominately Muslim country, and the Muslim culture of these youths is similar to that of their parents' generation before the revolution (in terms of keeping with a secular mindset and still respecting and even practicing their religion).

12 The role of the spiritual leader of the country is to uphold the Islamic values of the revolution. He also exercises veto power over the Islamic Majlis (congress) and the president.

13 In summer 2000 everything from entertainment to philosophy magazines featured articles that debated the differences between faith and belief. The reform movement was especially interested in these notions as they propose new ideas about a public versus private religion. Faith falls into the category of one's private beliefs versus practice, which is public and involves public spaces like the mosque.

14 A cultural producer who once worked at the Ministry of Islamic Guidance and wrote educational textbooks told me that the revolution's mistake was making rules a priority over belief. Was the Ministry of Islamic Guidance then the belief department or the rule department? He continued by saying that people cannot be made to follow rules that they do not believe in.

15 Zoroaster lived some time between 1400 and 1200 BC and was the first to proclaim that salvation is possible for all, both the humble of mankind as well as the heroes of legend. He composed hymns called Gathas to glorify the Creator, to which were later added the writings known as Avesta. Among his teachings are the doctrine of a resurrection after death; the existence of the soul; the existence of heaven and hell (and

an intermediate state, or limbo, between the two); the end of time and the world after; the struggle between the forces of good and evil; and a universal last judgment. Zoroastrian metaphysics provides the proto-type for the doctrine of the logos (the Amesha Spenta) and that of the angels. Zoroastrians regard fire as sacred. There are today some 30,000 Zoroastrians left in Iran, mostly in Tehran and Yazd, and in India there is a population of some 130,000, largely in Bombay and the Gujrat (see Bearman, *The Encyclopedia of Islam*).

16 *Takiyya* is to dispense with the ordinances of religion in cases of con-straint and when there is a possibility of harm. Al Tabiri says: "If any-one is compelled and professes unbelief with his tongue, while his heart contradicts him, in order to escape his enemies, no blame falls on him, because God takes his servants as their hearts believe" (quoted in Bear-man, *The Encyclopedia of Islam*, 134). Of course, what is in the heart is hid-den but what is on the tongue is revealed. Much of this is based on in-tention; how can one interpret another's deepest intentions but by their word and actions?

17 Taussig's "public secret" is information that is not acceptable to voice and yet is something that everyone knows.

18 This is why every fraction of an inch of hejab that is pushed back to show more hair points to a lack of authority of the state as vested by the people who wear the hejab (ostensibly out of individual belief, even though it is required by law). If the clergy really wants to know whether people be-lieve in the kind of Islam that requires a hejab, they could simply allow women to choose not to wear the hejab. In doing so, the clergy risks the chance that a majority of women will choose not to wear the hejab, which then will point to a lack of belief in the brand of Islam being propagated by the state.

19 In depicting Furugh's work Bani-Etemad uses her own documentary footage shot in squatter areas of southern Tehran, as well as scenes of characters from her fiction films (primarily about the south of the city). In one scene Furugh runs into a girl from a factory where she had been filming her documentary in search of the ideal mother. The girl is an actual character from Bani-Etemad's film *The Blue Veil*, which is about a woman and her young sister in a factory (the same factory where Fu-rugh films). Post-revolution Iranian cinema has become renowned for its unique style of neorealism, especially the signature mark of Abbas Kiarostami who somehow always brings himself (as a character) or the camera or the crew into the film to remind us that film is fiction, or that life is like a film. Bani-Etemad also does this by linking the southern and northern parts of Tehran to show the universality of human suffer-ing and the ways in which the lives of Tehran women supersede notions

of class and religion in their struggle to live in a harshly regulated and patriarchal society. This also shows the ease of moving from documentary footage to fiction film without the created reality or the represented reality changing in tone to show continuity between fiction and fact.

20 In Iranian cinema behavior and dress must adhere to the same rules of public conduct: women are fully veiled (even in their beds) and there is no touching between men and women (even a mother and her son). We never see her hug Ramin or even touch his forehead.

21 Until fall 2001, classes on sexual education were only permitted for those who had applied for marriage licenses.

22 The state becomes a strict parent that equates all things on the same grand level (for example, staying out too late equals stealing). Thus teenagers who are brought in from parties are locked up with criminals (an excellent example of this is shown in the film *Women's Prison* by Manijeh Hekmat). If nothing is permissible, then once a small rule is broken and the child is already condemned as he or she would be for a big mistake, the line has already been crossed and nothing has any relative value — thus making everything permissible.

23 It is not clear how these parents found the whereabouts of their children, as often the komiteh will not tell the parents where their child is. Most likely one parent followed the van in his or her car and informed the others. It is often the case that parents will arrive at a party to gather their child to find that he or she was arrested.

24 To punish the parents, the komiteh will often demand the deed to the house, which they keep until the court hearing is over or the komiteh are properly bribed.

25 Again we will see how the notion of the Hegelian state comes to play in the choices that parents must make in handing the care of their children over to the state (whether or not they allow the state to teach its brand of morality to their children). There is a resistance on the part of the secular middle classes to allow the state to play the role of parent. A fissure results when these parents refuse to condone teachings on morality that appear on television, at school, and in public. A wonderful exception is portrayed on screen in the movie *The Girl in Sneakers*. A young woman who gets caught with a boy is almost released by the komiteh officer, who wants to let her off with a warning, when the parents step in and ask the state to punish the two children, thereby putting her in a worse position than the boy (as she is subjected to a virginity test, which happened frequently prior to Khatami's presidency).

26 James Siegel's *A New Criminal Type in Jakarta* questions the category of "criminal" and the idea of criminal types. His work can be considered in terms of places like Iran where ordinary citizens are often treated

like criminals for engaging in what they deem as ordinary behavior but what the state defines as improper or non-Islamic behavior and therefore illegal. Siegel claims that, in Islam, tradition does not produce law but rather produces *adat*, or customary law or ways of behaving (in Persian *adat* means habit). During the revolution in Iran criminal acts became nationalists acts; there seems to be a moment of suspension during revolutions where criminality and nationalism are blurred. Violence, or criminality, becomes justified because the end justifies the means and because "criminal" becomes "revolutionary," and even if both acts involve killing, stealing, and bearing arms they do so as differently defined categories, which seems to make all the difference. Siegel says that the state takes on the form of a criminal in order to obtain power. Siegel's work concentrates on teenage criminals, who remain outside of the law because the law is considered an adult activity. These young adults mirror yet remain outside of the adult world. And as such they remain outside of comprehension. Are they insane or disturbed? Children tend to be brought too quickly into the adult world as either criminals or victims. Based on Siegel's research we see that early childhood victims often end up becoming criminals. As I read Siegel's discussion of reform schools, I mused that there are few such schools in Iran, as every school is potentially treated as a reform school. Or perhaps in Iran there are few reform schools because their existence would point to a failure on the part of an Islamic society, where society, the public schools, and the family are supposed to adequately discipline youth. As is the case in Iran, foreign influence is what Indonesians blame for corrupting youth. Siegel says, "It is at the point of articulation between the family and the nation that failure is located" (75). (This is a Hegelian notion; as I noted earlier, for Hegel the state is not only modeled on family but it becomes a surrogate family. War, the ultimate nationalist activity, is thus not criminal.) Justice is done when less-fortunate members of society (the amoral criminals) are rescued from the failure of the assimilative powers of the nation. This is the case in Iran where any act against Islam is considered a criminal act and where justice (e.g., floggings and prison tenures) is considered reform. Without criminals there would be no law. So, in Iran, the Islamic police's existence is the state's expectation of resistance to Islamic law (the same police that deal with regular crimes).

There seems to be a need for recognition that is inherent in many crimes (this would be true especially of youth), and yet the self-consciousness, according to Siegel, does not occur until the police (or therapist) shows up. The new criminal type, as defined by Siegel, has a power that is independent of the state and calls attention to itself without ever affecting the recognition that would make it an accepted part of the nation. Siegel concludes that, despite everything, the presence of the police means safety. After the Islamic revolution when Iran was somewhat of a police state, crime decreased in Tehran. Now with economic and political instability crime has increased—people are starving and addicted and thus are killing and stealing to make ends meet.

27 In Iran there is constant paranoia that anyone might be a potential undercover Islamic police officer. The difference here between democratic systems with undercover police is that they are supposed to elicit a feeling of safety, whereas in Iran the police only conjure feelings of paranoia and discomfort from thinking that at any moment one's actions might be considered illegal.

28 My aunts were constantly encouraging me to wear bright colors, "To hell with all this mourning," they would say.

29 A culture of secrecy enforces the notion that one must not confide in or trust anyone else.

30 One of the main problems for Tehrani youth is the lack of places to go in order to expend energy. In a city of over seven million where the majority are apartment dwellers, a feeling of claustrophobia and pent-up energy plagues a generation that has little access to public space. (In the film, for example, we see Ramin using a punching bag in his bedroom.) These youths have had to keep stress inside in order for it not to spill over into unacceptable places. In psychological terms, they become the receptacle of family feelings and of the state's anger toward them, which is acted out in their transgressions. Like a schizophrenic they carry with them different consciousnesses. Unlike the Columbia University dorm residents (who at the moment are interrupting my writing with their "shout out"), they are not allowed to yell out the window and have it deemed acceptable and cathartic. In Iran there is no outlet for energy. Exercise is available to those with money, but, even for them it is not always easy to access. Parks are polluted and guarded and it is hard to jog in a rupush and russari even though we see Furugh jogging in a park while covered from head to toe (the film was made in winter when it is not too hot to jog in such heavy clothing). Mohsen Makmalbaf claims that with no place to let off steam, youths will eventually implode or explode. Driving fast is thus an outlet.

31 This is one of the first films to bravely show both a Basij barricade and komiteh cars picking up the youth at a party (these scenes are now more commonplace in movies). Violence toward the Basij, however, would be unacceptable in a film. Though in summer 2000 there were more than a few incidents of mysterious murders of Basij on the streets, Tehran is not dangerous in terms of street crimes, especially violent acts like murder. By a peculiar circularity, however, as the Islamic nature of the city begins

to fade and there are less komiteh (if for no other reason than budget cuts and bad pay), there are more crimes (owing to a failing economy)—the komiteh bribe while other thugs mug.

32 Despite the Western feminist interpretations, young boys, not girls, are bothered most by the komiteh. In a state where a young man should be exemplifying the ideals of a Basij, young secular boys (or punks, as the komiteh sees them) are a greater threat than a woman whose hejab slips an inch.

6. MAJNUN'S MASK

1 This was apparent in the research study (which I was allowed to read but not photocopy) conducted in 2000 by Tehran University on the quality of life for youth under the age of twenty-five.

2 I would like to thank my colleagues who thoughtfully pointed out (at an SSRC conference in Beirut) that I was perhaps too quick in using terms like schizophrenia, which (and I agree) resonate with certain contemporary theorists or medical terminology that might be misleading. My purpose in using the term schizophrenia and in addressing the issue in general, is to use the language and ideas in the way I encountered them in Iran (Iran today is steeped in postmodern literature and psychology). People (parents mostly, along with some youths and teachers) were continually telling me that young people who were raised in the Islamic republic were "bi hoviat," or "do shakhsiyat"—that is, without identity or with split and double identities. As an anthropologist I insisted that one could not be without identity; that there must be some identity—perhaps not a strong sense of self, but an identity nonetheless. The struggle, the attempt, the desire to know the self . . . this is a strong struggle with identity.

3 I have noticed that each "generation" of youth (that is, groups that are five years apart) looks at the next generation and notes their "craziness." Increasingly more youths are beginning to point it out in their peers and, as I present later in journal entries, in themselves.

4 For further readings on the children of substance abusers, see Black, *Double Duty*.

5 Twelve-step programs and therapy have become very popular in Tehran.

6 The video footage here seems displaced or appropriated, and yet it superimposes two different effects of war. The first is the subtle aftermath of war: not just the sacred memory that has to do with Islam, but the aftermath that involves drug use, pooch, or a different kind of bi khodi. The video is one like many made by the *Revayat-e Fath* production group for the precise reason of remembering the horrors of the war and what

the Basij suffered. Here, the footage is oddly placed by a secular film-maker, Masoud Kimiyai (who is married to the famous pre-revolution pop singer Googoosh), in a movie about the nonexistent (except in his head) secular student movement.

7 Farokzad might be described as the Sylvia Plath of Iran. She is still one of the most popular poets among youth today, even thirty years after her premature death.

8 Statistics come from a report by Mohammad Ali Zam, head of Tehran's Cultural and Artistic Affairs; 2000, Tehran.

9 This vignette is compiled from a few similar stories I have heard from hikers in Darband.

10 From *Kar va Kargar* (*Work and the Worker*), quoted in *The Daily*, Spring 2000. In more than one film I have seen a scene where either a man or woman wanting to call the opposite sex must find someone of that gender to make the call. In *The Circle*, young soldiers ask a woman to make a call, while in *The Girl in Sneakers* a teenage girl who is trying to reach her boy-friend has a man call him from the pay phone. Artistic and personal views are expressed more freely through blogging; there are international and national exhibitions of the work of young Iranians; the theater is in full bloom; and the cinema has younger, newer directors, and of the group I worked with in my research, over two-thirds of those who are now in Europe and the United States doing postgraduate work intend to return to Iran when they are finished.

11 The point here is that while the identity that most people choose to project is often performative of the context; in Tehran, youth have no choice but to perform a specific identity for a specific situation. These days, writing Web blogs is the most popular outlet for frustrations, hopes, dreams, and secrets.

12 I tried for nine months to get an interview with a psychologist to discuss the general trends seen in young patients. But because I did not have direct contacts it was impossible to find a doctor who would trust me—even through semiformal contacts it was impossible. At one point my cousin gave me the number of her friend's father who runs group therapy in the mountains of Tehran where he clandestinely mixes boys and girls. She told me that they would meet and play music and light a fire. But when I called him at his home, he told me to call him at Tehran University—where no one ever picked up the phone. In another instance a nurse I met on a four-day hiking trip spoke to me for hours about her job at a psychiatric hospital, during which she told me information about the types of youths who came to her hospital after suicide attempts and the response of the hospitals, which has been mainly to administer medication. She offered to speak with one of the doctors who was leading

group therapy for youths at the hospital and get permission for me to interview the doctors or even sit in on group therapy. But something happened when she went to ask the doctor, because he neither gave her permission nor did she agree to speak with me ever again.

13 This vignette is based on a number of different people's experiences that were relayed to me. I consolidated and fictionalized them to protect the various women involved.

14 On the 23rd of September 2000, Iran's 20 million schoolchildren received their first sex education lessons. The deputy education minister, Rahim Ebadi, was reported to have told a seminar that health matters during puberty were an important question for both sexes, and that if nothing were done to help inform boys and girls, there would be a crisis. In the past, sex education has been regarded as taboo in Iran. In 2005 in London I met Sara Nasserzadeh, who gave the first sex education classes in Iran. Her classes began in 2001 as private workshops for women, advertised by word of mouth. She had separate workshops for engaged, married, and single individuals, as well as consultations for men over the phone, which she later stopped because, in her words, "it could get problematic." She described these courses as follows: "Topics I would cover were: knowing their bodies (which always had some surprises for them), relationship with the opposite sex and same sex in general, masturbation, female and male genital organs and their functions, different methods of contraception which were available in Iran from different sources (pharmacy, doctors, family planning clinics, etc.), and the cons and pros for each of them, sexual relationship with a partner (physical and emotional aspects), STDs, abortion and its available methods in Iran (legal and illegal), first sexual experience; dilemmas around hymen (being a virgin when you get married is still important in Iran), how to explore their sexual desire and how to respond to it, how to please thier partner's sexual desires while enjoying themselves, and sexual relations while pregnant and after giving birth. Among the participants there were very religious people as well as sex workers. I also had a few specialist doctors in my classes. The classes were held in my own apartment and some sessions in a private institute which had some classes for success, etc. I got the training from reading textbooks, which I brought myself from outside the country (you can't send them by post and need to import with a passenger's luggage). My husband is a doctor, so he was a great help to me regarding the anatomy section of the class. Internet was helpful too; also my colleagues from outside the country were very helpful in sending me information via e-mails. Questions from pupils ranged from, What would happen to someone if they only had anal sex? Or is anal sex and oral sex the only ways to keep your hymen? Are STDs includ-

ing HIV transferable via oral sex as well? Most of the knowledge came from porno films and adult channels in satellite" (from my interview with Sara Nasserzadeh, London, 2005. See also Azarmina, and Nasserzadeh, "Access to Sexual Health Information in Iran"). In the summer of 2005 I attended half of the required sexual education classes a couple must take in order to get a marriage license, and the main emphasis before segregating the crowd was on birth control and pregnancy. Later, the couples were segregated for more specific information.

15 According to Nasserzadeh: "Elective abortion was never legal after the revolution (medical abortion has been); I don't know about before. There was a fatwa by Ayatollah Khameini (supreme leader of Iran) in which he said If some one wants to have an abortion it should be before the soul is blown to the baby's body (some time around four months), but even at this time the doctor should write a note to say that either the mother or the child is in life-threatening danger. In this case they can abort their babies. As far as I know, when someone wants to abort her baby, the father of the baby should sign a consent form. I am not sure if it's still the case or not. On the time that I was there, unmarried people were afraid to go to clinics and hospitals, so they either go to get the injections from the black market (if it's early enough to abort their babies in this way) or go to a family doctor or someone who would do it for them confidentially" (from my interview with Sara Nasserzadeh, London, 2005).

16 Condoms are available in drugstores, and boys (and usually girls) are not given a hard time for buying them. Girls can get birth control without a prescription. (Given the increasing problem that Iran is having with HIV, it is amazing that one of Iran's supposedly socially minded film directors, Abbas Kiarostami, would go to Africa to make a film on the AIDS virus (*ABC Africa*), when one at home would have been most useful.) One sad commentary is the situation of a young boy who had contracted HIV but had no idea he had it, or how one contracts it. He claimed to be a virgin because he was too humiliated to admit that he had been raped in prison (interview with a Tehran doctor, summer 2000). Recently the campaign to educate the public has been strengthened and AIDS/HIV awareness posters appear throughout the city, especially in highly traversed areas like transportation hubs. Further, the World Health Organization and Iran's Ministry of Health have teamed up to combat HIV, and now there are Web sites where one can go and read in Persian the stories of HIV-affected Iranians as well as learn about testing and prevention.

17 In Tehran there is easy access to hymen reconstructive surgery, and many young people use other methods of intercourse that do not break the hymen (I was told that anal intercourse is especially popular).

18 In 2000 a statistical report leaked to the press noted that prostitution

had increased 635 percent among high school students and the rate of suicide in the country had exceeded the record by 109 percent in the years 1998 and 1999. The report added that divorce is on the rise and that the average age of prostitutes has dropped to twenty years old, compared with twenty-seven a few years ago (Zam, 2000). In Jafar Panahi's film *The Circle*, the only scenes found unacceptable and thus censorable by the Iranian government came in the last twenty minutes when a young woman, unremarkable in appearance, is picked up for prostitution. This scene is more benign than one at the beginning of the film where an older woman actually prostitutes herself, or at least where there is the strong implication that she is selling sex. But because the scenario at the end is closer to what is really going on in Iran, it was considered more damning.

19 Another problem in reading space comes with the idea that certain spaces are never demarcated because they are taboo: e.g., red-light districts or corners where drugs are sold. In this way they are decentered because they are not supposed to exist and therefore have no center, which makes them diffuse and all-encompassing: the red-light district, for example, is nowhere and thus everywhere.

20 This statement was repeatedly made by Khameini on Iranian television.

21 *Fear and Trembling* is especially popular due to its discussion of sacrifice.

22 The young people's opinions expressed here are from a questionnaire I distributed in 2000.

23 Amanpour did a disservice to the reformist movement by showing exactly what the clergy were claiming: young Iranians as a group of youth who only want reforms that will allow them the freedom to drink, wear miniskirts, listen to rap music, and be with their boyfriends or girlfriends. For the wealthy Westernized youth that Amanpour interviewed, these things already exist under the surface.

7. THE GHOST IN THE MACHINE

1 This was also the case with the Center for Educational Development for Children and Young Adults, which gave birth to directors such as Abbas Kiarostami.

2 It is important to note here that this discussion of films critical of the war is not a critique of the Islamic ideal of a sacred defense or what was originally fought for, but rather that the war carried on beyond that point and that the promises made to the soldiers were not kept.

3 Confessional political essays and books like those by former revolutionaries turned reformists (most notably Akbar Ganji) were popular hits in Iran.

4 My experiences of Hatamikia's films have been in packed movie theaters in Tehran, where I have been fortunate enough to be present for the release of each of his most successful and controversial films: *Kharkeh to Rhine*, 1994; *The Scent of Yusef's Shirt*, 1996; *The Glass Agency*, 1998; and *The Red Ribbon*, 2000. I was even lucky enough to participate in his film *The Deadly Wave* (2002), which was banned by the government, about a U.S. tanker in the Gulf (I played the American voice on the radio transmitter from the tanker).

5 From my interview with Hatamikia in Tehran, 1997.

6 When I first saw Kamal Tabrizi's comedy *Leili Is with Me* (Tabrizi is a former Basij and friend of Hatamikia) I was shocked at the satirical way in which the war was portrayed. The story is a comedic sequence of events in which a photographer tries, unsuccessfully, to get out of an assignment at the front. The comedy continues when he finally reaches the war front and tries in vain to avoid going all the way to the actual line of martyrdom. Finally, a sign that points to the front line is turned around in the wind and he ends up in the trenches with the men waiting to die. All of the stereotypes of the crazy young boys at the front come into play, especially in the character of a teenager who, unlike the photographer, will do anything to get to the front and die, but is restrained by his fellow battalion members who claim that he is too young and must wait his turn. His efforts, like the photographer's, are thwarted by the outside player we call chance, or God, who keeps him away from the front line. To me, the entire scenario seemed mocking and politically incorrect for Iran. I interpreted the laughter of the audience and the mockery of the characters as some sort of blasphemous critique, and I was shocked that it would be allowed in the theater, and even more shocked to hear Mohammed Attibai, the head of Farabi Film Foundation's International office, tell me that it was the next big film for export. Why send abroad such a personal film that could easily be misinterpreted by a foreigner as a mockery of the war? In any event, they never did manage to get it to the United States. Almost ten years later, I had the chance to interview the actor who played the photographer. I gave him my initial impressions and he told me that contrary to how I had interpreted the film it was actually an affirmation of martyrdom. It showed that even in the face of adversary one would make it to one's fate and, in the end, find happiness (which the photographer does, in the camaraderie of his fellow soldiers). Even so, while that may have been the intention of the filmmaker, most secular Iranians I spoke to about the film agreed that it was poking fun at the "crazy Basij." It is also interesting to note that, while done in jest, the title (which is also a line in the film) refers directly to Leili and Majnun and the importance of the inner image—the guided

beloved that moves one toward the front and onto the correct path, the protector.

7 Islamic clerics are expected to marry and raise children.

8 At this time, there were a number of Basij turning up murdered or missing in Tehran—people were no longer scared to take the law literally into their own hands.

9 Most youth I asked said that they would go to war to defend Iran: even if it was in the name of Islam, if Iran was at stake they would go.

10 Many of Mehdi's comments are reminiscent of ones I heard from Hatamikia and from people in the *Revayat-e Fath* group in interviews. It is clear that he takes great inspiration from their teachings.

11 The most poignant example of this on film is *Crimson Gold* (written by Abbas Kiarostami and directed by Jafar Panahi) about a former Basij and his struggles in everyday life.

12 Editorial, 1997.

13 *The Glass Agency* was dismissed by American critics (so enamored of Iranian neorealist cinema) as nothing more than an attempt to make an Iranian version of Sidney Lumet's *Dog Day Afternoon*. Hatamikia went on to make other imitations, like the *Red Ribbon*, which looks a lot like *The English Patient*. His ability to translate an American film scenario for an Iranian audience and make it look like the Iran-Iraq war points to the universality of war; an issue overlooked by film critics.

14 "Hauntology" is introduced in Derrida's *Specters of Marx*.

15 Zekr is an important act done in preparation for martyrdom and in remembering martyrs during various times of the year.

16 For further readings on ghosts and modernity in anthropology, see Ivy, *Discourses of the Vanishing*.

17 Virilio, 61.

18 Ibid., 4.

19 Many POWs were sent to treatment centers abroad. Hatamikia's film *From Kharkeh to Rhine* explicitly deals with this situation. *The Glass Agency*, as noted above, is a controversial film about a pair of war veterans who go to desperate measures to seek treatment for war wounds.

20 Khomeini, *Islam and Revolution*, 226.

21 Hatamikia says he tries to address the pain of the returned soldiers who spend years in POW camps or in rehabilitation centers abroad dreaming of their triumphant homecoming, which then never materializes on the grand level they imagined. Instead, according to him, they return to a disillusioned population that would prefer to forget the war. "This is a population that turns their faces away from the sight of a man in a wheelchair rather than to congratulate or thank him for fighting in the war," says Hatamikia. He describes postwar Iran as a place where

people are suffocating: "People could not work (due to the skyrocketing unemployment rate) or see the future. Everyone was suffering, everyone was waiting for a miracle, and there was nothing they could do but wait, *entizar* [waiting is an important concept in Shiism that implies waiting for the hidden Imam]." The film, made shortly before Khatami came to office, illustrates the hopelessness inherent in the difficulties suffered by the country before Khatami arrived on the scene.

22 Derrida, *Specters of Marx*, 9.

23 This is very similar to Majnun's mad cries at Leili's tomb, to the effect of: Oh unopened blossom, you died young and left me alone, was this world too small that you had to go hide under dirt? Are you comfortable in this dark grave or are you still troubled by my love? (Nizami, *The Loves of Laili and Majnun*, trans. Atkinson, 110).

24 Derrida, *Specters of Marx*, 51.

25 Ibid.

26 In the end it is Shireen who sees, or finds, Yusef at the front.

27 Yunis/Jonah is the boy in the story that appears in both the Bible and the Quran who is swallowed by a whale. He remains alive in the belly of a whale and is later spouted out.

28 Or perhaps they engage in the kind of bi-khodi described in chapter 6 in terms of Iranian youth and their troubles with drugs and suicide. Hatamikia says, "We move away from God, and we forget ourselves, move away from ourselves—with alcohol. The drunk German in *From Kharkeh to Rhine* is just one example of self-loss, bi-khodi" (from my interview with Hatamikia in Tehran, 1997).

29 Deleuze, *Negotiations, 1972–1990*, 34.

8. REFORMING IDENTITY IN POST-KHATAMI IRAN

1 This student left Iran for post-graduate study in France.

2 See Varzi, "Iran Gardi."

3 When visuals become benign, the state becomes the object of scrutiny.

4 Address to the nation, April 24, 2000, Seda Sima (the Islamic republic of Iran broadcasting).

5 Interview in Tehran, 2000.

6 Abdul Karim Soroush was a key ideologue in the Ministry of Education and President Khatami was the Minister of Culture; Mohsen Makhmalbaf's evolution can be traced from that of a revolutionary to a reformist by watching the thematic development of his films, and Ibrahim Hatamikia, as noted in chapter 7, once worked with Avini's project at the front. Makhmalbaf began his career with films like *Boycott*, which portrayed his own experiences as a young revolutionary in the shah's pris-

ons. His next acclaimed work was on the war, titled *Marriage of the Blessed*, which also engaged in a critical view of the war and the struggle of veterans to reenter society. His films continued to emphasize social issues, and they are as critical of society during the revolution years as they had been before. Finally, in films like *Gabbeh*, Makhmalbaf moved over toward the reformist project of redefining Iran in terms of its nomadic and non-Islamic cultural heritage, where the very texture and emphasis on color in the film is a move against the all-black backdrop of a revolutionary Tehran.

7 Jafar Panahi's *Crimson Gold* is a wonderful portrayal of a war veteran (who plays himself) trying to make ends meet in postwar Iran.

8 Interview in Tehran, 2000. This resonates with the theorists of secularization who define a religious state in terms of making the public space a religious space. See Asad, "Religion, Nation-State, Secularism."

9 This is why empirical research is important to the project, as I demonstrate below.

10 In a presentation at the University of Washington in 1997, Abdul Karim Soroush, the controversial Islamic thinker, claimed that in Iran there has been a shift from a Cartesian subject position to an Islamic one, which will enable Iran to move away from an Islamic republic to an Islamic democracy based on a nation of independent Islamic subjects.

11 My training in anthropology has led me to be skeptical of a monolithic and essential "Iranian" or "Islamic" identity. I contend that no strong monolithic Islamic identity exists in contrast to the image that we have of Iran—even on the surface. What exists is a state of imposed "normalcy" in the context of the black mourning banners commemorating martyred imams and the imposing billboards of bloodied war martyrs and maimed POWs from the Iran-Iraq war.

12 Speech on Seda Sima, spring 2000 (my translation). Years later, this continues to be relevant.

13 Instead of taking polls, which people rarely answer correctly anyway, a day without mandatory Islamic covering would expose the percentage of the population who might choose not to wear Islamic cover. This, of course, is a dangerous idea, because masses of uncovered Iranian women would shatter the illusion of a strong Islamic Republic. In 2005 women are getting away with wearing the minimum requirements.

14 In 2000, the Department of Social Welfare stated that unemployment had risen in the last four years from 9.1 percent to 16 percent, while unofficial figures put it at almost double that figure. The department also stated that nearly one-fifth of all Iranians were living below the poverty line—in other words, making less than an average of one dollar per day. Meanwhile, personal savings have disappeared with the decreased

value of the rial. The rial was close to 300 to the dollar when I was in Iran in 1993, but had more than tripled to almost 1,000 to the dollar in 2000.

15 Indeed, the war gave purpose to many boys who lacked direction. As noted earlier, Avini's project alone gave boys from villages and the south of the city, who were never given a chance to speak or be heard, an opportunity to be in the limelight and voice their feelings.

16 As noted in chapter 6 and elsewhere, the government never trusted this generation, and their parents never trusted the government to deal with them properly, so ultimately they were left without anyone's trust.

17 This view can be thought of in light of Hegel's discussion about a higher purpose for work; see the Hegelian reading of the war outlined in chapter 2.

18 Here, I would disagree; as noted in previous chapters, spirituality (self-hypnosis and meditation classes, Jung classes, Sufi music, self-help culture, Hafiz's poetry) has the function of escape and protest.

19 The study took ten months and the efforts of sixty researchers. The form of the research was a questionnaire with yes or no answers, and the resulting report included many charts and tables with statistics.

20 Namaz Jumeh, or Friday prayers are as political as they are religious — recall from chapter 2 that during the war they served as forums to encourage boys to martyr themselves.

21 Note that theater is fast becoming one of the most popular (and avant-garde) forms of entertainment. I saw a production of Genet's *The Blacks* that used body language to the absolute limit of Islamic possibility.

22 The theme of this questionnaire came at an interesting and important time, as the Basij who are those most likely to engage in public disciplining have become the brunt of a rare show by the general public of not just anger but violence. In spring and summer 2000 more than a few incidents of violence toward Basij, some resulting in death, were reported on the radio and in papers.

23 I heard endless tirades on the hypocrisy of classmates coming from religious families who owned bootlegged videos and western clothes; further, they could enjoy these things without the fear of the authorities because they were the authorities.

24 And, again, the components of outward identity and belief in an ideology are easier to measure than belief or faith in religion, because ideology is public and visible whereas faith is invisible.

25 To see how concerned people are with surfaces, all one needs to do is walk through Tehran and take note of the noses bandaged as a result of recent cosmetic surgery, as well as the more straightforward evidence of botox and makeup.

26 The hours of material appearing on blogs alone gives an idea of the struggle of Iranian youth.

CONCLUSION: MEHDI'S CLIMB

1 See Varzi, "The Caravan."

2 The 2000 jungle is an area near the Caspian Sea.

3 In summer 2000 the filmmaker Mohsen Makmalbaf told me in an interview at his office in Tehran that this generation has the same identity as his generation, and that the only difference is the way they dress (he is a father of five children, including the wonder woman of her generation, Samira Makmalbaf).

4 From my first visit to Iran when I went on a weekend ski trip I learned that reading a novel or using a Walkman were considered rude practices because the time was all to be spent with the group. Indeed, the group went to the slopes together, ate together, and everyone went to sleep at the same time. Any time spent listening to music or reading (usually poetry read out loud) was also done as a group. (Note that this situation has changed slightly in recent years.) Now individualism and being different has become hip to the point that the moment something different appears everyone catches on and it becomes a trend (this is not so different from capitalist societies where businesses like the Gap market "uniqueness"; in Iran, however, it is the youths who pick up the trends and follow them rather than the capitalists telling people what to wear). Mehdi mentioned to me in an interview that Iranian society is a follower society and that there is no room for individualism even if it is something that his generation fancies themselves practicing.

EPILOGUE

1 As noted earlier, the reform movement is imbedded in this language: talk centers around moving toward faith and a society where religion should be a personal decision and not a public mandate. The collective thus becomes a group of faithful individuals that together bring about an Islamic democracy.

2 Five years after I took Mehdi's climb, he found me at my University of London office, as SOAS, where I was on the faculty of the Anthropology department. He informed me that none of the members of my dowreh in Tehran had stayed on—and only a couple continued to study engineering—three of them were in the UK, two in France, and several more in the United States.

Abbas Amanat, "The Study of History in Post-Revolutionary Iran: Nostalgia, or Historical Awareness?" *Iranian Studies* 22 (1989): 3–18.

Abedi, Mehdi, and Gary Legenhausen, eds. *Jihad and Shahadat: Struggle and Martyrdom in Islam*. Houston: Institute for Research and Islamic Studies, 1986.

Abrahamian, Ervand. *Iran between Two Revolutions*. Princeton, N.J.: Princeton University Press, 1982.

———. *Tortured confessions: prisons and public recantations in modern Iran*. Berkeley: University of California Press, 1999.

Al-Ahmad, Jalal. *Gharbzadighi [Westoxification]*. Tehran: Azad, 1962.

———. *Lost in the Crowd*. Translated by John Green, with Ahmad Alizadeh and Farzin. Washington, D.C.: Three Continents Press, 1985.

Algar, Hamid. *Religion and State in Iran*. Berkeley: University of California Press, 1969.

Althusser, Louis. *Essays on ideology*, London: Verso, 1984.

Andrews, Walter G. "Singing the Alienated 'I': Guattari, Deleuze, and Lyrical Decodings of 'The Subject in Ottoman Divan Poetry.'" *Yale Journal of Criticism* 6.2 (1993): 191–219.

Arjomand, Said Amir. "The State and Khomeini's Islamic Order." *Iranian Studies* 13.1–4 (1980): 147–64.

Arkoun, Mohammed. *Rethinking Islam: Common Questions, Uncommon Answers*. Translated by Robert D. Lee. Boulder: Westview Press, 1994.

Asad, Talal. "Religion, Nation-State, Secularism." In *Nation and Religion: Perspectives on Europe and Asia*, edited by Peter van der Veer and Hartmut Lehmann. Princeton, N.J.: Princeton University Press, 1999.

Attar, Farid al-Din. *The Conference of the Birds*. Translated by Garcin de Tassy and C. S. Nott. Boulder, Colo.: Shambala, 1971.

Avini, Morteza. *Revayat-e Fath*. Video. Tehran: Revayat-e Fath, 1986.

———. *Yek Tajrobehyeh Mondegar*. Tehran: Rivayat-e Fath, 2000.

Azarmina, P., and S. Nasserzadeh. "Access to Sexual Health Information in Iran." INASP Newsletter, no. 27 (2004).

Barnouw, Erik, *Documentary: a history of the non-fiction film*. New York: Oxford University Press, 1992.

Bataille, G. *Eroticism: Death and Sensuality*. San Francisco: City Lights, 1986.

Bearman, P. J., et al., eds. *The Encyclopedia of Islam*. Leiden, Netherlands: Brill, 2000.

Benjamin, Walter. *Illuminations*. New York: Schocken Books, 1968.

———. *Reflections*. New York: Harcourt and Brace, 1978.

Black, Claudia. *Double Duty: Dual Dynamics within the Chemically Dependent Home*. New York: Ballantine Books, 1990.

Butler, Judith. *The Psychic Life of Power: Theories in Subjection*. Stanford, Calif.: Stanford University Press, 1997.

Canetti, Elias. *Crowds and Power*. Translated by Carol Stewart. New York: Noonday Press, 1962.

Certeau, Michel de. *The Practice of Everyday Life*. Berkeley: University of California Press, 1984.

———. *The mystic fable*, translated by Michael B. Smith. Chicago: University of Chicago Press, 1992.

Chelkowski, P. J. *Ta'ziyeh: Ritual and Drama in Iran*. New York: New York University Press, 1979.

Chelkowski, P. J., and Hamid Dabashi. *Staging a Revolution*. London: Booth-Collins, 1995.

Chittick, William. *The Sufi Path of Knowledge: Ibn al-Arabi's Metaphysics of Imagination*. Albany: State University of New York Press, 1989.

Clifford, James and Marcus, George E., editors, *Writing culture: the poetics and politics of ethnography*. Berkeley: University of California Press, 1986.

Corbin, Henry. *Creative Imagination in the Sufism of Ibn Arabi*. Translated by Ralph Manheim. Princeton, N.J.: Princeton University Press, 1969.

Corbin, Henry, and Allamah Tabataba'i. "The Imams and the Imamate." In *Shi'ism: Doctrines, Thought, and Spirituality*, edited by Nasr, Seyyed Hossein, Dabashi, Hamid, Vali Reza, Seyyed. Albany: State University of New York Press, 1988.

Deleuze, Gilles. *Negotiations 1972–1990*. New York: Columbia University Press, 1990.

Derrida, Jacques. *Specters of Marx: The State of the Debt, the Work of Mourning, and the New International*. Translated by Peggy Kamuf, introduction by Bernd Magnus and Stephen Cullenberg. New York: Routledge, 1994.

Durkheim, Emile. *The Elementary Forms of Religious Life*. Translated by Joseph Ward Swain. New York: Macmillan, 1912.

Eagleton, Terry. *Ideology: An Introduction*. New York: Verso, 1991.

Fischer, Michael. "Becoming Mullah: Reflections on Iranian Clerics in a Revolutionary Age." *Iranian Studies* 13.1–4 (1980): 83–117.

——. *From Religious Dispute to Revolution*. Cambridge, Mass.: Harvard University Press, 1980.

Fischer, Michael, and Mehdi Abedi. *Debating Muslims: Cultural Dialogues in Post-modernity and Tradition*. Madison: University of Wisconsin Press, 1990.

Foucault, Michel. "Iran: The Spirit of a World without Spirit." Translated by Alan Sheridan. In *Politics, Philosophy, Culture: Interviews and Other Writings, 1977–1984*, edited by Lawrence D. Kritzman. New York: Routledge, 1988.

——. *Language, Counter-Memory, Practice: Selected Essays and Interviews*. Edited by Donald F. Bouchard. Ithaca, N.Y.: Cornell University Press, 1977.

——. *Madness and civilization; a history of insanity in the Age of Reason*. Translated by Richard Howard. New York: Vintage Books, 1973.

——. *The Order of Things: An Archeology of the Human Sciences*. New York: Vintage Books, 1973.

Girard, René. *Violence and the Sacred*. Baltimore, Md.: Johns Hopkins University Press, 1977.

Glasse, Cyril. *Concise Encyclopedia of Islam*. London: Stacey International, 1989.

Hashtroodi, Seyyed Yasser, ed. *Hello My Country: Ten Interviews with the Iranian POWs Redemption*. Tehran: Huzeh Honari, 1988.

Hatamikia, Ebrahim, dir. *The Glass Agency*. Screenplay by Ibrahim Hatamikia. Iran: Farabi Cinema Foundation, 1997.

——. *Kharke to Rhine*. Screenplay by Ibrahim Hatamikia. Tehran; Germany: Farabi Cinema Foundation, 1992.

——. *The Scent of Yusef's Shirt*. Screenplay by Ibrahim Hatamikia. Tehran: Farabi Cinema Foundation, 1996.

Heidegger, Martin. *The Question Concerning Technology and Other Essays*. Translated by William Lovitt. New York: Harper and Row, 1977.

Ivy, Marilyn. *Discourses of the Vanishing: Modernity, Phantasm, Japan*. Chicago: University of Chicago Press, 1995.

Kennedy, Duncan F. *The Arts of Love: Five Studies in the Discourse of the Roman Love Elegy*. Cambridge: Cambridge University Press, 1993.

Khaisrallah, As'ad E. *Love, Madness, and Poetry: An Interpretation of The Majnun Legend*. Beirut: Orient Institute der DMG, 1980.

Khalil, Samir al. *The Monument: Art, Vulgarity, and Responsibility in Iraq.* Berkeley: University of California Press, 1991.

Khomeini, Imam [Ayatollah]. *The Imam and the Ommat.* Tehran: Ministry of Islamic Guidance, 1981.

——. "Imam Khomeini-RA Voice Chat." http://khoemeini.com/ GatewayToHeaven/imamKhomeiniVoiceChat.htm. 2002.

——.*Islam and Revolution: Writings and Declarations of Imam Khomeini.* Berkeley, Calif.: Mizan Press, 1981.

Kojève, Alexander. *Introduction to the Reading of Hegel: Lectures on "The Phemenology of the Spirit."* Translated by James H. Nichols Jr. Ithaca, N.Y.: Cornell University Press, 1969.

Lefebvre, Henri. *The Production of Space.* Translated by Donald Nicholson-Smith. Cambridge: Blackwell, 1991.

Loftus, Elizabeth. *The Myth of Repressed Memory.* New York: St. Martin's Press, 1994.

Malinowski, Bronislaw. *Magic, Science, Religion.* New York: Beacon Press, 1953.

Marcus, George, and Michael Fischer. *Anthropology as Cultural Critique: An Experimental Moment in the Human Sciences.* Chicago: University of Chicago Press, 1986.

Ministry of Islamic Guidance. *Captivity and Prisoners of War in the Battle of Truth against Falsehood.* Tehran: Ministry of Islamic Guidance, 1984.

——. *The Imposed War: Defense vs. Aggression.* Tehran: Ministry of Islamic Guidance, 1983.

Mitchell, W. J. T. *Iconology: Image, Text, Ideology.* Chicago: University of Chicago Press, 1986.

Mottahedeh, Roy. *Mantle of the Prophet.* New York: Simon and Schuster, 1985.

Nettler, Ron. *Sufi Metaphysics and Qur'anic Prophets: Ibn Arabi Thought and Method in the Fusus Al Hakim.* Cambridge: Islamic Texts Society, 2003.

Nicholson, Reynold A. *Rumi: Poet and Mystic.* London: George Allen and Unwin, 1950.

Nizami, Ganjavi. *Haft Paykar.* Translated by Julie Scott Meisami. Oxford: Oxford University Press, 1995.

——. *The Story of Leili and Majnun.* Translated by R. Gelpke. Zurich: Bruno Cassirer, 1966.

——. *The Loves Of Leili and Majnun.* Translated by J. R. Atkinson. London: David Nutt, 1894.

Pandolfo, Stefania. *Impasse of the Angels.* Chicago: University of Chicago Press, 1997.

Pascal, Blaise. *Pensées and other writings,* Oxford; New York, Oxford University Press, 1999.

Penault, David, *The Shiites: ritual and popular piety in a Muslim community*. New York: St. Martin's Press, 1992.

Plato. *Phaedrus*. Translated by R. Hackforth. Cambridge: Cambridge University Press, 1952.

———. *Symposium and Phaedrus*. Edited by Stanley Appelbaum. New York: Dover Publications, 1993.

Quran [Holy Quran]. Cairo: Harf Information Technology, 1998.

Rahnema, Ali. *An Islamic utopian: a political biography of Ali Shari'ati*. London; New York: I. B. Tauris, 1998.

Ram, Haggy. *Myth and Mobilization in Revolutionary Iran: The Use of the Friday Congregational Service*. Washington, D.C.: American University Press, 1994.

Rouch, Jean. *Cine-Ethnography*. Translated by Steven Feld. Minneapolis: University of Minnesota Press, 2003.

Schimmell, Anne Marie. *I Am Wind, You Are Fire*. Boston: Shambhala, 1992.

Shariati, Ali. *Marxism and Other Western Fallacies: An Islamic Critique*. Berkeley, Calif.: Mizan Press, 1980.

Siegel, James T. *A New Criminal Type in Jakarta: Counter-Revolution Today*. Durham, N.C.: Duke University Press, 1998.

Sontag, Susan. *On Photography*. New York: Delta, 1977.

Sreberny, Annabelle. *Small Media, Big Revolution: Communication, Culture, and the Iranian Revolution*. Minneapolis: University of Minnesota Press, 1994.

Surush, Abdal-Karim. *Reason, Freedom, and Democracy in Islam: Essential Writings of Abdolkarim Soroush*. New York: Oxford University Press, 2000.

Tabrizi, Kamal, dir. *Leili Is with Me*. Screenplay by Reza Maghsudi. Tehran: Farabi Cinema Foundation, 1996.

Taussig, Michael. *The Magic of the State*. New York: Routledge, 1997.

———. *Mimesis and Alterity: A Particular History of the Senses*. New York: Routledge, 1993.

———. "Physiognomic Aspects of Visual Worlds." In *Visualizing Theory: Selected Essays from V.A.R.*, edited by Lucien Taylor. New York: Routledge, 1994.

Weber, Max. *On Charisma and Institutional Building*. Chicago: University of Chicago Press, 1968.

———. *The Protestant Ethic and the Spirit of Capitalism*. New York: Charles Scribner's Sons, 1958.

Varzi, Roxanne. "The Caravan." *New York Press* (January 4, 2000): 1.

———. "A Ghost in the Machine: The Cinema of the Iranian Sacred Defense." In *The New Iranian Cinema: Politics, Representation, and Identity*, edited by Richard Tapper. London: I. B. Tauris, 2002.

———. "Iran Gardi." *Public Culture* 11.3 (1999): 557–69.

———. "Refugee." *American Magazine* 50.3 (1999).

Virilio, Paul. *War and Cinema: The Logistics of Perception.* New York: Verso, 1989.

Zam, Mohammad Ali. Report as head of Tehran's cultural and artistic affairs, Tehran, 2000.

Ashura ("Day of Blood"): Basij revolutionaries and, 103, 241 n.97;
description of, 52, 99–103, 121,
241 n.87; fictional films of war
and, 99–101, 102, 241 nn.87, 88,
89, 91; film documentaries of war
and, 102–3; Muharram ceremony,
51–54, 229 nn.14, 15, 19; *Revayat-
e Fath* (documentary series) and,
103; war veterans and, 196
Assabiya (unity), 40
Attar, Farid al-Din, xiii–xiv, 33
Avini, Mohamad, 80, 81–82, 86,
102, 228 n.5
Avini, Shahid Morteza: as architect
of physical and imaginary spaces,
96, 193, 235 n.30; authority
and, 95–96; *baten* (inner self)
and, 78, 79; belief in vocation
or calling of Basij revolutionaries and, 80; biography of, 96,
235 n.30; casualty of film crew
at the war front, 76, 232 n.2;
death of, 232 n.2; faith and, 76,
78, 79, 133, 232–33 n.3; Islamic
reality in war documentaries
and, 78–79, 233–34 n.11; Jahad-
e-Sazandegi organization and,
77; majmu'eheyeh haghighat
(truth films) and, 77–78; and
martyrdom of individual versus
mass sacrifices, 93, 238 n.58;
on mystical atmosphere at war
front, 20, 80, 83–85; namus
(chastity/purity/honor/sacred
defense) and, 80; on neorealism
genre, 88; propaganda films and,
78, 233 n.7; reality and, 5, 16,
87–88; subjectivity and, 93, 96,
239 n.75. See also *Revayat-e Fath*
(documentary series)

Bani-Etemand, Rakhshan, 147–48,
248–49 n.19
Basij revolutionaries: about,

221 n.18, 228 n.3; Amir
(composite revolutionary),
45–47, 56–58, 67, 72–75, 227–
28 n.1, 228 n.2, 230 n.30; Ashura
("Day of Blood") and, 103,
241 n.97; barricades in streets
by, 153, 251–52 n.31; beliefs and,
19, 80, 220 n.10; disillusionment and criticism of Iran-Iraq
war by, 176–77, 179–80, 193,
257–58 n.6, 258 n.11; Khomeini
and, 16, 221 n.18; mysticism
and, 20, 45–47, 80, 85, 227–
28 n.1, 234–35 n.27; interaction
between youth and, 177–80;
production of persuasion and
motivation to join, 56; propaganda and Islamic reality in war
documentaries, 234 n.12; Revayat Fath production of films
about suffering of, 252–53 n.6;
shahadat (martyrdom) and, 19,
47; violence toward, 153, 179,
251–52 n.31, 258 n.8, 261 n.22;
vocation or calling of, 80. See
also soldiers
Bataille, George, 70
Baten (inner self/belief): Avini's
philosophy of documentary
filmmaking and, 78, 79; identity and, 5, 207; power and, 215;
and reality, 7; riya (deception)
and, 198–99; Sufism and, 198;
zaher (outer self) and, 108, 144,
206
Beliefs: Avini's belief in vocation or
calling of Basij revolutionaries,
80; Basij revolutionaries and,
19, 80, 220 n.10; faith versus,
145, 246 n.1, 247 n.13; Islamic
republic of Iran and, 145; and
mistake of Iranian revolution,
247 n.14; Pascal on practice
generating, 140, 145; rules and,
146, 247 n.14; youth and, 12,

Khomeini, Ayatollah Ruhollah (cont.)
47; basic laws of Iran and, 41,
42; cemetery of war martyrs
and photographic image of, 23–
24, 27, 225 n.31; charismatic
leaders and, 38, 227 n.53; clergy,
mandate of, 41–42; cultural
revolution and, 42–43; executive branch and, 41, 42; exile of,
226 n.42; ghazal poetry and, 34,
225 n.36; government of jurist
and, 42, 227 n.61; hidden/absent
master and role of, 35–37, 226
nn.45, 47; home of, 38, 40; imam
title and, 37–38, 80–81, 226
n.48, 239 n.72; Iranian revolution and, 38; on Islamic republic,
41; judiciary system of Iran and,
41; khod (self) and, 34, 225 n.38;
last will and testaments and,
223 n.15; legislative branch and,
41, 42; lover/beloved and image
of, 36, 37, 81, 234 n.18; martyrs
in murals and photographic
image of, 223 n.15; mausoleum
of, 38–39; as mystic interpreter
and guide, 34, 37; mysticism
and, 19, 20, 37; nation-state and,
37, 226 n.49; omniscience, and
images of, 27, 223 n.15; photographic versus painted images
and, 27, 222 nn.7, 8; pilgrimages
and sites associated with, 39, 40;
political issues and, 24, 26–27,
37; propaganda and, 24, 221 n.1;
quote on "affliction caused by the
tongue," 1; resaleh amaliyeh (instruction books for life) and, 83;
return to Iran of, 6, 37, 219 n.2;
sayings painted on walls about
namus (chastity/purity/honor/
sacred defense), 227–28 n.1;
shahadat (martyrdom) and, 82–
83, 219 n.4, 234 n.19; Shiite
Islam and memory of shahadat

(martyrdom), 50; soldiers' uniforms and, 223 n.15; state versus
family and, 69; tariqa (mystical
path) and, 34, 225 n.37; tawil
(Shiite hermeneutics) and, 34,
35; Velayat-i-faqih: Hukumat-i-
Islami (Guardianship of the Clergy:
Islamic Government!), 41
Khoramshahr, Hemase, 233 n.9
Kiarostami, Abbas, 199, 248–
49 n.19, 256 n.1, 258 n.11
Kierkegaard, Søren, 173
Kimiyai, Masoud, 252–53 n.6
Kojève, Alexander, 48, 66–72,
228 n.6
Komiteh (Islamic police): absolute
power of, 42; bribes and, 39, 150,
247 n.9, 249 n.24, 251–52 n.31;
criminal acts against Islam and,
249–51 n.26; Khaneqahs (place
for ceremony of zekr-Ali) and,
221 n.23; and notification of
parents about arrests of youth,
149–50, 249 n.23; safety issues
and, 249–51 n.26; Sharia-style
courts and, 42; sisters of Zahra
and body checks for women by,
245 n.31; undercover officers
and, 251 n.27; virginity test of
women and, 249 n.25; women's
dress codes and, 111, 245 n.31;
youth, and coping with, 116–17,
151

Land without Bread (film), 238 n.61
Language issues, 36, 47, 79,
238 n.61
Laws: adat (customary laws), 249–
51 n.26; citizen's arrest, 244
n.23; criminal acts equated with
nationalism, 151, 249–51 n.26;
criminal types, 151, 249–51 n.26;
punishments as reform and,
249–51 n.26; ritualistic behavior
and, 145; Shiite, 38, 227 n.63;

value system of infractions, 249 n.22; Velayt-e Faqih (basic laws of Iran established by Khomeini), 41, 42, 203; youth and, 249–51 n.26. *See also* Komiteh (Islamic police)

Layli and Majnun (Ganjavi), 6, 243 n.14

Leadership issues: Ali, and religious leadership combined with temporal power, 41; clergy as spiritual leader of country, 247 n.12; harmony with leader versus concept of majority rule/voting, 212–13; and invisibility of secular youth, 7; Khameini as prayer leader during Iran-Iraq war, 229 n.24; Khomeini as absolute leader of Shiism, 35; Khomeini as charismatic leader, 38, 227 n.53; Rafsanjani as prayer leader during Iran-Iraq war, 56, 229 n.24; subordination to leaders with use of images, 26, 221 n.3, 222 n.4; Weber on charismatic leaders, 38; women as prayer leaders, 203

Lefebvre, Henri: and nation based on ideology, 242 n.6; on seen defines obscene, 108; on space, 242 n.5

Leili Is with Me (film), 231–32 n.59, 257–57 n.6

Lost in the Crowd (Al-Ahmad), 8

Lover/beloved: journey of khodi (self) toward bi-khodi (self-annihilation) and, 33; Khomeini's image and, 36, 37, 81, 234 n.18; marriages versus concept of, 179, 258 n.7; master/slave relationship versus, 65–75; mental images and journey toward, 35; Sufiism, and journey toward, 6, 28, 35, 222 n.14; and union with God, 43

Lumet, Sidney, 258 n.13

Madness (majnun), 31, 32, 47, 224 n.22, 225 n.29

Madness and Civilization (Foucault), 230 n.34

Magic of the State, The (Taussig), 242 n.6

Majmu'eheyeh haghighat (truth films), 77–78, 233 n.9

Majnun (madness), 31, 32, 47, 224 n.22, 225 n.29

Makhmalbaf, Mohsen, 157, 251 n.30, 259–60 n.6, 262 n.3

Makmalbaf, Samira, 88, 98, 237 n.38, 262 n.3

Man With a Movie Camera (film), 92

Marriage of the Blessed (film), 259–60 n.6

Marriages, 132, 169, 170, 179, 196–97, 258 n.7

Martyrdom. *See* Shahadat (martyrdom)

Martyrs: and culture of survivors, 62; foundation, 227–28 n.1; images in cemetery of war martyrs, 23–24, 230 n.36; individual versus mass sacrifices, 93, 237 n.42, 238 n.58; murals and images of, 7; photographic image of Khomeini and murals with images of, 223 n.15; uniqueness of, 62

Marx, Karl, 3, 8, 36, 130, 220 n.6, 226 n.43, 246 n.41

Marxism and Other Western Fallacies (Shariati), 220 n.6, 228 n.5

Masnavi (Rumi), 32

Master/slave relationship versus lover/beloved, 65–75

May Lady, The (film), 147–53

Mehdi's climb story, 209–13

Mellat (citizen), 36, 42, 146. *See also* Islamic subjects

Men: communication between women and, 166–67, 253 n.10; dress codes and, 42, 111–12, 244–

revolution Iran and, 248–49 n.19;
reality constructed in film documentaries and, 88, 97, 235–
36 n.37; riya (deceit) and, 88–89
New Criminal Type in Jakarta (Siegel),
249–51 n.26
New York Times (newspaper), 230–
31 n.37
Nietzsche, Friedrich, 106
Noheh (religious music), 122,
244 n.24

Pahlavi, Mohammad Reza, 6, 9,
53–54, 55, 219 n.2, 226 n.44,
227–28 n.1, 229 nn.19, 23
Painted images, 27, 62, 222 nn.7, 8,
227–28 n.1. *See also* Murals
Palm d'Or, 199
Panahi, Jafar, 255–56 n.18, 257 n.4,
260 n.7
Pandolfo, Stefania, 231 n.38
Paranoia, dangerous public space
for youth and, 140–42, 246 n.6,
251 n.27
Parenting issues, 149–50, 151,
153–54, 249 n.23, 251 n.28, 261
n.16
Pascal, Blaise, 140, 145
Persian mysticism, xiii
Photography, 27, 62, 63–64,
222 nn.7, 8, 230–31 n.37,
231 n.38
Plato, 64, 65
Poetry, 2–5, 34, 222 n.4, 225 n.36
Political issues: arrests for joining political organizations, 2,
219 n.1; censorship and, 4–5;
constitution of Iran, 42, 227
n.63; emancipation from oppressor and, 132; government of the
jurist, 42, 227 n.61; insanity and,
155–56; Islam as political force,
8; Muharram ceremony and, 52–
53, 229 n.14; nation-state and,
7, 65; rage and nation building,

53, 55, 229 n.15; revolutionary
council, 42, 227 n.63; shahadat
(martyrdom) as state policy, 47;
Shiite law and, 227 n.63; state
versus family, 65–66, 68–69, 72,
149–51, 159, 231 n.44, 249 n.25,
249–51 n.26; voting and, 206–7
Pooch (Farokhzad), 164
Pooch (nothingness/darkness),
163–64, 252–53 n.6
Poru (selfish), 119, 144 n.22
Post-revolution Iran: culture producers in, 196, 199; MIAs and,
186–87; neorealist genre and,
248–49 n.19; POWs and, 182–87,
189, 258 nn.19, 21, 259–60 n.6;
survival issues and, 175. *See also*
Film documentaries of post-
revolution Iran
Poverty issues, 260–61 n.14
Power: baten (inner self/belief)
and, 215; images and individual,
7; religion intersection with,
7, 146; tactility and physical
acts of population under control of political power, 133, 138,
246 n.3; vision intersection with,
7, 132–33; zaher (outer self) and,
215
Practice of Everyday Life (de Certeau),
221 n.17
Private Islamic culture: public
Islamic culture versus, 196–97;
and youth in Iran, 141–42, 204,
207–8, 261 n.23, 262 n.26
Private secular culture: alienation
as intellectually Western and
Muslim, 8; fortune-telling and,
134–36; Islamic identity and, 197;
Islamic rituals and submission
to Islamic republican government by youth, 143, 247 n.11;
Persian classical music training
and, 136; public Islamic culture
and, 132, 137–38, 147–53; public

Private secular culture (*cont.*)
laws of conduct and, 140; riya
(deceit) and, 144–46, 215; self-
help classes and, 136; theater
and, 137, 203, 253 n.10, 261 n.21;
Web blogs and, 202, 253 nn.10,
11
Production of persuasion, 56–59,
230 nn.28, 30
Propaganda: Avini and, 78, 233 n.7;
Basij revolutionaries and,
234 n.12; culture producers in
post-revolution Iran and, 199;
and desensitization from repeated exposure, 130, 246 n.43;
faith and Islamic reality in war
documentaries, 76, 78–79, 233–
34 n.11, 234 n.12; fictional films
and war, 98, 240–41 n.86; film
documentaries of war and, 77–
78, 233 nn.7, 8; images and, 24,
130, 221 n.1, 246 n.42; images inhabiting the mind and, 107, 129,
243 n.11, 245 nn.37, 38; Iranian
population and, 88, 237 n.38;
Khomeini and, 24, 221 n.1; Nazi
propaganda films, 239 n.71;
riya (deceit) and television war
documentaries, 93; television
programs about Iran-Iraq war
and, 77, 86–87, 93–94; youth
and, 127–28, 245 n.34
Prostitution, 10, 171, 254–55 n.14,
255–56 n.18
Psychological issues: hyperawareness, 126, 159; hypervigilance,
126, 128, 159, 245 n.35; khod-
koshi (suicide), 10, 164–66, 232
n.63; khod-sazi (self-help/self-
reconstruction) and, 10; madness
(majnun), 31, 32, 47, 224 n.22,
225 n.29; personas of youth
and, 167–68, 253 n.11; pooch
(nothingness/darkness), 163–64,
252–53 n.6; sanity and madness

in historic or social contexts,
230 n.34; therapy and, 167–68,
252 n.5, 253–54 n.12; twelve-step
programs, 252 n.5
Public discipline/encouraging good
behavior (amr be maruf), 141,
204, 261, n.22
Public Islamic culture: amr be
maruf (public discipline/encour-
aging good behavior) and, 141,
204, 261 n.22; culture of sameness and, 146–47; identity and,
147; Islamic identity, and appearances of, 195, 198, 260 n.11; and
Islamic republic of Iran, 146–47,
194–95, 259 n.3; nay as monkar
(discouraging bad behavior),
141; parenting issues and, 151,
251 n.28; private Islamic culture
versus, 196–97; private secular
culture, and intersection with,
132, 137–38, 140, 147–53; prohibition and definition of, 147;
public secrets and, 147, 199,
248 n.17; riya (deceit) and private
secular culture versus, 144–45,
146, 215; rules of Islamic republic and effects on, 140–42;
and youth in Iran, 141–42, 204,
207–8, 261 n.23, 262 n.26

Quran, 59, 63–64, 65, 231 n.38

Rafsanjani, Hojat al Islam Hashemi,
56, 222 nn.7, 8, 229 n.24
Rational self (nafs), 30–34,
223 n.17, 224 n.25, 225 n.38
Reality: Avini on, 5, 16; baten (inner
self/belief), and construction
of, 7; constructed in film documentaries, 86–87, 238 n.55;
contemplation of images and,
32; faith and, 193; film images
and, 80, 85–89, 225 n.34; hyperreality, 128–30; Islamic cultural

project of Khomeini on spiritual, 85–86, 96; veils (*pardeh*) and, 5, 80; zaher (outer self) and, 7

Red Ribbon (film), 258 n.13

Reform movement: eslah talaban (students of reform) and, 195, 196; Islamic identity and, 195, 198, 199, 206, 215, 260 n.12, 262 n.1; Islamic republic of Iran and, 195, 198; riya (deceit) and, 195, 215; Soroush and philosophy of, 197–98, 260 n.10; spirituality and, 202, 215, 261 n.18

Religious events: chants repeated about memory of glorious death, 47; as excuse to cover other acts, 122–23, 244 nn.24, 26; hey'ats (religious gathering), 20; Ta'zieh ceremony (reenactment of events at Karbala), 99, 121–22, 229 n.18, 241 n.95; youth's fraternization at, 121, 122, 244 n.24. *See also* Ashura ("Day of Blood")

Resalat (newspaper), 181

Revayat-e Fath (documentary series): 66, Ashura ("Day of Blood") and, 103; audience participation and, 94–95, 239 nn.63, 64; authority and authenticity issues and, 95–97; camera/cameraman and, 89, 92–93, 96–97; and casualty of film crew at the war front, 76, 232 n.2; and clichéd displays of piety, 89–90, 237 n.47; description of, 76–77, 232 n.2; directing film and, 92, 238 n.55; editing film and, 91–92; faith and, 76, 78–79, 97, 232–33 n.3, 240 n.82; fear of combat and, 97, 240 n.82; film crew and, 95–96, 239 n.67; interviewing and, 90–91; Karbala battle and, 91; language dubbed over action and, 94, 238 n.62; majmu'eheyeh haghighat (truth films) and, 78; martyrdom and,

84; mystic journey and, 79–80; news about Iran-Iraq war and, 234 n.12, 242 n.100; Rafsanjani's speeches and, 229 n.24; rowzeh kahn (singer of story of martyrdom) and, 91, 94–95, 237–38 n.51, 239 n.93; sound and, 89, 94; techniques for projecting reality and, 89–104; training of film crew and, 90, 96, 239 n.70; and war front as place for mystical atmosphere/practices, 83–84, 179–80, 258 n.10. *See also* Film documentaries of war

Revolution in Iran. *See* Iranian revolution

Riefenstahl, Leni, 239 n.71

Rivayat Fat'h production, 80, 86, 235 n.33, 252–53 n.6

Riya (deceit/deception): 6, 159, 198–99; akhlaq (Islamic character) and, 154; eslah talaban (students of reform) and, 195; film documentaries of war and, 88–89, 237 n.43, 239 n.77; propaganda television war documentaries and, 93; public Islamic culture versus private secular culture and, 144–45, 146, 215; reform movement and, 195, 215; taqlid (emulating a religious teacher through imitation) and, 153

Rossellini, Roberto, 235–36 n.37

Rouch, Jean, 220 n.12

Rowzeh kahn (singer of story of martyrdom), 50, 51–52, 91, 94–95, 237–38 n.51, 239 n.93

Rules: beliefs and, 146, 247 n.14; collective public identity versus private individual identities, 132, 138–40; Ministry of Culture and, 247 n.14; paranoia and, 140–42, 246 n.6, 251 n.27; preexisting consent to follow, of Islam, 140, 246 n.5

Rumi, Jalal al-Din (Mawlana): biography of, 223 n.16; on death, 59, 84; hidden master and, 34; on love and self-annihilation, 30; *Masnavi*, 32; on nafs (rational self), 30; and rays of sun, 234 n.18; on reality and imagination, 32, 224 n.27; on shahid (martyr of love), 30

Sacred defense/chastity/purity/ honor (namus), 46, 227–28 n.1

Sacrifice: confrontation with death in act of, 70; mass, versus martyrdom of individual, 93, 224 n.25, 237 n.42, 238 n.58; as veil for another violent intention, 48–50, 66, 71, 72, 232 n.63

Saddam-Yazid title, 55

Satellite dishes, chador (outer garment) and, 122, 125

Saving Private Ryan (film), 237 n.49, 240 n.85

Scent of Yusef's Shirt, The (film), 181–84, 185–92, 257 n.4, 259 nn.26, 27

Schimmel, Anne Marie, 223 n.16

Schizophrenic existence of identity-less (bi-hoviyat) youth in Iran, 10–11, 147, 153, 156–57, 173–74, 252 nn.2, 3

Secrecy, culture of, 6, 147, 151, 199, 248 n.17, 251 n.29

Secular Iranians. *See* Private secular culture

Self (khod). *See* Khod (self)

Self-annihilation (bi-khodi). *See* Bi-khodi (self-annihilation)

Selfish (poru), 119, 144 n.22

Self-loss, path of, 70, 193, 231–32 n.59

Sepah Pasdaran (Revolutionary Guard), 233 n.9

Sexual relations: birth control and, 170, 255 n.16; hymen recon-

structive surgery and, 255 n.17; interpersonal relations outside marriage and, 148–49, 166–67, 169–71, 249 n.20, 253 n.10, 255 n.17; men and, 43, 148; sex education of youth, 148–49, 169–70, 249 n.21, 254–55 n.14, 255 n.16; virginity of women and, 170, 249, n.25; women and, 43, 148

Sex workers, 10, 171, 254–55 n.14, 255–56 n.18

Shah, The. *See* Pahlavi, Mohammad Reza

Shahadat (martyrdom): bi-khodi (self-annihilation) and, 219 n.5; cemetery of war martyrs, 23–24; culture of, in film documentaries, 86, 235 n.33; Iran-Iraq war and, 6, 54, 61–62, 175; Islamic republic and, 6; jihad (holy war) and, 6; Khomeini and, 82–83, 219 n.4, 234 n.19; master/slave relationship and, 66–68; Namaz Jumah (Friday prayers) and, 203, 261 n.20; nation building and, 65–75; religious references and, 219 n.4; *Revayat-e Fath* (documentary series) and, 84; sacrifice as veil for another violent intention and, 48–50, 66; sanity and madness and, 61, 230 n.34; secular references and, 219 n.4; Shi'i Islam and, 19; as state policy, 47; state versus family and, 65–66, 68–69, 72, 231 n.44; Sufiism and, 19; survival issues versus, 175; war protestors and, 232 n.63; war veterans and, 196; work and, 66

Shahid (witness/martyr of love), 30, 223–24 n.17

Shah Nameh (Book of Kings), 45

Shariati, Ali: initzar (waiting for hidden imam) and, 37; and

107, 112–13, 129, 242–43 n.9, 243 nn.10, 11, 245 nn.37, 38; images of martyrdom and revolution in, 104, 106–7, 128–29; industrial modernity and, 130, 246 n.41; Islamic public space, and youth in, 108, 128–30; Jordan Street, 119–22, 245 n.39; original perceptions of space and, 115, 243 n.18; pedestrians and public space of, 115, 130, 243 n.16; remaking space by youth of Iran and, 116; as revolutionary space, 6–7, 108–16, 242 n.3; scenes of destruction and, 242 n.1; street names and, 106, 242 n.1; unconscious perceptions of space and, 116; youth as subjects turned into Islamic objects in, 7, 108, 112–13, 142–44, 242–43 n.9, 243 n.10, 247 n.9

Television programs: majmu'eheyeh haghighat (truth films) and, 233 n.9; propaganda about Iran-Iraq war and, 77, 86–87, 93–94; riya (deceit) and Iran-Iraq war propaganda, 93. See also Revayat-e Fath (documentary series)

Theater, private secular culture and, 137, 203, 253 n.10, 261 n.21

Truth: bi-khodi (self-annihilation) and, 33; film documentaries of war and, 86; majmu'eheyeh haghighat (truth films), 77–78, 233 n.9; restoration of khod (self) or nafs (rational self) and, 33; U.S. media and, 235–36 n.37; Vertov and, 86

Tudeh Party, 2, 219 n.4

Ummat (Moslem society/community), 38, 40

Unemployment/employment issues, 260–61 n.14

Union with God, 43

United States: Army commercials and, 237 n.42; Khameini and, 56; media and, 235–36 n.37; propaganda and, 235–36 n.37, 237 n.42; reality TV and, 235–36 n.37

Unity (assabiya), 40

University entrance system, 14, 221 n.15

Valiyat-I fagih (Islamic state). See Islamic republic of Iran

Vasiyat-namehs (last wills and testaments), 17, 58–59, 223 n.15

Velayat-i-faqih: Hukumat-i-Islami (Guardianship of the Clergy: Islamic Government) (Khomeini), 41

Velayt-e Faqih (basic laws of Iran established by Khomeini), 41, 42, 203

Vertov, Dziga, 86, 92, 235–36 n.37

Veterans, war. See War veterans

Vietnam, formal combat training of soldiers in, 237 n.49

Violence issues, 48–50, 66, 80, 234 n.14

Virilio, Paul, 101

Vision: intersection with power, 7, 132–33; intersection with religion, 7; subject/object dichotomy and, 115, 243 n.14

Walkman/iPods, secondary use of space and, 124, 244 n.29

War: Islamic cultural project of Khomeini on spiritual reality of war, 85–86, 96; MIAs and, 186–87; namus (chastity/purity/honor/sacred defense) and, 45, 46, 50, 228 n.10; POWs and, 182–87, 189, 258 nn.19, 21, 259–60 n.6; religious fanatics and, 47–48, 228 n.4; sacrifice as veil for another violent intention and,

ROXANNE VARZI is an assistant professor of anthropology
at the University of California, Irvine.

Library of Congress Cataloging-in-Publication Data
Varzi, Roxanne
Warring souls : youth, media, and martyrdom in post-revolution Iran /
Roxanne Varzi.
p. cm.
Includes bibliographical references and index.
ISBN 0-8223-3709-6 (cloth : alk. paper)
ISBN 0-8223-3721-5 (pbk. : alk. paper)
1. Mass media and youth—Iran. 2. Youth—Iran—Attitudes. 3. Mass media—
Political aspects—Iran. 4. Popular culture—Political aspects—Iran. 5. Islam
and politics—Iran. 6. Islam and culture—Iran. 7. Iran-Iraq War, 1980–1988—
Influence. I. Title.
HQ799.2.M35V37 2006
302.2308350955—dc22   2005034368